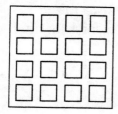

Helping Children Explore Science

A Sourcebook for Teachers of Young Children

MARY JO PUCKETT CLIATT
JEAN M. SHAW

The University of Mississippi

Merrill, an imprint of
Macmillan Publishing Company
New York

Maxwell Macmillan Canada
Toronto

Maxwell Macmillan International
New York □ *Oxford* □ *Singapore* □ *Sydney*

We dedicate this book to our parents, Lucy and Allen Puckett, and Edith and Don R. Mueller, and to Harold C. Hein, Professor Emeritus of Secondary Education.

Cover Photo: David Young-Wolff/PhotoEdit
Editor: Linda A. Sullivan
Production Editor: Stephen C. Robb
Art Coordinator: Raydelle M. Clement
Production Buyer: Patricia A. Tonneman

This book was set in Century Old Style by Ruttle, Shaw & Wetherill, Inc. and was printed and bound by Book Press, Inc., a Quebecor America Book Group Company. The cover was printed by New England Book Components.

Macmillan Publishing Company
866 Third Avenue
New York, NY 10022

Macmillan Publishing Company is part of the Maxwell Communications Group of Companies.

Maxwell Macmillan Canada, Inc.
1200 Eglinton Avenue East, Suite 200
Don Mills, Ontario   M3C 3N1

Library of Congress Cataloging-in-Publication Data

Cliatt, Mary Jo Puckett.
    Helping children explore science : a sourcebook for teachers of young children / Mary Jo Puckett Cliatt, Jean M. Shaw.
        p.   cm.
    Includes bibliographical references and index.
    ISBN 0–675–21325–8
    1. Science—Study and teaching (Elementary)   2. Education, Elementary—Activity programs.   I. Shaw, Jean M.   II. Title.
LB1585.C53   1992
372.3′5044—dc20   91–23412
                                                            CIP

Printing: 1   2   3   4   5   6   7   8   9   Year: 2   3   4   5

Photo credits: Nancy P. Alexander

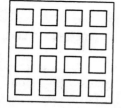

Preface

SCIENCE is an area of significant concern—today, more than ever. A basic science background is vital for people to function in the modern world. The economic development and stability of our country and even the entire world greatly depend on an enlightened understanding of science and practical application of scientific principles. Developing an understanding of science and a scientific attitude must begin early in one's life. To make science meaningful to young children, it needs to be blended into the entire curriculum. Science is a natural part of all of life; it doesn't exist in isolation. Because science permeates all aspects of life, science can help children develop as whole beings.

Because young children have such active curiosity about the world around them, teaching science to them can be a joy. Although helpful, an extensive scientific background is not absolutely necessary for adults to do a good job of teaching science. In fact, teachers can learn along with their students. Additionally, science learning should be active. That is the nature of the subject; it is also the way young children learn best. When children are actively involved in learning science, they enjoy it. They build positive attitudes toward science and develop confidence in working with it.

The purpose of this book is to provide concepts and related activities on a wide variety of science topics for teachers of young children. As children participate in these activities, they will use different science processes as ways of learning.

This book is written for preservice and in-service teachers of four through eight year olds. The content of the book would also interest parents and others who work with young children. Administrators, science supervisors, staff developers, and science teachers working with students at other age levels will find their own particular uses for this book.

ORGANIZATION OF THE BOOK

The book is organized in the following manner. In chapter 1, we present background information about science, the nature of young children, and appropriate ways to teach science to young children. Chapter 2 introduces the science processes. This chapter includes discussions and related activities explaining various processes such as observing, classifying, and communicating. In teaching science, it is extremely important to guide children's thinking by asking stimulating questions. Evaluating children's progress is equally important. Thus, chapter 3 deals with questioning and evaluation techniques appropriate for young children and for teachers of science. Chapter 4 addresses the question, How can you make a classroom run smoothly when you are using active approaches? The content focuses on management of science in an active classroom, exploring topics such as techniques for organizing materials, media, and learners working in different group sizes.

The focus of the book then shifts to science subject matter areas, specifically concepts and activities appropriate for young children. Chapters 5 through 8 deal with the life sciences. We start with the human body (chapter 5), move to animals (chapter 6), on to plants (chapter 7), and finish with nature (chapter 8). Chapters 9 and 10 include concepts related to the earth, its weather, and space. In chapters 11 through 13, we discuss the physical sciences. Water, air, and light are the topics for chapter 11; while heat, sound, and machines are introduced in chapter 12; and, finally, we discuss magnets and electricity in chapter 13.

In each of the first four chapters we present a different aspect of teaching science to young children. We have included many concrete examples to help our readers assimilate the principles discussed in the chapters and to help them relate these principles to their own experiences.

In the chapters that include science curriculum areas, we introduce four or more concepts related to each topic. Each concept includes two or more activities to make that concept meaningful to young children. In each activity we provide a list of science processes that children could use; we give instructions for conducting the activity, related questions to stimulate children's thinking, and suggestions for evaluation.

Each chapter concludes with a "Now It's Your Turn" section. The section includes a variety of suggested projects intended to make you think creatively, apply your ideas with children, do some further independent research, or implement a small personal development project. The "Now It's Your Turn" section provides the readers with opportunities to assimilate the ideas presented in each chapter by putting those ideas into practice.

HOW TO USE THIS BOOK

Teachers and preservice teachers might wish to study the book in a sequential way from cover to cover. They might also use isolated chapters to bring new units into their early childhood classrooms or to enrich and supplement the units they already have in their textbooks and curriculum plans. Educators might also plan staff development sessions using portions of the book.

ACKNOWLEDGMENTS

Many people helped us complete this book. Nancy P. Alexander provided photographs. Sandra Allen and Shirley Messer ably typed the manuscript. Tammie Brown gave us clerical assistance. Jean's daughter, Victoria E. Shaw, helped to compile the index. Our students shared ideas with us and helped us refine these ideas as we worked with them and young children out in the schools. Friends and family members supported us in numerous ways. Our reviewers—Shareen Abramson, California State University-Fresno; Catherine Blount, Cuyahoga Community College; Audrey Boyd, Guilford Technical Community College; Aimee Howley, University of Charleston; Mark Malone, University of Colorado at Colorado Springs; and Julianne Nutting, Lane Community College—helped us refine our ideas and added strength and quality to the chapters. Our editors, David Faherty and Linda Sullivan, greatly facilitated our work. Thanks also to production editor Steve Robb and art coordinator Raydelle Clement.

Mary Jo Puckett Cliatt
Jean M. Shaw

Oxford, Mississippi

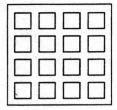

Contents

Chapter 3

Questioning and Evaluation in Science   43

Chapter 4

Organizing and Managing the Classroom   67

Chapter 5

The Human Body   87

Chapter 6

Animals   121

Chapter 7

Plants   141

Chapter 8

Nature   165

Chapter 11

Water, Air, and Light   225

Chapter 12

Heat, Sound, and Machines   255

Chapter 13

Magnets and Electricity   281

Index   306

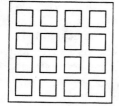

Chapter 1

Science for Young Children—Why, What, Who, and How?

ON a warm summer evening two teachers discussed their upcoming school year. As their conversation tapered off, each became lost in her own thoughts about the science programs she would be responsible for teaching.

Meg, who was scheduled to teach four year olds in their prekindergarten year, looked forward to teaching science. She pictured a group of children busy at the water table and the many ways they could experiment with water. Meg thought about inviting children to share their discoveries with others and of ways she could build the children's vocabularies as they worked. She pictured the children taking a walk and examining soil and weeds near the schoolgrounds. Meg imagined engaging the children in creative movement, then having them feel and stretch their muscles as they tried different ways of using their bodies. She saw teaching science as using the children's natural energy and curiosity to find out more about themselves and their world.

Kelly's brow furrowed as she imagined teaching science to her second graders. Her past experiences with science had not been very positive. She felt insecure about some of the facts that were included in her science textbook. She knew how some of the children's attention wandered as their classmates read from the book. Kelly had tried letting the children collect and sort rocks, but thought they got too noisy as they worked with the rocks. She did not have a microscope or test tubes in her classroom, and so she hesitated to plan more science experiences with her children. She wondered if it was worth it to expose second graders to science anyway. Wasn't it too difficult for the students? Wasn't it boring?

As you read these vignettes, did you find any elements of your own feelings and attitudes? Has your own schooling in science made you feel confident and eager or are you somewhat fearful and apprehensive at the thought of teaching science to young children? Many people have mixed feelings. You may be among them.

Even if you are hesitant about teaching science, we hope that you acknowledge that science is an important area for young children to explore. Science is an area that virtually everyone can learn more about. Its study can be intriguing and rewarding for both children and teachers. The purpose of this book is to help you become more confident in presenting science to young children in meaningful ways.

To get you started, this chapter provides background information on a variety of topics. We will discuss the importance of science and present some definitions of science. We will describe learner characteristics and discuss the need for individualization in teaching. Based on the work of psychologists and science educators, we suggest a variety of appropriate methods and guiding principles for teaching science. In an effort to present science in a meaningful way, we encourage educators to blend science with other curricular areas. Thus, this initial chapter will provide some background information on the "whys, whats, whos, and hows" of teaching science to young children.

WHY IS SCIENCE IMPORTANT?

Science touches every area of our lives. Without scientific advances in health care, nutrition, and prevention of disease, most of us would not be alive. We would not enjoy heated and air-conditioned homes with electric appliances and comfortable furniture. We would be engaged in life-sustaining labor that would not permit us free time to visit with others or enjoy technological entertainment devices such as television. It is hard to imagine a world without the influences of science.

Science helps people understand themselves and the world around them. Surrounded by interesting phenomena, it is natural for people to describe, try to explain, and to investigate regularities and unusual events. Knowledge of science helps people to be more aware of and more appreciative of their surroundings. Even young children can explore the living things around them and begin to understand their uniqueness as living beings. They can observe and communicate about the soil, rocks, weather, and sky. Through concrete experiences they can begin to learn about physical forces and energy forms such as magnetism, light, and sound. Through experimentation young children can explore the properties of water and heat. The early childhood years are prime times for children to begin their work in science.

Science is important for the decision making that is involved in responsible citizenship. Old and young citizens need scientific knowledge to make informed decisions about the problems facing people in our complicated world. Educators can help even young children build knowledge and caring attitudes to prepare them for the roles they will assume as citizens of their country and world.

Science is essential to people as consumers, as producers, and as innovators. To compete in a rapidly changing global economy, each country and society needs citizens who are well informed and scientifically literate, citizens who possess science process skills, and who can work together to solve problems. Science programs for young children can help to build a foundation in each of these areas.

Science contributes to people's health and well-being. Good habits and healthy lifestyles can begin as young children learn about and practice good diet, regular exercise, and proper rest. Healthy people live longer than do unhealthy ones. Good health contributes to people's enjoyment of life. New scientific discoveries add to our knowledge base about health and prevention of diseases. Study of science is essential to people's physical and mental health.

Science is important because it contributes to children's development in all areas. Science strengthens children's intellectual growth; it builds knowledge and provides opportunities for children to use intellectual skills such as classifying, predicting, and ordering. Because science provides so many interesting opportunities to work with objects and events, children are stimulated to use and build communication skills. Indeed, communication skills are a natural and important part of science. Children can use and refine their large and small motor skills in a wide variety of science experiences. Thus, science enhances physical growth. Young children, like scientists, can often work together as they explore science topics; as they work together children build social skills. Involvement in science calls for creativity in children. Science lets them be creative in their thinking, their actions, and in creating products. Study of science can support emotional growth as children build positive feelings and attitudes.

For these many reasons science is truly an important curricular area for young children, but there is another reason that science is important for them. It is intriguing and fun. Moreover, making science interesting and meaningful is easy and exciting!

WHAT IS SCIENCE?

What comes to your mind when you hear the word "science"? Do you picture yourself in your high school biology lab? Do you think of a college lecture class? Do you remember collecting and discussing weather data in elementary school? Do you recall a definition of science presented by one of your teachers? Before you read further, take a moment and jot down your own definition of science.

Many authorities have developed definitions of science. For example, Paul Blackwood (1964) asserted that "Science is what scientists do." Blackwood added that scientists describe, predict, and explain. Jacobsen and Bergman (1987, p. 2) defined science as "humanity's quest to know . . . the investigation and interpretation of events in the natural, physical environment and within our bodies." In these definitions, we see three aspects of science. The definitions imply the active, investigative nature of science. They outline some content of science: science deals with the natural, physical world and with the human body. The authors of the definitions hint at scientific attitudes—those of people's curiosity and persistence.

In light of these definitions of science, what should be our goal for teaching science to children? Katz and Chard (1989), in discussing categories of learning goals for children, describe four types of goals: knowledge, skills, dispositions, and feelings.

Knowledge includes ideas, facts, concepts, and information. *Skills* include physical, social, communicative, and cognitive behaviors such as working and playing alone or with others, and conveying ideas through oral language and writing. Katz and Chard define *dispositions* as "relatively enduring habits of actions or tendencies to respond to categories of experience across classes of situations," and state that "desirable dispositions include curiosity, humor, generosity, and helpfulness," (p. 31). Katz and Chard advocate designing the curriculum in ways that promote the simultaneous acquisition of knowledge, skills, and desirable dispositions. *Feelings*—emotional or affective states—include children feeling accepted, comfortable, and competent. Feelings also concern children sensing that they are contributing members of the class group. Considering Katz and Chard's discussion of appropriate goals, we advocate an active curriculum that provides opportunities for children to engage in concrete experiences. This type of curriculum enhances the development of children in each of the goal areas discussed by Katz and Chard.

We see science as a blend of content, process, and attitudes (dispositions and feelings). In their study of science, people deal with topics from the life and health sciences, earth and space sciences, and physical sciences. As they work in science, people also use a number of processes or ways of investigating. Among these are observing, predicting, communicating, and experimenting. Attitudes affect people's eagerness and abilities to work with science. Curious, interested people are more likely to work cooperatively to find the answer to a scientific question than are people who are afraid, hesitant, and uninterested in science.

Science is a blend of content, process, and attitudes.

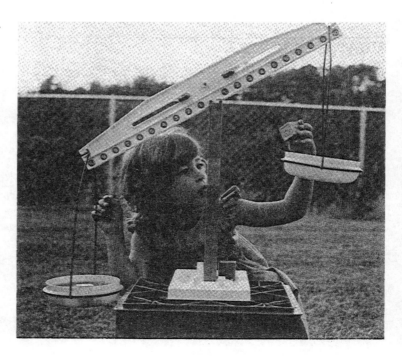

Let's look at some examples of how science content, process, and attitudes fit together.

Five-year-old Pablo plays with a car in the wet sand. He pushes it, but the car doesn't move far. Pablo smooths the sand and tries again, but the car still doesn't move freely as he pushes it. Pablo looks around and asks his teacher if he can use some strips of stiff paper from the art center. He places the strips on the sand and pushes the car along. It moves freely. Pablo looks satisfied and pleased. He shapes the sand into hills and valleys and lays his "roads" in place. Pablo narrates, "Up and down . . . barroom, 'room, 'room" as he moves his car along.

Pablo has solved a problem. He has tried several approaches, assessed the effects, and kept on investigating until he found an acceptable solution. In doing so, Pablo used several processes of science. His attitudes of persistence, independence, and confidence that he could solve the problem were similar to those shown by professional scientists as they search for a cure to a devastating disease. Pablo worked informally with some science content, too. He observed the inhibiting effects of wet sand and applied the idea that an object moves more freely on a firm, smooth surface than on a wet, mushy one.

Eight-year-old Alicia and Cassie have brought earthworms to their third grade class. Alicia holds one of the worms in her hands and tells her classmates how she read and observed that earthworms have no eyes, but they do have mouths. She describes where the girls found the worms. Cassie demonstrates how the worms want to wiggle off a dry paper towel but seem more comfortable and relaxed on a damp towel. She predicts that the worms will prefer a shady to a sunny area and then shows her classmates how the worms behave when they are placed in the shade and sun. When a classmate suggests that they cut the worm in half and see what will happen, Alicia and Cassie retort, "No! They're living things. We're taking them back to the garden."

Alicia and Cassie found some interesting creatures and learned more about their bodies and habits from reading and observing. Based on her prior experience, Cassie predicted how the worms would behave in different light conditions; she checked her prediction. The girls demonstrated a respect for life and will act on their beliefs by returning the worms to a suitable environment.

As you proceed in your study and use of this book, reflect on the ways content, process, and attitudes are related. Virtually every activity we present will illustrate a science concept and deepen children's understanding of the concept. We present a thorough discussion of science processes in chapter 2; we also list the processes that could be used in all subsequent learning experiences. Development of positive attitudes toward science is inherent in most learning activities. Teachers can generate interest by providing hands-on work for children that gets them involved, by making science relevant to children's lives, and by themselves showing interest and enthusiasm for science. Encouraging children to be persistent, cooperative, and thorough is another part of the teacher's work in building positive attitudes toward science.

WHAT ARE OUR LEARNERS LIKE?

To make science meaningful to the children we teach, we need to have a clear perception of our children. What are the learning needs and characteristics of young children? How are these characteristics alike or different from those of older students?

First of all we must realize that young children learn and develop as whole people. Their cognitive, affective, physical, social, aesthetic, and personal-emotional areas are all intricately intertwined. Children cannot grow in one area without other areas being affected. When children develop cognitively, they also develop affectively. Their social development can greatly influence their emotional development. Children's abilities and eagerness to learn will be closely related to their self-concepts. The interrelationship of these areas in a child's life can result in positive influences on the child's entire growth as well as negative influences. Educators must constantly be aware that they are responsible for the development of the whole child and that in influencing one area, they will most likely influence several other areas.

Young children grow through the same predictable stages but at different rates.

Children help to prepare a breakfast featuring homemade butter. They learn best through involvement with concrete experiences.

While researchers and child development experts can give us information on certain developmental characteristics representative of each age, we know that all children at a given age will not fit the norm. Certain four year olds who may be advanced intellectually for their age may be quite immature socially or physically. Educators should be aware of the characteristics of the age child they teach. At the same time they need to be prepared to make allowances for the differences that might be found in their classroom because children do grow emotionally, socially, physically, and intellectually at different rates.

Young children learn best through active involvement with concrete experiences. They learn by talking with others about their experiences. Piaget tells us that "the young child embodies two puzzling qualities—while he readily learns a great deal, he is paradoxically, rather difficult to teach" (Chittenden, 1969, p. 19). Young children construct their own knowledge of things and events around them by using their five senses and by manipulating and experimenting. As they talk to one another about their experiences, their learning is clarified and gains new meaning.

Young children are curious and eager to learn when the teacher fits the learning environment to their interests, their needs, and their levels of maturity. Educators must be sensitive to their young learners. They must understand that young children learn best what is meaningful to them. "Artificial sequences set up by adults for learning topics" (Shaw, Cliatt, Emerson, Leigh & Perry, 1990) lack meaning for children. Children learn best in environments that are natural, relaxed, and free of competitive elements rather than in settings that are highly structured and tightly organized.

Young children have different learning styles. Some learn best through visual modes; others are primarily aural, tactile, or kinesthetic learners. Some learners are global, incorporating all five senses to gather information. To be effective, educators need to be aware of each student's primary learning style. Teachers need to introduce new concepts and ideas in ways that are easiest for children to assimilate. While they will want to focus on children's dominant learning styles, they will also take care to cultivate and stimulate children's weaker modes of learning in order to help these modes develop. In most learning experiences children need to use several learning modes.

The previous information tells us about some general learning characteristics of young children; however, this picture does not adequately represent all of our young children. Often we work with children who leave us with a sense of failure—children whom we never reach—children who are isolated and even rejected by our society.

What do statistics tell us about this segment of our population? We know that a very large percentage of our children are at risk. Duckett (1988) described at-risk children as those who live in poverty, those who are the "children of children" (p. 167)—those with teenaged mothers, and those who cannot speak English. Duckett pointed out that minority children are not necessarily at risk: "Poverty is a more influential factor than race."

One of five children in America lives in poverty. Children born into poverty have higher risk factors such as "premature birth, low birthweight, malnutrition, recurrent and untreated health problems, physical and psychological stress, child abuse and learning disabilities" (Committee for Economic Development, 1987).

Among poor children in our nation, 43.1 percent are black, 37.7 percent are Hispanic, and 16.1 percent are white (Chafel, 1990). By the year 2020, 48 percent of our school-age children will belong to ethnic minority groups (Carbo, 1987).

Statistics reveal some alarming factors about our at-risk children. Everyday, 2,795 teenagers get pregnant, 1,106 teenagers have abortions, 1,295 teenagers give birth. Every 8 seconds during our school day a child drops out of school; every 26 seconds a child runs away from home. Children are abused or neglected every 47 seconds; the number of children abused or neglected each day averages 1,849 (Children's Defense Fund, 1990).

Drug abuse has become a national crisis. Nearly 2.2 million Americans are hard-core cocaine addicts. We've read many reports relating drug abuse to crimes committed against our children. However, our children have become drug abusers themselves. Every 7 minutes a child is arrested for a drug offense (Children's Defense Fund, 1990).

Many of our families have disintegrated and our children are left devastated. These are some of the children we work with daily. They are children who have lost their innocence—who come to us with numerous problems, pressures, and distractions. Forty of our fifty states have made a concerted effort to raise the standard of education, but these at-risk children need counselors and other support services before they can concentrate on their schoolwork and become effective class participants.

Are our at-risk learners any different from our average young learners? Our at-risk learners come from more extreme backgrounds than our so-called normal learners. Nevertheless, teaching practices that are appropriate for average children are usually appropriate for our at-risk children. Young, at-risk children thrive on many of the same hands-on concrete experiences that are so appropriate for the rest of the class. Teachers need to use many of these hands-on learning experiences tailored with minor adjustments to fit the individual needs of the learners in their classrooms.

WHAT DO PSYCHOLOGISTS AND EDUCATORS SAY ABOUT SCIENCE FOR YOUNG CHILDREN?

To teach children effectively, we must be aware of the ways they think about things and their typical levels of understanding. Psychologists and educators offer much information about children. Especially pertinent to science education is the work of psychologists and educators Piaget, Bruner, Gagné, and Cohen and his colleagues. You have probably read about these authors' works. Let's take a look at some of their ideas that apply to science for young children.

Jean Piaget.   The well-known Swiss psychologist, Jean Piaget, and his many follow-ers outlined four stages of intellectual development. They also described five factors that promote learning.

Most children ages four to eight, the age span addressed in this book, are in Piaget's preoperational or concrete operational stages. These stages follow the sensory motor stage. In the sensory motor stage, children learn to focus on and manipulate objects. They repeat actions and achieve permanence.

In the preoperational stage, children are typically ages two to six or seven. They begin to use language and other symbols. The preoperational stage is a period of rapid vocabulary growth. Children learn words from conditioning and as the result of experience. They learn to draw and interpret pictures. By kindergarten and first grade, most children can draw representationally in a rudimentary way. They begin to write letters, words, and numerals. All these symbols, along with spoken words, add to preoperational children's communication abilities.

Actual experiences with science materials are essential to children's language development. As children handle, act on, and talk about material, language becomes meaningful. Children remember what they can understand and begin to relate experiences to other experiences. With meaningful language learning, a disposition for learning and exploring is inherent in children.

Because of their language and perceptual abilities, preoperational children can observe and describe properties of objects. They usually concentrate or "center" on one characteristic of an object, such as color, and have trouble taking into account other factors. Preoperational children have not developed an understanding of the concept of conservation. This means, for example, that they do not understand that a number of objects can be rearranged and still have the same number.

Similarly, most preoperational children may be shown two identical balls of clay and agree that they contain the same amount of material. Yet, when one ball is flattened, a child might say there is more clay in the ball because the "pancake" is thinner. The child does not consider that, though the pancake is thinner, it is also wider, or that no clay was added or taken away. If one clay ball is formed into a "hotdog," the child might say the hotdog contains more clay than the ball because it is longer. Preoperational children do not mentally reverse their thinking to "see" that the pancake or hotdog could be reformed into the original ball.

Preoperational children are beginning to be able to arrange objects in order according to their characteristics. For instance, they could arrange potted plants in order from tallest to shortest or order leaves from darkest to lightest. The number of objects with which they can work, however, is limited. Preoperational children typically have trouble inserting new objects into a series. When they work with ordering, they must compare objects side by side; they cannot order a whole group without making several direct comparisons.

Young children can make simple classifications but find multiple classifications difficult. Their understanding of space is restricted to that of the immediate environment. Children are just beginning to understand time concepts such as before and after; their understanding of hours, days, seasons, and years is very limited.

Science experiences for kindergarteners and first graders, then, must be firsthand and must involve experiences with many objects. To develop young children's language, they must be surrounded with meaningful spoken and written words, and must have numerous opportunities to use language.

Six or seven year olds typically enter the stage Piaget described as concrete operational. Development through this stage usually continues through age eleven or twelve. Children in this stage develop abilities to think logically, but more readily through concrete means.

For example, suppose you had no experience in handling magnets and someone told you facts about a magnetic field: "A magnetic field surrounds a magnet. This field can act like a magnet. When iron filings are sprinkled around a magnet, the filings arrange themselves into a pattern of lines. These lines are called lines of force and they show where the magnetic field is located and how it is arranged. More lines of force are found near the poles of the magnet, where the magnetic force is the strongest, than at the nonpole areas of the magnet." Is all this language clear? Would it be if you were a seven year old with little previous experience with magnets? Probably not! What would clarify the stated facts for a youngster? Concrete experiences with various magnets are essential if children are to gain understanding of concepts such as magnetic attraction or magnetic fields.

With many experiences, concrete operational children develop ideas of conservation of number, matter, length, area, weight, and volume. They are therefore ready for concrete and carefully sequenced experiences with measurement.

Concrete operational children are able to classify objects and pictures of objects with which they are familiar. To enhance their growing flexibility in thinking, they can be given objects to classify many different ways. Concrete operational children can devise their own classification schemes as well as work with those suggested by others. They can deal with various subclassifications.

Children's mathematics abilities are growing rapidly, and first- through third-grade children can use their math skills in science situations. They can add and subtract, tell time on a clock, and understand longer time periods such as days, weeks, months, or years.

Concrete operational children's thinking is becoming more and more sophisticated. They can begin to understand simple causal relationships; discriminate between solids, liquids, and gases; visualize relative positions of objects as seen from the point of view of another person; and use concrete models explaining scientific phenomena. Their growing skills in using art materials and measuring tools let them develop construction projects more independently than before.

Because they are increasingly familiar with symbols—written words, graphs, and numbers—concrete operational children can keep records of observations and experiments. They can learn to interpret diagrams, especially when the diagrams are of familiar objects.

Young children have not yet achieved Piaget's final stage of formal operations. Indeed, Piaget believed that most adults seldom think completely on the formal or abstract level. When faced with new or difficult situations, most adults think better on a more concrete level. Piaget described formal operational people as being able to think in abstract terms—beyond their own personal experiences. Formal operational people can consider all possible combinations of factors in an experiment. They enjoy thinking about hypothetical situations and can relate one abstraction to another.

Piaget's research indicated that five factors are involved in promoting learning.

1. Physical experience—manipulation of real materials.
2. Social experience—interaction with others, confronting the ideas and views of others.

3. Logical-mathematical experience—activities involving comparing, grouping, taking apart and putting together, seriating, and counting.

4. Equilibration—a mental state of balance in which people take in new information and organize it into both their existing and changing mental schemes.

5. Maturation—the passing of time.

Educators can attend to the first four factors with hands-on science experiences for children. Actual experiences let children handle materials and objects. As children work in groups with the teacher's guidance, they have social experiences. In hands-on work, children use the logical-mathematical process that Piaget deemed so important. As they problem-solve and experiment, the process of equilibration is enhanced. Hands-on experience is truly suited to Piaget's conception of intellectual development.

Jerome Bruner.　American psychologist Jerome Bruner complemented Piaget's work by stressing the role of discovery inherent in hands-on science. Bruner suggested that allowing learners to discover information and to organize this information was necessary for learning the techniques of problem solving. He advocated that, whenever possible, children should be given the opportunity to discover concepts for themselves. Bruner discussed four advantages to learning by discovery:

1. Discovery learning helps children learn how to learn. It builds inquiry and problem-solving skills that are applicable to new situations.

2. Discovery learning is self-rewarding. It shifts motives away from learning for the sake of satisfying someone else to learning that produces self-satisfaction and pride.

3. Discovery learning builds decision-making and problem-solving skills.

4. Discovery learning results in knowledge that is more easily remembered and recalled than rote learning.

Bruner described three modes of presentation. His *action* (or enactive) mode concerns actual contact with real objects. This mode or presentation is very appropriate for young children. Bruner's *imagery* (or ikonic) mode concerns the uses of models, pictures, and diagrams as representations for objects. This mode helps learners to relate graphic forms and experiences. Finally, Bruner's *language* (or symbolic) mode, relies on words and other symbols to convey meaning. Experiences involving the use of the action and imagery modes complement and should accompany the language mode.

Robert Gagné.　The work of another American psychologist, Robert Gagné, is also pertinent to planning science activities for elementary students. Gagné believed that elementary school science should be taught and learned as a process of inquiry. Children should have many opportunities to generate ideas and to test them in laboratory situations in the classroom. Gagné advocated teaching skills such as observing, describing, classifying, measuring, and inferring as crucial to problem solving. Such skills are important because they are used throughout a person's lifetime.

Human Brain Research

Based on currently available research about human brain functioning, Cohen, Staley, and Horak (1989) suggest that the brain is very complex and that no two individuals learn in exactly the same way. They draw several implications for science education:

- Retention and recall of knowledge are heightened when learners are engaged in multisensory experiences with real objects.

- Because of a wide range of individual differences, it is probably unnecessary to spend much time and energy trying to figure out different children's learning styles. It might be more productive, when teaching science, to offer a wide range of options for students to become engaged in and to express their learning. This way children will be able to find activities suitable to their individual learning styles.

- Interesting, pleasurable experiences must be offered to engage students in learning. Repetitive tasks, work sheets, and drill and practice exercises may actually disengage parts of the brain (the reticular formation and limbic system) from the learning process.

- Sensory exploration and manipulation of objects must be accompanied by discussion. Children need to talk, demonstrate, and interact. When children talk about what they are doing, concept and language development are enhanced.

- Children need opportunities to engage in a variety of modes of interactions with objects and other people. Engagement modes might include listening or reading, sensory explorations, experiments, observing demonstrations, brainstorming, discussion, drama, nature walks, and simulations.

- Children must have opportunities to express the results of their engagements. Expressive modes might include talking, reporting, making models, drawing, or conducting experiments and explorations on their own.

Implications

Based on the work of Piaget, Bruner, Gagné, and Cohen and his colleagues, we advocate the following principles.

- Present science as a way of finding out rather than a body of facts to be memorized. Emphasize science process, as well as content and positive attitudes.

- Adapt science experiences to children's developmental levels. Otherwise, learning will be rote, or will not occur at all.

- Emphasize learning by doing and discovering how things work using direct observation and experimentation.

- Stress verbalization about ideas and events. Encourage interactions among children.

- Provide adequate time for children to deal with concepts. Allow children to manipulate materials, think, talk, and use a variety of expressive forms to show what they are learning.

HOW CAN EDUCATORS ACHIEVE EXCELLENCE IN TEACHING SCIENCE?

Educators and the media have focused attention on the need to improve science education in our country. In this section, we present results of studies and recommendations by the National Assessment of Educational Progress Science Committee, The National Science Teachers Association, a National Research Council committee, and researchers Penick and Johnson.

National Assessment of Educational Progress Study

The science committee of the 1986 National Assessment of Education Progress (NAEP) studied the nature and impact of school science as well as the techniques that teachers used. The committee also studied students' attitudes toward science. Though the NAEP researchers (Mullis & Jenkins, 1988) collected data on nine-, thirteen-, and seventeen-year-olds, these data provide information that have implications for young children.

In general, results from the NAEP study are dismal. The authors of the NAEP study pointed to the need for improvement in science education in our country. United States students' performance compared unfavorably to that of students in other industrialized countries. Science proficiency varied greatly when subgroups were compared by race and gender. In general, girls' achievement lagged behind that of boys; disparities increased as students' ages increased. Despite recent gains, the average proficiency of black and Hispanic students was lower than that of their white peers. NAEP data also showed that more than two-thirds of the third-grade teachers in the study spent less than two hours per week teaching science; 11 percent of the third graders reported having no science instruction at the time of the assessment. NAEP results showed a positive relationship between students' use of science equipment and their proficiency in science. Though most teachers in the study believed that laboratory classes were more effective than nonlaboratory classes, they reported lecturing as their primary teaching technique.

The authors of the NAEP report (Mullis & Jenkins, 1988) reflected that examination of scientific enterprise in general provides features that educators might emulate. Scientists investigate and use science processes. "An effective science learning system would provide students with opportunities to engage in these activities, and encourage science teachers to model them in their classrooms" (p. 12). Scientists believe that people can investigate the regularities of the real world and make decisions and inferences based on knowledge and data. Students can also be expected to investigate causes and effects in their environment and use evidence to support their conclusions. Successful scientists exhibit traits of curiosity, creativity, and dedication. They find joy, and take pride, in their discoveries. Educators can nurture these traits in children.

The NAEP study authors also recommend that additional studies be performed on the effects of hands-on work on achievement and on the relationship of amounts of science instruction to students' science learning. They recommend longitudinal studies as a means of investigating these relationships. Mullis and Jenkins point to the need to engage students in more observation of natural phenomena and to engage students in gathering, analyzing, and communicating about data both as a means of strengthening mental processes and as a means of building understanding. They address the need for bringing the "spirit of science" to dull classrooms. Finally, they express the need for better teacher education so that teachers can effectively engage students in relevant, meaningful experiences.

National Science Teachers Association Criteria for Excellence

The National Science Teachers Association (NSTA) began a project called "The Search for Excellence in Science Education" in 1982. Based on criteria developed for rewarding excellent programs, NSTA officials developed *Criteria for Excellence* (1987). This document includes statements about qualities of excellent programs of different levels and science subject matter areas. It addresses criteria for students, curriculum, instruction, and teachers of science in grades K–6. Some of these criteria (which also apply to science instruction for younger children) follow.

In an exemplary science program:

- students
  - acquire effective health habits,
  - recognize people's relationship to the environment,
  - bring varied . . . resources to problem solving;
- curriculum
  - provides planned programs for all students, emphasizing hands-on learning,
  - presents knowledge and experiences that students can apply to their lives now and in the future;
- instruction
  - offers many problem-solving activities applicable to the daily life of students,
  - provides enough materials for all students to conduct experiments,
  - integrates science into other content areas on a regular basis;
- teachers
  - learn new methods and ideas and try them,
  - provide varied experiences with the content, processes, and other dimensions of science,
  - provide experiences from many sources, including the life, physical, and environmental sciences, technology, and current community and societal problems.

Educators may consider these criteria in evaluating existing programs at their own schools or in assessing their own teaching philosophies and performances.

National Research Council

The Committee on Indicators of Precollege Science and Mathematics of the National Research Council developed a report (National Research Council, 1988) on the state of science education in our country. The report's authors drew conclusions and made suggestions for the improvement of science teaching and learning. They based their recommendations on two premises: "All students need the knowledge and reasoning skills that good science and mathematics education provides" (p. 1), and many factors influence teachers and students and determine how much learning takes place.

The committee called for teacher responses to changes in the curriculum and the "use of hands-on experiences involving concrete materials, laboratory experiments, and computers" (National Research Council, 1988, p. 11). The committee drew attention to developing research on the nature of children's learning—how children must actively construct knowledge for themselves through interaction with the environment and through formal and informal teaching. The report highlighted the need for equipment and materials for student investigations and stressed the need for the development of higher level thinking skills.

Research Within Reach

Science educators Penick and Johnson, in *Research Within Reach: Science Education* (Holdzkom & Lutz, no date), presented characteristics of exemplary science programs at the elementary level. The characteristics included devoting more time to science than the national norm; teacher enthusiasm and "ownership" of programs; and teacher development through reading, attending workshops and conferences, and taking courses. Exemplary science programs also "emphasize hands-on science, inquiry strategies, and student decision making" (p. 17).

The authors of *Research Within Reach* also stressed the need for a "well-coordinated science curriculum that balances process skills and content; that provides students with opportunities to identify and solve problems" (Holdzkom & Lutz, p. 18). The authors highlight the role of laboratory work in which students develop "manipulative and observation skills, scientific concepts, positive attitudes, and skills of cooperation and communication" (p. 8).

WHAT ARE SOME METHODS FOR PRESENTING SCIENCE IN MEANINGFUL WAYS TO YOUNG CHILDREN?

Teachers have available many techniques for teaching science to young children. Each method is suitable for different purposes. Following are descriptions of some of these methods.

Exposition

In the expository method, the teacher or some authority presents information to the students without any interaction between the teacher and the children. An example of exposition is a lecture. An exposition technique may be used with a teacher, a textbook, or a film, but the basic purpose is to give out information. Exposition is often used when the teacher wishes to give directions, to present background information, or to summarize a lesson. The expository method can be interspersed with questions to give the teacher feedback on children's understanding of the information being covered. This technique is quite appropriate for review sessions and presentation of new material. For example, as you summarize for the children the different parts of a plant, you might insert questions asking children to name roots, stems, or leaves of plants that we eat. A diagram of the expository method might look like that in Figure 1.1.

Figure 1.2 shows an expository technique interspersed with questions.

Discussion

In the discussion method, children and teachers talk back and forth, but the children talk as much, if not more than the teacher. They interact, not only with the teacher, but also with each other. For example, a tornado has caused considerable damage in the town. Children come to school full of stories related to the damage done by the storm. At different times during the discussion the teacher redirects the discussion with questions related to sights, sounds, and feelings before and after the storm. At another time he asks children about the safety precautions they took during the storm. A diagram of a classroom in which a discussion was occurring might look like Figure 1.3.

The Socratic Method

In the Socratic method, teachers develop children's understanding of a concept by asking questions. These questions are guided in such a way as to solicit the information from the children rather than from the teacher supplying the information. For the Socratic method to be effective, the children need some previous background experience related to the concept. The teacher needs to be aware of the children's background knowledge, and should be ready to adjust questions or plan a back-up activity if the questions do not call forth the appropriate answers. An example of the Socratic method follows. The kindergarten class has come from a visit to the zoo. The teacher asks, "What makes a good pet?" Through guided questions and answers, the children finally arrive at the conclusion that a good pet would be one that is safe and one that you could easily care for. The teacher then asks the children to name zoo animals that

Figure 1.1
The expository method.

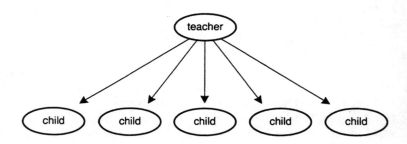

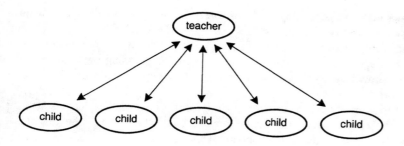

Figure 1.2
An expository technique interspersed with questions.

might be good pets. Barney suggests that a seal would make a good pet. The teacher asks, "Is he safe?" Several of the children reply, "yes." She responds with the question, "But how could you care for it?" For a while the children are silent. They ponder this dilemma. Hui Hui finally adds, "He's too big for your bathtub. Besides, how could you bathe with a seal?" Barney says, "I have a swimming pool. He could live there." "But how are you going to feed it?" adds Urma. Barney seems stumped by this inquiry. After a thoughtful pause he comes up with, "I'll give him fish. My mother can buy fish at the supermarket!" The teacher responds, "Can you afford it? Will it be too expensive?" "No," replies Barney, "we'll be able to feed him." "Then can we say the seal will be a good pet?" asks the teacher. "Yes," the children say in unison. "Is the seal safe?" "Yes." "Can Barney take care of him?" "Yes," they reply. In this example, the teacher used the Socratic method to get children to make an evaluative judgment on what makes good pets.

Demonstration

In the demonstration method, the adult or a child stands before the group and shows how something works. In this method the teacher or the demonstrator is the only one who is actively involved. The others act as observers. There are times when this method can be useful—when the teacher needs to give directions by demonstrating,

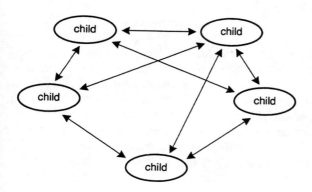

Figure 1.3
The discussion method.

when an experience has the potential to create safety hazards, when the class lacks enough equipment for everyone to be involved, or when the teacher wishes to open a lesson in a motivating or dramatic way. Teachers make use of the demonstration technique when they show children how to clean a carrot by scraping away from the body or when they show how to trap air in a glass by inserting the glass upside down straight into the water.

The demonstration method can be altered to become more of a problem-solving situation in which the teacher does the active work but the children tell the teacher what to do in an effort to solve the problem. This adaptation is called *discovery demonstration*. Discovery demonstration, which is a simplification of J. Richard Suchman's inquiry training model (1966), is a technique that is more suitable for older children.

Guided Discovery

When teachers use the guided discovery method, they allow the children to take the dominant role in the learning process. The children work with materials using the science processes to develop their own knowledge. Teachers guide the children to substantiate their findings by asking questions, but they accept children's final conclusions whether they are scientifically correct or not. The major emphasis here is using the science processes in a hands-on approach to learn information. Guided discovery is an appropriate approach for young children. The teacher may employ the guided discovery method as he arranges the water tray with different objects for the children to determine which objects float or sink. The teacher sets up the problem, but the children are free to solve the problem in their own ways. The teacher may ask questions to help the children form conclusions based on substantial evidence.

Exploration

Before young children can learn effectively from the guided discovery approach they often need time to explore—especially if the materials are new. In exploration, the children are free to experiment with the materials in their own ways. The teacher has no hidden agenda as to what he wishes the children to learn. He doesn't even interrupt them with questions to guide their thinking in a certain direction. The children are free to explore and follow any avenue down which their curiosity might lead them. Children need adequate time for exploration.

Let's look at the water play activity used as an example for guided discovery. The teacher using this method wanted the children to work with the materials to find out which things float and which ones sink. In the guided discovery approach the teacher guided the children's thinking with questions. The exploration method will be quite different. The teacher sets up the water play tray and puts the materials out. He may hope that the children discover certain information as they work with the materials, but he has no assurance. He should not impose his preconceived ideas upon the children. One child may explore ideas about objects that float or sink, another child may experiment with pouring water from one container to another, and another might be intrigued with displacing water by blowing air through a straw. Children may use the materials in many different ways while they are at the water table. They are curious to determine what they can do with the materials and what limitations the materials have. The only fair question in exploration is one that helps the children extend the ideas they are exploring. The teacher may also verbalize what the children are doing to give them a clearer understanding of their actions.

HOW DO WE COORDINATE SCIENCE WITH OTHER AREAS OF THE CURRICULUM?

Perhaps the first question we should ask is, "Should we coordinate science with the other curricular areas, and if we should, how do we do it in a natural way?" First of all we need to remember that none of life is segmented; all parts of life flow and blend together in a very natural way. The same principle is true with science.

When children use the science processes, they must often use their math skills. They sort and classify, they measure and order phenomena in time and space perspectives, and they communicate using mathematical terms. Science becomes math and math becomes science. As they observe interesting aspects of science, they talk to one another and ask questions. They draw pictures and write about their observa-

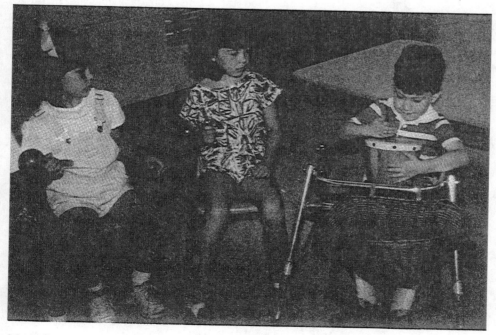

Music time creates a natural opportunity for children to explore sound.

tions. They sing and dramatize to demonstrate the changes they observe in nature. Which of these actions use science processes and which use language skills? They blend together in a very natural way.

Social studies may also become a natural part of children's science investigations. As children work together in small groups on science projects, and as they learn to give up their desires for the good of the entire group, they gain social skills needed for working effectively as citizens in a larger community. When children learn about ways to properly care for their bodies, they often learn about health care workers who help them care for their bodies. As they learn concepts related to social studies, they learn about science.

Science should be coordinated with all of the areas of the curriculum because it does not stand alone. As teachers allow it to blend with other subjects in a natural way, and as they teach science in context with social studies, language arts, and math, learning in the classroom will be meaningful and motivating. Children gain a wider perspective of learning—one which stretches beyond the classroom into all of life.

NOW IT'S YOUR TURN

In this chapter we have presented some background information that we think is necessary for educators as they think about teaching science to young children. After your study of the chapter's contents, you can profit from applying the material, evaluating some of its aspects, and doing further research on your own. "Now It's Your Turn" is intended to encourage you to extend the material in this chapter. Choose two or more of the following options to deepen your knowledge and stretch your mind.

1. Review our discussion of the three interrelated aspects of science—content, process, and attitudes. Observe a child at work on a science activity. Describe the content the child was working with, any science processes (for example, observing, predicting, classifying) the child used, and any attitudes she displayed.

2. To deepen and extend your knowledge of children, observe a child or group of children different from you in terms of socioeconomic status, race, religion, or language used in the home. Note the child's or children's behaviors and the ways educators direct and motivate the child. Discuss your observations with a small group of teachers, reflecting on what you learned and how the things you learned may be of use to you in the future.

3. Review our discussion of learners and the psychological basis for hands-on science. Observe another child working on a science project. Describe characteristics that the child exhibited and relate at least three of those characteristics to the ones we described.

4. Review our discussion of teaching methods for science. Select three different science activities and choose the most appropriate method for each. Make a chart like the following one. Write at least three entries.

Activity Name	Key Words To Describe Method	Advantages	Disadvantages
1. _____	1. _____	1. _____	1. _____
2. _____	2. _____	2. _____	2. _____
3. _____	3. _____	3. _____	3. _____

5. We have asserted that science is easy to integrate with other curriculum areas such as art, music, langue arts, mathematics, and social studies. Choose a science topic that you might teach to young children. Plan ways to integrate activities from at least three other subject areas.

6. We have presented some highlights from the work of Piaget, Bruner, Gagné, and Cohen, Staley, and Horak. We have discussed some implications for the teaching of science. Read more about one of these authorities or choose another authority whose work relates to science teaching. Plan ways to share your findings with your colleagues.

7. In the section entitled "What Is Science?" we asked you to jot down a definition of science. Reread your definition and critique it after completing this chapter. Add to or adapt your definition if you wish. You might wish to keep your definition and refine it even further as you proceed through this book.

8. Some educators advocate identifying and planning to accommodate each child's learning style. Others assert that it is sufficient to provide a variety of learning activities so that children can choose those that best suit their learning styles. Still others advocate providing many multisensory activities to promote children's learning. Read more about learning styles. State and defend your position on providing activities for children's learning styles.

9. Design and complete another activity to enhance your background in teaching science to young children.

REFERENCES

Blackwood, P. E. (1964, September). Science teaching in the elementary school. *Science and Children*, 21–25.

Carbo, M. (1987). Reading styles research: What works isn't always phonics. *Phi Delta Kappan, 68*(6), 431–435.

Chafel, J. A. (1990). Needed: A legislative agenda for children at risk. *Childhood Education, 66*(4), 241–242.

Children's Defense Fund. (1990). *Children, 1990: A report card, briefing book, and action primer* (pp. 3–4). Washington, DC: National Association for the Education of Young Children.

Chittenden, E. A. (1969). What is learned and what is taught. *Young Children, 25*(1), 12–20.

Cohen, H. G., Staley, F. A., & Horak, W. J. (1989). *Teaching science as a decision making process* (2nd ed.). Dubuque, IA: Kendall/Hunt.

Committee for Economic Development. (1987). *Children in need: Investment strategies for the educationally disadvantaged.* New York: Committee for Economic Development.

Duckett, W. (1988). An interview with Harold Hodgkinson: Using demographic data for long-range planning. *Phi Delta Kappan, 69*(3), 166–170.

Holdzkom, D., & Lutz, P. B. (no date). *Research within reach: Science education.* Washington, DC: National Science Teachers Association.

Jacobsen, W. J., & Bergman, A. B. (1987). *Science for children: A book for teachers.* Englewood Cliffs, NJ: Prentice-Hall Inc.

Katz, L. G., & Chard, S. C. (1989). *Engaging children's minds: The process approach.* Norwood, NJ: Ablex.

Mullis, I. V. S., & Jenkins, L. B. (1988). *The science report card: Elements of risk and recovery: Trends and achievement based on the 1986 national assessment.* Princeton, NJ: Educational Testing Service.

National Research Council. (1988). *Improving indicators of the quality of science and mathematics education in grades K–12.* Washington, DC: National Academy Press.

National Science Teachers Association. (1987). *Criteria for excellence.* Washington, DC: Author.

Shaw, J. M., Cliatt, M. J. P., Emerson, P., Leigh, L. M., & Perry, J. (1990). *Continuity of learning for four- to seven-year-old children: A position statement.* Little Rock, AR: Southern Association of Children Under Six.

Suchman, J. R. (1966). *Putting inquiry into science: Learning inquiry development program.* Chicago: Science Research Associates.

Wolfinger, D. M. (1984). *Teaching science in the elementary school: Content, process, and attitude.* Boston: Little, Brown.

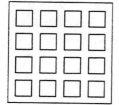

Chapter 2

Science Processes for Young Children: Ways of Exploring, Ways of Learning

A S you think about science for young children, what ideas come to your mind? Do you picture young children growing plants, working with magnets, or learning about different factors that cause rain to fall? Science *is* a body of knowledge. Young children can successfully begin to explore themes and content from the biological sciences, earth and space sciences, and physical sciences. Science, however, is more— it is investigating, wondering, questioning, and finding out. As young children (and adult scientists, too) work in science, they constantly use *science processes* to help them explore and learn.

In this chapter, we will develop and extend your understanding of the following science processes:

- Observing,
- Measuring and using numbers,
- Communicating,
- Ordering,
- Classifying,
- Predicting,
- Inferring,
- Using time and space relationships.

Getting young children to use science processes is important. Young children can use these processes every day. They can use them in science activities, in other school situations, and at home. Use of the processes contributes to young children's intellectual growth. The processes can make children more aware of their surroundings and can sustain and enhance curiosity, a powerful motivator for learning. Attention to science processes also balances a science program for young children. Such attention emphasizes *how* material is learned as well as *what* is to be learned. Awareness of process also promotes an appropriate, "hands-on, minds-on" approach to teaching science. Such an approach is sometimes missing when educators think of science only as content—a body of facts to be learned. In the following sections, we will describe and illustrate each science process, discuss its importance, and then provide examples of experiences in which young children can use each process.

OBSERVING

Observing is *gaining information through the senses*. People often use the sense of sight to observe, but observing often requires more than a casual glance. It requires a careful, thoughtful look at phenomena. The other senses are used in observing, too. Hearing can help us determine whether an unseen child in the hall is running or walking. Often we make observations about "what's cookin' " by using the sense of smell alone. Some people admire a velvet dress by looking at it; others are compelled to extend their observations using their sense of touch. Taste can help us observe whether a "white grainy substance" in the kitchen is salt or sugar. Often people use several senses or all five as they observe.

Observation provides us with *firsthand, direct knowledge*. Reading about a science topic is a valuable way to learn, but it is not observation. Reading can introduce or extend observation.

Observation may be *qualitative* or *quantitative*. *Qualitative* observations deal with the qualities or characteristics of objects and phenomena. Qualitative observations may include noticing color, texture, odor, shape, size, or sound. Qualitative observations may be referenced or compared. For example, children may observe that a rock has a smooth surface, but that the surface is not as smooth as window glass. We might remark that January weather is cold—even colder than December's. *Quantitative* observations include some type of measures or numbers. Children may have gathered lots of rocks; counting the rocks and seeing that there are nineteen quantifies the observation. We might picture the relationship between two children's heights if we know that Malika is taller than John. If we quantify the situation—Malika is about 110 cm (43 inches) tall while John is just 80 cm (32 inches)—the picture of the relationship may be even clearer.

Finally, observations may include *acting on objects*. Children may manipulate objects or test the effects of action on the objects. Children may see that a sample of dirt seems crumbly; they can rub their fingers in the dirt to see if it actually crumbles. They may smell a rock and detect only a slight odor; but after acting on the rock by wetting it, they may notice a stronger, more distinctive, musty odor.

Where appropriate, children should be encouraged to act on objects. Adults will need to provide guidance, however, to be sure that acting on objects is appropriate and safe. For example, the children may gently pet a classroom animal, but should not

This child is using his observational skills. He looks at and feels inside the crayfish hole.

act on its fur with scissors! They may observe newly mown grass with many senses but should not act on the grass by rubbing it into their clothes or eyes.

Children will need guidance and practice if they are to become skillful observers. Adults should guide children as they observe, encouraging them to use all the aspects of good observation—using the *senses*, gaining knowledge *firsthand*, making both *qualitative* and *quantitative* observations, and *acting on objects*.

It is important for educators to help children extend their observation abilities. Observation is used every day, everywhere. Observation is one of the primary ways that children learn. Observation also conveys to children the ideas "I can learn independently. My own observations supplement what I can learn from others and from pictures and books."

Opportunities for meaningful observations abound. Following are some examples of situations with rich potential for observation.

Observing Leaves

Leaves have many characteristics that make them easy to observe. They are readily available in most places. They have such varied properties. To encourage children to observe, let them go for a walk and collect a variety of leaves. Encourage children to *look* at the leaves and notice different aspects such as colors, sizes, shapes, edges, and veins. Ask them to *feel* the edges of leaves, the surface texture, and the vein patterns. Children might want to observe by *smelling* fresh leaves. Help them crumble a few fresh leaves to see if the odor is more evident. Ask children to suggest a few ways they might observe leaves by *listening*. They might drop leaves or crush dry leaves and notice the sounds. Choose some edible leaves such as spinach, lettuce, and parsley for using the sense of *taste*. Children can compare the way these leaves taste when cooked or eaten raw. They can also describe the textures they feel with their tongues.

As the children use their different senses and describe the leaves, they will be using *qualitative* references. Encourage them to observe leaves in *quantitative* ways. Also, you may ask questions such as "How many lobes does this leaf have? How many different leaves can you find with hairy surfaces? Measure the span of these leaves. How does it compare with the length?"

Children can make many good observations by *acting on* leaves. They might determine whether leaves will float or sink. They could drop water on various leaves to find out how different surfaces respond to the water. They could watch leaves being burned and notice that leaves react differently to fire. Some leaves will crackle. Some will disintegrate quickly. Other leaves will emit different odors as they burn.

☐ ☐ ☐   Observing the Properties of Water

Water has an instant appeal to most children. One of its appeals is that it captivates all of our senses. Set up a water tray area, and see how many ways you can entice your children to use their senses. What better way to learn about water than through *firsthand, direct knowledge*. Applying the sense of *sight,* children can stir the water and observe the circular movement. They can make waves or observe the water's surface when it is smooth and placid. Children can pour water through containers and materials such as sieves, funnels, and loosely woven cloth to see the different effects.

To capture the sense of *hearing,* encourage children to find how many different sounds they can make with the water—slow drips, fast drips, stirring sounds, pouring sounds, different sounds made by objects dropped in the water, and sounds made when the water is slapped.

Provide bowls of water with varying temperatures. Let children *feel* and talk about the difference in hot, warm, cool, and cold water. They might wish to arrange the bowls of water from hot to cold. Children will enjoy feeling the force of water as it is poured from different heights. Remember that we can feel with several different parts of our bodies—elbows, feet, cheeks, as well as hands. On a rainy day children can feel even rain dripping on their tongues. Rain also offers an opportunity for children to use their sense of *smell.* Encourage children to smell the rain and describe what they smell.

To help children observe the *taste* of water, make different solutions with water—a mild salt solution, a mild sugar solution, lemon water, and plain water. Allow children to take a sip of each liquid, describe the taste, and identify which liquid is plain water. In this case the liquids look the same; only their sense of taste can help children find the plain water.

Provide different-size containers into which children can pour water. Let children find out how many small containers of water it will take to fill a designated large container. As children measure the water, they are using *quantitative* terms. As they pour water into different containers and do various other experiments they are *acting on* the water to find out more about its properties.

USING NUMBERS AND MEASUREMENTS

Young children can *use numbers* in many ways as they work in science. Opportunities for counting are abundant. For example, children might find sixteen large shells and twelve smaller shells in the classroom shell collection. They might cut two carrots into eight pieces to feed to a rabbit. As children keep track of the growth of plants over a period of time, they may use numbers for dates and for the measurements of the leaves of the plants.

Often *graphs* can be used to help children organize and report data from science situations. For example, second- and third-grade children could fill in a predrawn thermometer picture (Figure 2.1) as the teacher helps them read and report the temperature each morning. Younger children could make a graph of weather predictions, pinning on clothespins to show what they think will happen (Figure 2.2).

Once graphs are made, the children should interpret them. The teacher might ask

How many jelly beans of each color are there? Using a graph helps us find out.

Figure 2.1
Temperature graph.

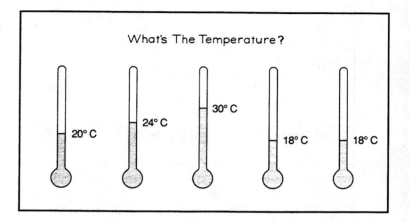

different children to talk about the graph, then fill in with questions addressing points the children did not deal with. On the clothespin graph, the teacher can guide the children to count the predictions in each category, compare the numbers, and decide how many children marked the graph in all.

Using numbers and measurements is an inherent part of making *quantitative observations*. Measurements may be nonstandard or standard. The teacher could help

Figure 2.2
Rain prediction graph.

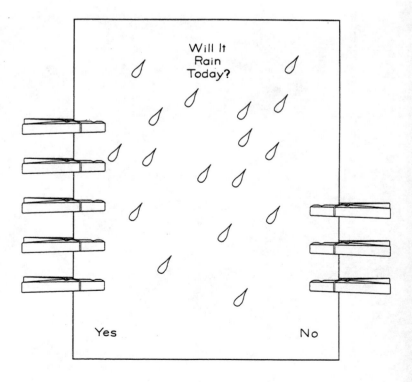

the children measure the length and width of a desktop in "hand widths" or in centimeters. The volume of a washtub may be measured in "jarfuls" or in liters. To determine the weight of a pine cone, the children might use a balance scale and express the weight in "crayons" or in grams.

As children investigate in science, math skills are applied and reinforced in natural, meaningful ways. Using numbers and measurements in science helps children communicate in clear, precise terms. Measurements and numbers skills, developed in science activities, lay a foundation that children will use through their entire schooling in science. Use of numbers and measurements is highlighted in the following activities.

Classroom Inventory

Practice counting and comparing with this easy activity. Let the children "take inventory" of objects in the classroom. You might divide the class into teams to investigate different aspects. One team might count floor tiles, another could count wooden objects, another could "inventory" window panes, and a fourth team could count books. Show each team how to make tally marks as they count. Children could use improvised clip boards for their inventory (Figure 2.3). Discuss how they might count in a systematic way so the children know what has already been counted and what is yet to be inventoried. When the inventories are complete, children can write their data on the chalkboard, compare numbers, and perhaps find the total of all the objects that were inventoried.

Balancing Act

To encourage children to gain experience in using a balance scale, let them see how placing heavy objects in a balance pan causes the pan to lower, while removing objects causes the pan to rise again. Let the children choose two objects, one of which is obviously heavier than the other. They should place one object—perhaps a shoe—on one pan of the scale and the other—perhaps a bracelet—on the other pan and observe what happens to the pans. Guide the children to switch the objects in the pans and see what happens.

Now use small paper cups filled with ingredients such as water, sand, paper bits, rocks, and styrofoam pieces. Let the children help you decide on other ingredients that might be used. Help the children make predictions for pairs of objects—perhaps the cup of sand will be heavier than the cup of water. Now test the predictions using the balance scale. Record your predictions and results on a chart.

COMMUNICATING

Communication is an essential skill because it is people's means of relating to others. People communicate with others often and in many different ways. Communication is a two-way process. It involves sending information and receiving it, too. *Spoken words,*

Figure 2.3
Inventory clip board.

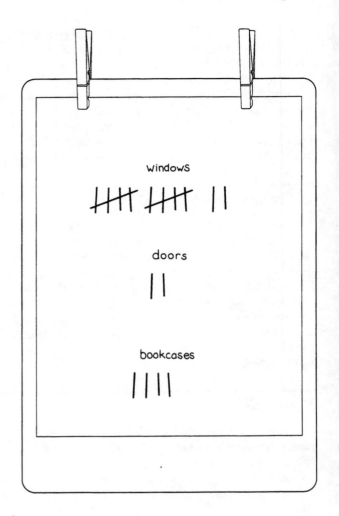

facial expressions, and gestures communicate our thoughts and feelings to others. People listen to what others say and interpret the gestures that others make.

Other communication forms include drawing and interpreting *pictures* and *diagrams*, making and reading *maps*, and creating and using *graphs*. All these forms help us symbolize ideas and relationships. *Written words* are another important symbolic communication form. Children refine their communication skills as they encounter stimulating experiences and as they express their feelings about experiences. Even children with limited English language ability are motivated to express themselves when they participate in appropriate science activities. When educators present meaningful science experiences and encourage children to use communication during and after their experiences, they help children build a rich vocabulary and conceptual base.

Communication and involvement in science are inseparable. The following descriptions of activities will help you see the potential for communication as an integral part of science activities.

Pet Projects

□ □ □

To help children learn to make graphs, let them draw pictures or bring photos of their favorite pets and put the pictures on a graph. Let children talk about the different pets they have at home. Then help them make a graph showing how many pets they have at home (Figure 2.4).

Bring a picture of an unusual pet. Encourage children to talk about the animal. Have them describe its different features, compare it to other animals, suggest ways to care for it, and tell why it might or might not make a good pet for them. Make an experience chart of the children's responses, or let children write their own responses after the discussion.

Mapping a Walk

□ □ □

Maps help us communicate what we observe. To help children learn how to draw a simple map, let them begin by making a group map of a walk that the class has taken. As the children walk, point out interesting sights and ask questions to help children

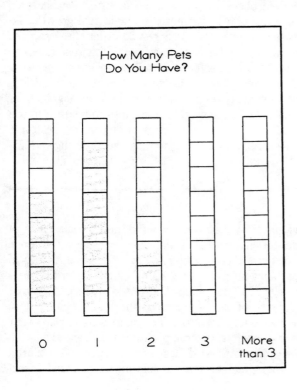

Figure 2.4
Graph of pets.

carefully notice things around them. Collect objects along the way. When you return to the classroom, discuss with the children the different phenomena you saw at various points on your walk. Show and talk about the different objects they collected. Help children make a map of their walk by telling what they saw in the order they saw it. Glue real objects from their collections on the map. In some places on the map children will want to draw a picture to show what they saw.

ORDERING

Ordering is *arranging, seriating, or grading objects along a continuum* on the basis of some characteristic of the objects. Ordering should be done considering many different characteristics. Children might test five magnets to see how many paperclips each will pick up. The magnets could be arranged according to their magnetic power—from strongest to weakest. They might arrange a collection of fresh vegetables in order from darkest to lightest colors. The students could also use a tape measure to measure around the widest part of each vegetable, then arrange the vegetables in order, from the one with the smallest circumference (girth) to the largest circumference. Other bases for ordering include height, weight, temperature, number, or time.

Learning to order things is important because it is one of several ways by which people organize the environment. References to ordering occur often in children's everyday lives. Practice in ordering contributes to children's intellectual growth. To promote flexible thinking, teachers should encourage children to order the same set of objects in many ways. After ordering vegetables on the basis of their circumference, for example, the children might order them from shiniest to dullest, tallest to shortest, or lightest to heaviest. After children have shown that they can order with facility, teachers might add another stage of complexity. For instance, once an arrangement is made, the teacher can introduce another object and ask the children to insert it in the appropriate place in the existing order. Ordering can often be a part of children's science experiences. The following activities describe ways to use ordering, an important science process.

☐ ☐ ☐ Ordering People

Children are interested in their own physical characteristics and the characteristics of others. This activity uses many different characteristics as bases for ordering. Choose five or six children. Let the others observe the children and suggest different ways to arrange them in order. They will probably suggest ordering by height or by length of hair. Let the children arrange themselves in order according to the characteristic that is suggested. You might also use lengths of feet (longest to shortest) or number of siblings (fewest to most siblings) as bases for ordering. The children could also order themselves according to the number of objects in their pockets. Children might also rearrange themselves in alphabetical order by first or last names. After the children have ordered themselves, ask another child or two to join the group and insert themselves in the right order. You might also let a small group secretly decide on a basis for ordering. Then let them arrange themselves and let the others guess how they are ordered.

Ramp Race

To help children practice ordering, let them have a ramp race with their Match Box cars. Remind children a day ahead to bring their cars for the race. Make a ramp out of a flat board braced with a shoebox. Let children take turns rolling their cars off the ramp and then measuring with a long piece of colored yarn how far their cars rolled. Let children cut yarn the length of each roll and tape the different lengths of yarn on a long piece of paper to make a graphlike form (Figure 2.5). Discuss with the children which cars rolled the farthest and the shortest distance, or if any cars went the same distance. Second and third graders will be able to measure the distance of their rolls with a centimeter tape. For variation, raise the height of the ramp and compare the lengths of the rolls with the heights of the ramp.

CLASSIFYING

Classifying is *making groupings* on the basis of observable characteristics or attributes. Children should classify objects using many different bases for grouping. They can group objects by color, size, shape, texture, magnetic attraction, weight, solubility, or

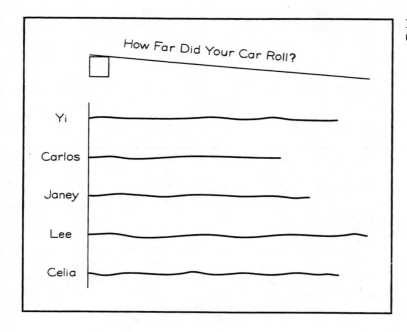

Figure 2.5
Graph for practicing ordering.

other characteristics. Because sets of objects can be grouped many different ways, educators should also ask children to classify the same set of objects one way, then another way. For example, children might collect trash during a walk around the block. (Make sure your trash is clean and safe.) After examining the collected trash, they might place it in categories—trash made of metal, plastic, and paper. After grouping trash by the material of which it is made, the children might "reshuffle" the trash and classify it in other ways—trash that is broken or whole, trash that is crumpled or not, or trash that is recyclable in the classroom or not.

Once classifications are made, older children will also be able to make some subclassifications or subgroups. In classifying a set of animal pictures, children might make two groups—animals with legs and animals without legs. They might next make subgroups, judging whether the animals in the pictures are wild or tame. The children can then notice that they have actually made four sets—wild animals with legs, wild animals without legs, tame animals with legs, and tame animals without legs.

Experience with classifying helps children develop and refine concepts. Classifying is essential for both basic and advanced work in science. Educators can take advantage of children's natural interest in classifying using activities such as those in the following section.

☐ ☐ ☐ Conductors and Nonconductors

Children can sort objects as to whether the objects conduct electricity or not. Make a little conducting board by hammering two nails partway into a piece of board or block (Figure 2.6). Place the nails about 2 cm apart. Attach wires to a dry cell and small light bulb and socket. Connect the wires to the nails in the conducting board as shown. The light bulb will not light because the electric circuit is incomplete. Gather a variety of small objects made of wood, paper, cloth, plastic, metal, and other substances. Have the children test each object by pressing it firmly to the nail tops. If the object conducts electricity, the circuit will be completed; the bulb will light. If the object is a nonconductor (or insulator), the bulb will not light. After testing each object the children can place the object into boxes labeled "objects that conduct electricity" and "objects that don't conduct electricity."

☐ ☐ ☐ Rock Groups

Encourage children to make a big collection of rocks. Show them how to classify rocks by different attributes—smooth/rough, big/medium/small, light/dark, shiny/dull, and so on. After children have practiced grouping in a variety of ways, show them how to make subgroups. For instance, make a chart using a big sheet of paper. Put the rocks in the center. Next, let the children classify the rocks in groups based on size—small, medium, or large. They can move the rocks to the appropriate places labeled on the chart. Make subgroups and move the rocks to the places where they belong: small rocks that are rough and small rocks that are smooth; medium-size rocks that are rough and medium-size, smooth rocks; large, rough rocks and large, smooth rocks.

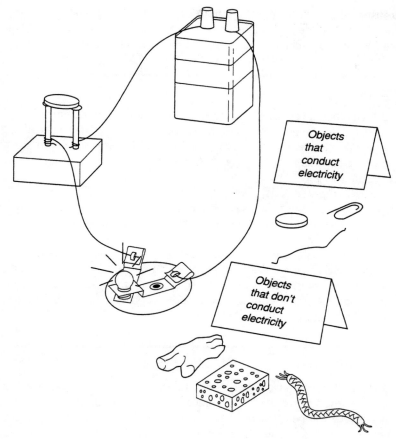

Figure 2.6
Experiment with conductors and nonconductors.

Objects that conduct electricity

Objects that don't conduct electricity

PREDICTING

Predicting is an important science process. Both scientists and nonscientists predict outcomes and events as a part of everyday life and in their jobs. People predict the weather and also pay attention to others who predict it. We predict how long events or chores will take as we go about our daily schedules. We predict others' reactions to situations or try to foretell consequences of our actions.

Predicting is *deciding in advance what we think will happen* in a given situation. People make predictions based on past experience and based on authority. For example, we have experienced the fact that it usually rains when there are dark, heavy clouds and high winds. When we see these phenomena, we expect rain. Perhaps we read on a seed package that the seeds need direct sunlight and heavy watering. We plant the seeds in a sunny spot and water them daily. Based on the seed company's "authority," we predict that the seeds will grow if given proper care.

Science offers many opportunities for children to predict. Children's interest in events is often aroused when educators ask them to predict in advance and when they allow children time to check their predictions. Activities such as the samples that follow can be used to encourage children to predict and check predictions.

☐ ☐ ☐ Weather Predictions

Make predicting the weather a regular part of classroom routine. At the end of each school day, for example, you might ask children to predict the next day's weather. Every Friday, you could ask children to predict the weekend weather, record their predictions, and then check them on Monday. Children can take turns acting as the class weather predictor.

As you make weather predictions, focus on different aspects: Will tomorrow's weather be warmer, cooler, or about the same as today's weather? Will it snow before Monday? Will our state have a tornado? What might the wind be like tonight?

Help children record predictions in various ways. You can mark weather predictions and actual weather outcomes on a large classroom calendar. You might use a clothespin graph to quickly let each child make a prediction. You could tally or record predictions on the chalkboard and then check the predictions at a later time. Be sure to allow time—it only takes a minute or two—to follow up on predictions and to let chldren tell why they are making their predictions.

☐ ☐ ☐ Predicting with Magnets

Using magnets can be a good way for children to practice their predicting skills. Gather objects made from a variety of materials. Let each child choose an object, predict whether or not that object will be attracted to a magnet, and place that object under the correct heading on a chart according to his prediction. Then let the child test the object with a magnet to see if his prediction was correct. If the prediction was incorrect, place a paper "X" over the object. Continue with each child—predicting, testing, and evaluating his or her prediction—until each object has been placed on the chart. After the objects have all been tested, let the children rearrange the objects and place them on the chart based on whether the objects actually were attracted to the magnet or not.

INFERRING

Inferring involves *making conclusions or generalizations* based on observations or experiences. Inferring involves thinking and reasoning rather than firsthand knowledge. A person may awaken at her regular time, but after noting that the room is unusually dark, infer that the weather outside is uncommonly cloudy. She may smell coffee and infer that her spouse is busy in the kitchen.

Suppose that pairs of second graders plant seeds and place some on a sunny windowsill and some in the closet. After a week, the children observe that the plants that received sun are tall and green, whereas the ones kept in the closet are limp and yellow. They may infer that sunlight helped the plants grow into healthy specimens, whereas lack of sun depressed the growth of some of the plants.

Prediction can often *precede* science experiences. Time to infer should *follow* science experiences. Teachers can help young children infer by asking them questions such as, "What did we learn from this? What conclusions can we make? What does this evidence tell us?" Inferring is important because it helps to conclude or "tie up" science experiences. It helps children go one step beyond "what happened," to "what did this mean."

Conscious attention to inferring heightens children's ability to use it. Activities such as those that follow highlight inferring as an important science process.

What's in the Box?   □ □ □

Children enjoy guessing games. With a little help from their senses, they can learn to make inferences or conclusions based on reasoning. Decorate a box. Put a "surprise" inside the box. Let children shake the box and listen to the sound, reach in and feel the "surprise" object without looking, or even smell to determine if it has an odor. You may wish to give some verbal clues about the object. Then encourage each of the children to make inferences about what is in the box based on the clues they have. Use the surprise box often. Let children bring objects to place in the box. Encourage them to think of a few clues to give their classmates.

Bone Detectives   □ □ □

Guide children to carefully observe the characteristics of bones and make inferences about those bones based on the evidence they observe. Collect several different types of bones. Let children number each bone to identify it. Then encourage them to carefully study each bone, making qualitative and quantitative observations. For instance, one bone might be very large, bleached, and brittle. Your young detectives might infer that this is an old bone that belonged to a cow or other large animal. Upon observing another small, flexible, Y-shaped bone, children might infer that it is the "wishbone" from a chicken that has just been eaten.

USING TIME AND SPACE RELATIONSHIPS

Awareness of time and space relationships is one of the foundations for learning in young children. Children learn concepts such as top, bottom, in, out, before, after, and now over a period of time. Learning is enhanced through meaningful experiences and conversations about those experiences.

As they work in science, people use many time and space relationships. Some changes occur in short *time periods,* others take days, weeks, months, or years to become apparent. Young children are beginning to refine their understanding of time. In the early childhood years, children grow dramatically in their abilities to comprehend and use time-oriented terms such as before and after. They learn to use clocks, calendars, and other devices that measure time. Science offers many different ways to extend and support their understanding in meaningful contexts. Children can watch with pride as a guinea pig, their classroom pet, grows large and healthy over a period of several months. On a hot day, children can watch an ice cube melt in a matter of minutes. Educators can help children appreciate how each has grown over the years by looking at baby pictures and toddler clothes and discussing the capabilities that children attain as they grow older.

Space relationships involve attention to *shape, relative position, movement,* and *symmetry.* As children examine seashells, many spatial concepts may be highlighted. Shells have several different shapes—oblong, circular, and spiral. Shells have outsides and insides that may be different colors and textures. Shells can be moved closer to or farther from each other; children may have found shells buried deep in the sand or close to the surface. Viewed from different angles, some shells are symmetrical; they are the same on both sides of an imaginary line. Other shells lack symmetry.

Appropriately planned science experiences can do much to enhance children's understanding of time and space relationships. The following examples will illustrate some uses of time and spatial relationships in intriguing activities.

Subtle Changes, Dramatic Changes

Draw children's attention to the many changes in the branches of a deciduous tree with this long-term activity. Choose a branch of a deciduous tree that is close to your classroom door or window. Mark the branch with a tied-on piece of yarn or ribbon. Starting in the fall, make regular observations of your branch, noting the number, size, positions, and colors of its leaves and textures of its bark. Encourage the children to draw and write about what they observe. Write dates on your observations. As the year progresses, make regular observations—perhaps every two weeks. Add other observations as the children suggest them or after unusual events such as the first frost or a heavy rainstorm. You and the children will notice both subtle and dramatic changes in the branch—from green to colored leaves, from leafy to bare branches, from buds to leaves. Discuss with the children the fact that what they have observed is part of a continuing yearly cycle of growth and change.

Evaporation Comparisons

Compare rates of evaporation and ways that liquids evaporate under different conditions. Pose different questions for children to investigate. For instance, will a circle of water evaporate faster on the counter or the chalkboard, or will the rate be approximately the same? Will water evaporate faster in a shady spot or a sunny spot? Will the water from a smooth, dampened paper towel evaporate faster than from a crumpled, dampened paper towel? Will a spot of water evaporate at the same rate as a spot of rubbing alcohol? Will a spot of water evaporate faster when it is fanned? Have the children plan what they will do to answer their questions, then proceed. While the children wait for evaporation to occur, draw their attention to measuring time, describing the shape and sizes of the "wet spots" they use, and describing the dry areas as they appear. Guide the children to make conclusions about what they have learned. See if the children can apply the information to everyday life. For example, "Flat towels dry faster than crumpled ones. That's why Mom asked me to hang up my wet towels." "It was hotter in the sunny spot. The water evaporated faster—that's like our dryer at home. The heat helps the clothes get dry."

FINAL THOUGHTS

In this chapter, we have discussed eight science processes for young children: observing, measuring and using numbers, communicating, ordering, classifying, predicting, inferring, and using time and space relationships. We have defined and discussed each process and have given examples of how children can use each process as they work in science.

Using science processes is an important part of working in science. These processes help people—both children and adults—to learn and to communicate with others what they have learned. Growth in ability to use the processes is developmental; that is, it grows over time. Second graders are more sophisticated than kindergarteners as they become engaged in the science processes such as observing or inferring, but both need guidance and practice if they are to enhance their abilities.

Almost any science experience is rich in potential for using several processes. When educators are oriented toward these processes, they see science as more than a body of facts. Science becomes an opportunity for children to practice learning how to learn.

NOW IT'S YOUR TURN

Now it's your turn to practice. Use the exercises in this section to help you internalize and apply the information from this important chapter on science processes. By working through these exercises—or similar ones you might create for yourself—you will understand the material more clearly.

1. Review the various aspects of making good, thorough observations. Think about how using measurements and numbers can increase the specificity of observations. Now choose something you could observe as you go about your regular schedule. Carry out an observation using all the aspects of observing. Use numbers and measurements as you observe.

2. Think about the many possible forms that communication can take in science. Choose a science topic that you will be teaching (or could teach) in the near future.

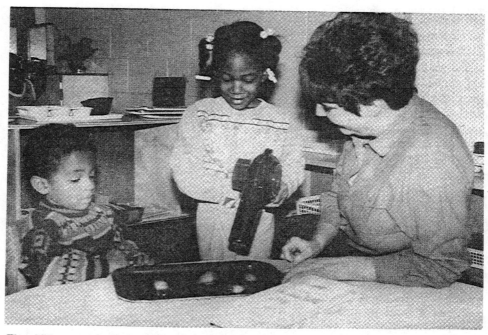

The children watch the ice cubes change shape as they melt. They can also determine how long it takes the ice cubes to melt.

Decide how you could have the children use at least four communication forms as they explore the topic.

3. Ordering and classifying are closely related, yet very different processes. Find some objects that you can both order and classify. For instance, you might find some unusual objects if you clean out your desk drawer or a kitchen cabinet. Order these objects along some continuum. Now take the same objects and classify them using a predetermined attribute. Be imaginative in your selection of objects and the way you organize them.

4. Predictions are made before an observation or experiment. Inferences are made afterward. Choose an observation or experiment you could carry out by yourself, on an adult level, or with children. Make and record at least one prediction. Write down the steps in your observation or experiment. Record at least one inference. Comment on how predicting and inferring enhanced the experience for you or for the children you teach.

5. Choose something in your everyday life and make some time and/or space observations. If your observation is time oriented, communicate your observations using a time line. If you focus on spatial relationships, draw a picture to show your findings. For observations that are both time and spatially oriented, find a creative way that clearly communicates your observations. Share your results with a friend.

6. Skim through an issue of *Science and Children*, the National Science Teachers Association's journal for teachers of preschool through middle-school children. Find an article that describes a science activity or series of activities. The "Early Childhood" column of *Science and Children* may be of special interest to you. See if the activity mentions using science processes and how the processes are used. Try to extend the use of processes that are described or think about the activity and how you could use additional science processes as you involve young children in the activity.

7. Choose at least four science processes that are described in this chapter. Plan a science activity in which you could involve your children using all the processes you chose.

8. "Why are science processes important? Isn't attention to basic facts and concepts in science enough for young children?" Suppose a parent of one of your students asked you these questions. Develop an answer.

9. Working with science processes can be a motivating experience. Suppose you have a child who has difficulty interacting with other children. Observe that child closely. Based upon your observations, plan a small-group science process activity that would encourage this child to participate with the group.

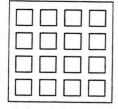

Chapter 3

Questioning and Evaluation in Science

THIS chapter includes material on two interrelated and vital parts of teaching science to young children. In the first part of the chapter, we will discuss effective questions and their uses in promoting science learning. In relation to questioning techniques, we will present ideas concerning Bloom's taxonomy and Rowe's wait time theory—both techniques used to encourage quality thinking (Bloom, 1956; Rowe, 1973). We will also suggest some guides for asking thought-provoking questions in the classroom. In the second part of the chapter, we will focus on evaluating children's progress in various aspects of science and on evaluating teacher effectiveness.

QUESTIONING TO PROMOTE SCIENCE LEARNING

Questions are a very important part of our lives. We use questions and answers to interact with one another. In the classroom, teachers consider questions to be a traditional and large part of their teaching responsibility. They use questions to stimulate thinking, to encourage children to express their ideas, and to get immediate feedback on chidren's understanding.

Questions vary widely in quality. Some questions lead us into dead ends, while others initiate high levels of thinking and wide varieties of interaction. Good questioning strategies need careful attention. The purpose of the first part of this chapter is to help you understand different aspects of questions. We will discuss the many ways educators can use questions in the classroom. Next, we will explore two distinctly different types of questions: divergent thinking questions and convergent thinking questions. Since Bloom's taxonomy provides a major framework for understanding the different levels of thinking, we will discuss different levels of questions in relation to Bloom's taxonomy. Next, we will review Rowe's wait time theory. Finally, we will suggest some guides for improving questioning techniques.

Different Purposes of Questions

We have many different reasons for asking questions. Sometimes we just want to get a listener involved. At other times we want to attract the listener's attention and set the focus for our topic. Questions help us understand what the listener already knows and what he or she is thinking. Some questions help us guide children's observations and investigations, whereas others are used for review and testing. Many times we use questions to promote interaction among children or to offer opportunities for children to share their personal experiences. There are many different purposes for asking questions—many more than those mentioned here. It is important for us to know the purpose behind each question. If we are aware of our purposes, our questions are more clearly defined and to the point. We are more likely to accomplish our goals.

Questions often *stimulate involvement*. Sometimes we adults do all of the talking. However, if we could share the limelight with our audience—if we could get children involved—we could enhance the learning situation for them. Children would be more interested and motivated. Good questions often call for a response from the listener. Involvement questions invite passive listeners to become active participants. Let's look at two different questioning techniques that stimulate listener involvement. Sometimes we ask questions of strangers to get an initial response and to get them involved in a conversation. For example, we ask, "Have you lived in this city long? Where are you from?" Questions like these can open the door to a conversation with many possibilities. In the classroom, our involvement questions are similar in nature but more focused on our subject matter. "Do you like rainy days or sunny days? What can you do on rainy days that you can't do on sunny days?" These questions are related to a particular topic rather than a person, yet they invite the listener to become an active participant in the discussion.

Questions help *set the focus* for a topic. They draw children's attention to a central theme. Focusing questions will help children to understand the purpose of the discussion. When purposes or goals are clearly set, they are more easily obtainable. By asking a focusing question such as "After reading about frogs, can you describe any unusual features they have to help them catch bugs?" we help children concentrate on one particular issue and weed out extraneous information. Often we ask focusing questions to generate interest. When we ask questions such as "How many of you have ever been frightened in a storm?" we are likely to get many eager responses. Often we can change the flow of thought and redirect it into another category by asking simple questions such as "When the tornado passed over, what sounds did you hear? How was it different from a normal day?" In these questions, we are moving the focus from the storms in general to tornadoes.

Questions help us *determine what children actually know*. When a patient visits a doctor, the doctor must ask many questions about the patient's symptoms in order to pinpoint and finally diagnose the problem. Teachers also must ask many questions to determine the depth of their students' understanding. Questions may be asked at the beginning of a course of study, or they may be used at the end of a lesson to determine how much the children have comprehended. Sometimes a few questions let us know if we need to step back and start at a simpler level. At other times our questions help us realize that children already fully understand a concept and that we need to move on to something more complex. For instance, in studying digestion, suppose we ask the question, "What happens to food as it enters our bodies?" By the children's responses, and in some cases by their lack of responses, we may realize that the question is inappropriate for their level of understanding. We change to a simpler level of questioning such as, "As food enters our bodies, how do our teeth help us? Does the saliva in our mouths make food easier to digest? How? After food is chewed, tell me where it goes next." If we find, by our initial question, that children already understand the concept of digestion, we move quickly to a higher level of questioning, such as, "How do our bodies use food? What part do the intestines play?" Adults must listen sensitively to children's answers and be flexible enough to change directions if their answers suggest a need for change.

We often use questions to *guide children's observations and investigations* and to lead them from lower-level responses to more complex levels. In guiding children's observations, we begin with very simple, open-ended questions—questions that encourage many responses. Our beginning questions will set the focus of the discussion. We might begin a study of levers with a question such as, "How do machines help us in life?" This question has many possible answers. Our next question should guide students to use a higher level of thinking as they investigate. Suppose we show the children a broom and a nutcracker. We say, "Look at these two levers. How are they alike in the ways they work? How are they different?" Throughout our study we give students many different levers to work with—scissors, hammers, seesaws. After students have observed various aspects of the levers, we lead them into another level of thinking about their observations. We ask them to make generalizations and draw conclusions based on their observations with a question such as, "What have you learned about levers from your investigations?" In this questioning sequence, we have drawn children's attention to the topic, we have encouraged them to closely observe, and finally, we have asked them to make some conclusions about their observations.

Remember that questions can also help serve as a *review*. The questions we ask can help children organize the information to which they have been exposed, pull out the main points, and summarize what they have learned. As mentioned earlier, a carefully worded question can help children form conclusions or make inferences— educated leaps from the known to the unknown. Review questions help children determine what they understand clearly and what they have yet to learn.

We also use questions to *promote interactions*. Children clarify their concepts through give-and-take interactions. Not only are interactions between teachers and children important, but interactions among children are also vital. Often children can gain a better understanding when a peer talks about a concept than when an adult explains it. Questions that promote teacher-child interaction are generally fairly easy, but teachers will find it more challenging to plan the right questions to generate peer interaction. In peer interactions, the teacher plays a minor role. The conversation moves from teacher-directed inquiry to child-to-child discussion. In planning their questions, teachers will have to work to generate high-quality interactions among children, but with practice, children's interactions can move from superficial, "gossipy" topics to more meaningful interactions focused on substance. Generally, if the topic is intriguing, the interaction will flow well.

Questions can give children opportunities to share *their personal experiences,* thus enhancing their self-concepts. Questions with this purpose in mind not only allow children to talk about themselves, but provide students with opportunities to get to know their classmates. These questions, if handled wisely, can help children understand that everybody has something worthwhile to share. Each time children have successful experiences sharing information openly about themselves, they are encouraged to share again and again.

PROMOTING CHILDREN'S THINKING IN THE CLASSROOM

Questions can do much to set the quality and level of thought in the classroom. When adults continually ask children simple, low-level questions, most children are content to respond with simple, low-level answers. However, when adults ask stimulating questions that call for problem solving or higher-level thought processes, most children rise to the occasion and, with encouragement, give thoughtful answers to the questions.

Raising the complexity of questions to promote quality thinking and higher-level thinking in children takes thought and planning by teachers. Most teachers ask thought-provoking questions only with conscious attention to the questioning process. In the following section, you will read information on several types and levels of thinking. You will study numerous examples of ways teachers can promote these kinds of thinking through good questions.

Convergent and Divergent Thinking

It's October and the leaves are changing color; there's a hint of cold weather in the air. It's a perfect time for Mrs. Liang to begin her unit on fall and its many seasonal changes. To get the unit started, Mrs. Liang has gathered several bright-colored leaves, different acorns, and two sweet gum tree balls in a bag. She lets her second graders take turns feeling inside the bag, choosing an object, describing and naming the object, then showing the object to their classmates. As they work, Mrs. Liang questions the children: "Is it hard or soft? Is it flexible or stiff? Tell us about its size. What other ways can you describe it? What is your specimen?" In this activity, Mrs. Liang has involved the children in both convergent and divergent thinking.

Convergent thinking involves coming to a single point or small number of points. Convergent thinking questions have one good answer or a small number of acceptable answers. When Mrs. Liang asked about the texture of the specimens, she expected the children to make a choice of hard or soft, flexible or stiff. When she asked children to name their specimens, the range of acceptable answers was relatively small.

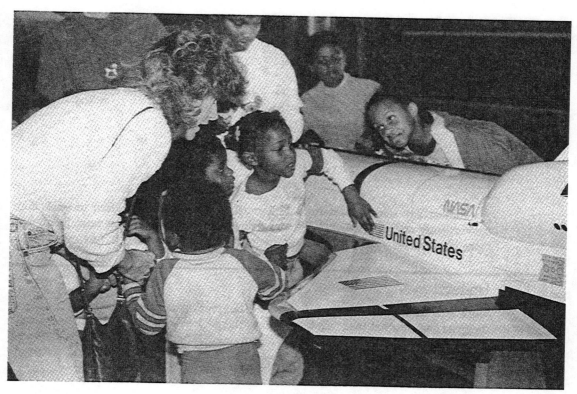

As the children observe this spaceship model, the teacher has many opportunities to ask both convergent and divergent questions.

Convergent thinking is important in the classroom. Often it focuses on names of objects and phenomena; qualities of objects such as color, texture, size, or shape; and answers to simple questions that involve comparison, time, number facts, or vocabulary.

In contrast, *divergent thinking* is involved in situations in which a wide range of answers are possible or desirable. Divergent thinking encourages people to explore in a number of different directions from a single starting point. Figure 3.1 illustrates some differences in convergent and divergent thinking.

When Mrs. Liang asked the children to describe the specimens' sizes, the question had several possible answers and so it involves divergent thinking. For example, if Kelly pulled out a ball from a sweet gum tree, she might respond: "It's smaller than a tennis ball. It's about the size of my big marble." Shawanda might add, "It's about two centimeters across. It's bigger than my thumbnail." There are many ways to describe the size of the sweet gum ball. Mrs. Liang also encouraged divergent thinking when she asked the children for other ways to describe the object.

Figure 3.1
Convergent and divergent
thinking.

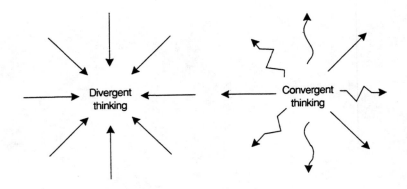

Almost any science activity has potential for encouraging children to think both convergently and divergently. Use the following examples. As you read them, add more convergent and divergent thinking questions of your own.

Understanding Shadows

Work with children outdoors on a sunny day. Let them stand still and see their shadows, then run and see that their shadows "follow them." Help children understand that light comes from the sun. Their bodies block some of the sun's rays and shadows can be seen. Help children clarify their thinking by asking both convergent and divergent questions:

Convergent Thinking Questions

- Where is the source of light?
- What blocks the sun to cause this shadow?

Divergent Thinking Questions

- Our bodies caused shadows today. What other things cause shadows?
- Tell me about shadows you've seen indoors. What was the light source? What blocked the light and caused the shadow?
- How can we change our shadows (make them longer, shorter, fatter, or skinnier)?

Investigating How We Breathe

Ask children to name some things their bodies do—every day, every minute. If they do not mention breathing, suggest that special parts of our bodies help us breathe all the time. We breathe constantly whether we are sleeping or awake, whether we are playing or resting. Tell children that air can enter their bodies in two places—through their noses and their mouths. Have children breathe in and out through their noses, then their mouths. Tell children that we can breathe slowly or deeply; we can breathe faster or take more shallow breaths. Have the children demonstrate.

Describe how air goes from the nose or mouth through the windpipe (trachea) and enters the lungs. Have each child demonstrate where these organs are located in their bodies. Have the children locate their diaphragms. Let them put their hands on their diaphragms and notice that when they breathe in deeply, their diaphragms move down and out. When they exhale deeply, their diaphragms move up and in. The diaphragm actually forces air out of the lungs through the trachea and nose or mouth.

Convergent Thinking Questions

- Where does air enter your body?
- What organ is here (demonstrate where the diaphragm is)?
- What does the diaphragm do?

Divergent Thinking Questions

- When are some times you breathe fast?
- When do you slow down your breathing?
- Besides breathing, what are some other things our bodies do constantly?

Bloom's Level of Thinking

Bloom (1956) and his colleagues developed a model of thinking. They pictured thinking as being in a hierarchy or on a number of levels. Some levels are higher or more advanced than others. In Bloom's model, higher levels of thinking build upon lower levels.

Figure 3.2 shows the way we picture Bloom's model. Study the figure, then read through the description of each level of thinking. Start at the bottom of the figure—at the most basic level of thinking.

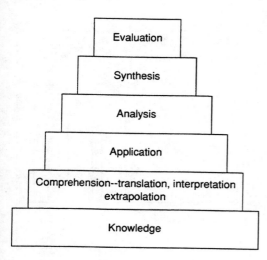

Figure 3.2
Bloom's model of thinking.

According to Bloom, *knowledge level thinking* is the most basic. It involves simple recall of facts or explicitly stated information. All other levels build on the knowledge level. When we ask children to recall names or facts that they have heard before, we ask them to think on the knowledge level. Without use of the knowledge level, oral and written communication would be very difficult.

Comprehension level thinking is slightly more advanced than knowledge level thinking. Comprehension involves building understanding. Comprehension level thinking may be of three basic types: translation, interpretation, and extrapolation. *Translation* involves changing information from one form to another. If children take part in a science experience, then draw a picture of their experience, they are translating information from one form to another. *Interpretation* involves putting information in one's own words or making simple comparisons. If children examine two insects, then compare and contrast them, the children are using comprehension level thinking in its interpretive aspect. *Extrapolation* means making conclusions about the unknown based on known data. Suppose children have planted seeds and cut strips of paper to represent the lengths of the plants as they grow. Their graph might look like the one in Figure 3.3. The children might use extrapolation to decide how tall their plants were on Saturday or Sunday. They might predict the plants' heights for the next day, then check their predictions.

When they solve simple problems or apply information previously learned to new situations, people use *application level thinking*. Perhaps the children have learned that their bodies need foods from four food groups and have named examples of foods from each group. They might use application level thinking to choose foods for a balanced meal.

Analysis level thinking, according to Bloom, involves dealing with relationships of wholes and parts. People may analyze how many parts form a whole or how a whole is comprised of many interrelated parts. For example, children may have studied different animal needs: food, water, and protection. They might be asked to analyze a picture that shows how an animal meets each of these needs. Children choose from

Figure 3.3
Plant growth chart.

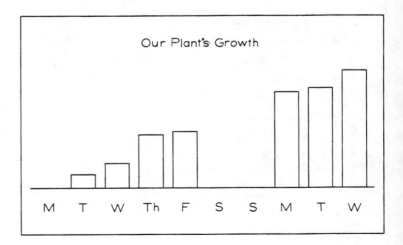

the whole, the picture, and identify the parts that show how the animal meets its needs for food, water, and protection.

Synthesis level thinking is creative or divergent thinking. With this type of thinking, people create new ideas or products, or put old ideas or products together in new ways. Children can use synthesis level thinking if they are provided with wood scraps, Styrofoam, toothpicks, paper, scissors, and other simple materials and are asked to make constructions that float. The children must draw on previous levels of thinking and produce original ideas. Children also use synthesis level thinking if they are asked to make a long list of things that float in water.

Evaluation is the highest level of thinking according to Bloom and his colleagues. Evaluation involves two steps: setting criteria for making judgments and then making judgments based on those criteria. After a unit on air, a group of children could be asked to plan and perform a skit about what they have learned. Before they perform the skit, the teacher might work with the children to decide how they will know if their skit was successful or not. The children might decide on several criteria for a good skit—it should provide information about air, it should make the other children pay attention, and everyone must remember their parts. After they perform the skit, the teacher could help the group members think about the criteria they established and whether the criteria were met. Thus the children have used evaluation level thinking; they have set criteria and used their criteria to make judgments.

As they plan activities, teachers must provide opportunities for children to think on all of Bloom's levels. Young children can begin to practice thinking on higher levels about concrete experiences, but teachers must challenge them to do so. With awareness of Bloom's levels and careful planning, educators can provide opportunities to encourage children to think on many levels. Children should practice the knowledge, comprehension, and application levels frequently, but analysis, synthesis, and evaluation will probably be used less frequently and on a more superficial level. Following is a description of several activities and ways teachers might encourage thinking on a variety of levels.

Examining a Square Meter of the Ground

A small section of the ground holds lots of interesting objects if we just take the time to examine it carefully. Help groups of three to five children stake off a square meter of ground. They can define the corners of a square with Popsicle sticks and stretch yarn around the sticks to make a square meter. Guide the children to place the square meters in different locations—perhaps one in a high-traffic area and one in a less trampled spot, one in the shade and one in the sunlight, or one on a flat surface and one on a hill.

Encourage the children to closely examine all the different things they can find in their square meter of ground. Use questions on various levels:

- What is this? What color is it? (Identifying a specific specimen—*knowledge.*)
- How are these two alike? Different? (Describing similarities and differences—*comprehension, interpretation.*)

- How could we classify these specimens? (Solving a simple problem—*application.*)
- What have we learned about our square meter of ground? (Pulling together many parts to form a whole—*analysis.*)
- Each of you may select three things from your square meter. We'll take them in the classroom and make something pretty from them. (Making a new product—*synthesis.*)
- Have we done a thorough job of examining what's here? What does "thorough" mean? (Setting criteria for "thoroughness," then using those criteria to make a judgment—*evaluation.*)

Wait Time—A Method for Encouraging Thinking

Rowe (1973), in her research concerning thinking in the classroom, found that when many teachers asked thought-provoking questions of children, they expected immediate answers from them. However, when teachers were trained to extend the length of time they waited before asking children to respond, the responses differed from when the "wait time" was just a second or two. When teachers waited five to seven seconds before expecting answers, children were able to offer higher quality answers than with the shorter wait time. Their answers were longer and more detailed. Children initiated more responses and interacted more with each others' responses.

Rowe also suggested that educators consider two wait time periods when asking children thought-provoking questions. A teacher should address a question to the entire group first and allow a wait time for all the children to think. Next, a teacher should call an individual child, then allow that child another wait time to think and phrase an answer. Rowe's study shows us the advantages of allowing children to think before we demand answers from them. Five to seven seconds may seem like a long time when adults stand before children, but, with practice, this pause can become a natural part of asking thought-provoking questions. The short "thinking period" that wait time provides can do much to improve the quality of children's thinking.

As you read the following descriptions of classroom activities and thought-provoking questions, think through some answers you would give to the questions. Hopefully you will see how a short wait time lets you generate a variety of possible answers. Notice that each question is also identified as convergent or divergent and according to the thinking level that it taps.

Bird Watching

Arrange some bird-watching experiences for children. Perhaps you can watch birds from a classroom window. Perhaps you can take the children to a park where the children can be seated in an area where birds are likely to appear. Observe the birds, noting their movements, what they eat, and how they interact. Back in the classroom, compare close-up pictures of two or more different kinds of birds. As you ask questions such as the following, be sure you allow enough wait time for the children to think about their answers.

- What did we learn about birds today? (*Divergent thinking*—many possible responses. *Comprehension-level thinking*—phrase answers in own words.)

- How are these birds alike? What are some ways they are different? (*Divergent thinking*—many possible responses. *Comprehension-level thinking*—similarities and differences.)

- When we go bird-watching, what are some ways we can encourage lots of birds to come near us? (*Divergent thinking*—many possible answers. *Application-level thinking*—solving a simple, concrete problem.)

Shadow Clock

Start this activity in the early morning on a sunny day. Use a ball of modeling clay and light-colored poster board as a base for a 30-cm (12-inch) ruler (Figure 3.4). Press the ruler into the clay so that it stands in an upright position. Set it in the middle of the poster board. Take the device—your shadow clock—outside and set it in a spot that will stay sunny most of the day. Let a child draw around the shadow that the ruler casts on the poster board. Help the children read the time on your watch and mark the time near the shadow. Return to the shadow clock several times during the day. Notice the position of the sun and the length and positions of the shadows. Draw around each shadow and mark the time each time you visit the shadow clock. At the end of the day, help the children look at the poster and make sense of the data.

- What happened to the shadows as time went on during the day? (*Convergent thinking*—concluding with a single point; few acceptable answers. *Analysis-level thinking*—looking at a whole set of data to notice patterns within the whole.)

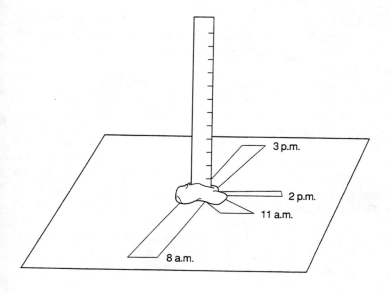

Figure 3.4
Shadow clock.

- Suppose we didn't have a watch. How could we use shadows like these to tell approximately what time it is? (*Divergent thinking*—several possible versions for answers. *Synthesis-level thinking*—creating new ideas.)
- What makes a good clock? Is our shadow clock a good one? (*Divergent thinking*—many possible criteria for a good clock. *Evaluation-level thinking*—setting criteria, then making a judgment.)

GUIDES FOR QUESTIONING IN THE CLASSROOM

Questions are an essential part of classroom interactions. Conscious attention to questioning techniques can help us ask productive, thought-provoking questions that gain children's attention and help them learn.

What are some qualities of good questions? Often they are *clear and brief*. Clarity helps children to focus and maintain attention. Clear questions let learners know precisely what we want to know. Brief questions avoid confusion; usually the longer questions are, the more chances learners have to become confused.

Good questions are *purposeful*. They play an important role in helping children learn. They directly address the ideas and skills teachers want children to learn. Such questions are asked using words children can understand.

Good questions are *thought-provoking*. They probe beyond the obvious and let children use the thinking skills of which they are capable. To lead to thought-provoking questions, teachers can often use a sequence of simple to more complex questions. Simpler questions get everyone involved and build confidence. More thought-provoking questions tantalize learners. They challenge and invite participants to clarify ideas, express a variety of thoughts, analyze facts, and make judgments.

In managing classroom interactions, teachers can use some general guides for questioning. The following paragraphs describe these guides.

Distribute questions widely throughout the class or group. Don't call on only the most willing or most verbal children. *All* students need to practice thinking skills, so be sure to make an effort to let eager children express themselves as well as draw out the more hesitant children.

Phrase questions to the entire group. When you call on an individual—"Patti, what is the weather like today?"—perhaps the other children feel free to "tune out." Rather, phrase the question, "Let's think of lots of words we can use to tell about today's weather. [pause] Patti, you start us out."

Don't repeat questions and answers. If teachers make it a habit to state questions only once, the children will learn the importance of careful listening each time a question is asked. Children easily fall into habits of inattentiveness if they know that questions will be asked again and again. The same is true of answers. Constant repetition of children's responses encourages inattentiveness. Instead, encourage children to speak audibly and listen to each other during verbal exchanges.

Build on children's responses. Instead of repeating children's responses, use them to extend children's thinking. If Hayley says it's a rainy day, build on that response by asking, "What kind of rainy day is it? Think of some more words to tell about the rain."

Use children's responses to help you make decisions about subsequent classroom questions and activities. Children's responses will tell you whether they are ready to move ahead in studying a topic or whether more work is necessary. Responses will tell you which child may be ready for enrichment activities and which child will need extra help to clarify thinking. Children's answers may give you clues about topics of special interest or points you wish to pursue.

Plan questions in advance. Be sure that questions relate to your objectives. Check your questions to see that you have included a balance between convergent and divergent thinking opportunities. Have you included questions on many levels? Most teachers will need to make a conscious effort to ensure that children think on the application, analysis, synthesis, and evaluation levels.

Take time to *evaluate your questions regularly.* After presenting your lessons, make it a habit to look back and see if you used a variety of thinking levels in your questions. See if you could clarify questions that confused the children. Did you add good questions to your original plans? Make notes on your questioning effectiveness. These notes will help you increase your awareness of questions in general. Notes can help you maintain and improve the quality of the questions you use the next time you teach a topic.

EVALUATION IN SCIENCE

Thus far in our book we have presented much information on *how* to teach science and *what* aspects of science topics are appropriate for young children to explore. We will continue these themes in subsequent chapters. Now, however, we will focus on evaluation in science. Evaluation asks not how or what, but *how well* the children have learned and *how well* we have taught.

Our means of evaluation should parallel our areas of emphasis in teaching. If we value and teach process, content, and attitudes, then we should evaluate these same aspects. We would need to develop means of assessing children's abilities to use processes such as observing, predicting, and classifying. We would also want to judge the number and quality of learning opportunities we have provided for children in these areas. Where we are concerned with content, we would need to use measures of children's abilities to remember, understand, and apply facts and ideas. We would want to judge our abilities to present content in understandable and interesting ways and to motivate children to master it. Finally, if we are concerned with children's attitudes, we will want to construct means of assessing their progress in areas such as interest, responsibility, and cooperation. We may want to examine our own attitudes and the attention we give to developing positive, scientific attitudes in children.

Purposes of Evaluation

Evaluation serves two main purposes. One is to *appraise children's achievement.* Such evaluation tells us whether or not we have accomplished objectives for process, content, or attitude development. Evaluation can also be *diagnostic.* When used for diagnosis, evaluation lets us know which children will need extra help and encouragement and which youngsters could profit from an extra challenge. Diagnosis helps us to accommodate both groups of children and individuals.

Evaluation may be formative or summative. *Formative evaluation* typically occurs during instruction. Classroom questions do much to tell us about children's understanding as they discuss different science areas. A quick glance around the classroom can be used as a means of formative evaluation of the level of interest and attentiveness. Listening to and watching children as they work often provides formative evaluation. One means of formative evaluation is signaling. Signaling means that each child in the group makes a nonverbal sign to respond to a question by the teacher. The teacher can glance around the group and quickly assess the children's understanding. For instance, the teacher might establish with the children that a "thumbs up" signal means yes, while a "thumbs down" signal means no. After looking at pictures of animals and discussing their characteristics, the teacher might ask second graders to signal answers to statements such as these: "Cows have cloven hooves. We drink milk from goats. A baby horse is called a colt or a filly."

Another means of formative evaluation is partner checks. The teacher pairs the children, has them discuss answers, and asks them to judge each other's answers. After partners have checked each other, the teacher may take a short time to listen to some of the answers. Partner checks puts responsibility on children for listening carefully; it conveys the idea that the teacher thinks each student is capable of making judgments.

Summative evaluation typically occurs after a series of learning experiences have been completed. Teachers may plan culminating projects or reports as means of summative evaluation. Sometimes tests serve as means for summative evaluation.

TECHNIQUES FOR EVALUATING CHILDREN'S WORK

Many techniques for evaluation are available in science. Different methods are suitable for different types of activities. We recommend a variety of techniques to tap and assess a variety of children's abilities and attitudes. Variety gives a broader picture than does a single measure or use of a single method of evaluation.

In this section, we will describe a number of techniques for evaluating children's work in science. These techniques will include evaluation of hands-on work, reports, recitation and discussion, project work, tests, and attitudes.

Hands-on work is an important part of science for young children. Evaluation of hands-on work is best done by teacher observation. If teachers know what to seek and use a checklist to record observations, the process is easy and systematic. For example, if teachers want to evaluate children's abilities to classify, they would identify specific behaviors that are parts of classifying. These behaviors could be listed on a checklist. As the children work with classifying experiences, the teacher might walk around and mark a checklist using + for exemplary work, a check for acceptable work, and − for work that needs improvement. They can leave the space blank for children if they do not observe the behaviors. The teacher's checklist might look like the one in Figure 3.5.

Do the children show interest in work with animals? Do they show respect for living things? Such questions can help a teacher evaluate hands-on work.

Behaviors	Children												
Makes groups consistently when given a basis for classifying.													
Names basis for classifying.													
Devises basis for classifying.													
Makes subclassifications.													
Other _____ _____ _____.													

Figure 3.5
A checklist for classifying skills.

Further evaluation of hands-on work may be accomplished by checking children's results. Often in hands-on work, children can draw pictures of results, fill in worksheets, or write a summary of what they learned. The teacher might look for completeness, care shown in making sketches and drawings, neatness, clarity, and reasonable results. Some variation in results is to be expected in hands-on work. Most teachers can help children produce high-quality written work by circulating as the children work, spot-checking work, and showing the children what they may do to improve their work.

Reports are often means of students demonstrating that they have learned something. Reports may be oral or written. They may be as simple as a kindergartner telling about a science book she has "read" or as complex as a second grader's elaborate drawing of Saturn's rings and a listing of facts gleaned from several books on planets. When judging children's reports, teachers will want to look for qualities such as clarity and accuracy of information, skill in language usage, and effective use of visual aids (as appropriate). For oral work, teachers may want to assess children's poise and enthusiasm. On written work, neatness and thoroughness should be considered.

Recitation and discussion occur every day in the classroom. Teachers will want to think about many factors as they evaluate children's contributions to discussions in the classroom. Who typically volunteers to answer questions? Who answers ably when called upon? Who uses elaborated responses and extensive vocabulary when responding? Who speaks willingly in small and large group settings or in one-to-one conversations? Who needs encouragement to participate more? Based on answers to these

Child-made pictures and projects are good ways for students to demonstrate what they have learned.

questions, teachers can plan strategies to help children improve their verbal skills and classroom discussions.

Project work can be used very effectively in helping children explore science. In project work, children make some sort of product applying information they have learned. It may be compiled and constructed individually or in large or small groups. Projects may range from art work with seeds or leaves to models of spaceships to the preparation of a well-balanced meal. When judging projects, teachers will want to identify some qualities that projects should exhibit, then check the project against these qualities. A sample project evaluation checklist appears in Figure 3.6.

Tests are traditional means of evaluating children's progress, but should be used sparingly in work with young children. Testing should be one of many means by which educators judge children's progress. The reading ability of most young children is limited, so when written tests are given, the instructions should be very simple or should be read aloud. Tests should be planned to cover main points of information that the children have explored. Teachers should consider making written tests a balance between objective questions, short-answer questions that require children to give

Qualities	Children								
Applies information.									
Conveys information clearly.									
Represents creative work.									
Neatly made.									
Clearly explained (as applicable).									
For group projects, was project work shared?									
Was work cooperative?									
Other _____ _____ _____.									

Figure 3.6
A checklist for evaluating projects.

examples or brief explanations, and questions to which children can repond with drawings or labeling of diagrams.

Evaluation of attitudes is important in science. Most teachers would like to think that they have sustained and deepened children's curiosity, interest, and responsible and caring attitudes. Though we cannot "get inside children's heads" and actually see what their attitudes are, we can make inferences about attitudes based on children's behaviors. As in other areas of science, evaluation of attitudes may be facilitated with use of teacher observations and checklists. A sample checklist is shown in Figure 3.7.

A more general checklist for recording teacher observations of children's work is found in appendix A. The checklist includes statements concerning children's progress

	Children										
Qualities											
Volunteers in discussion.											
Volunteers for activities.											
Does additional work.											
Given a choice, chooses science.											
Asks pertinent questions.											
Demonstrates deep involvement in work.											
Brings in additional items related to topic.											
Expresses interest.											
Cares for equipment and books.											
Cares for living things (plants, animals).											
Other _____											

Figure 3.7
A checklist for evaluating attitudes.

on science content, processes, and attitudes. It also includes a general "other" category dealing with children's creativity, willingness to respond, completion of work, and neatness. The checklist provides space to include names of all the children in a class. Teachers might mark the checklist daily or weekly. Comparison of checklists completed early and later in the year will help educators make judgments about children's behavior patterns over a period of time.

METHODS OF EVALUATING THE TEACHER'S WORK

Evaluation of teacher effectiveness is just as important as evaluation of student achievement. Teacher evaluations help teachers improve. People have a hard time seeing themselves objectively, but teacher evaluations help educators take an objective view of many aspects of their teaching techniques. Most schools today have inaugurated a very complete system for evaluating teachers. Administrators should advise teachers in advance about the factors on which they will be evaluated. Will they be evaluated through a statewide assessment instrument? Will their effectiveness be judged by their students' standardized test scores? What is the principal's perception of a good teacher? Teachers can be more effective when they have a clear understanding of what is expected of them. Besides mandatory teacher evaluations that occur in the classrooms, teachers need to initiate other evaluations to analyze their teaching techniques.

Who can help teachers evaluate? Their *colleagues* can often help. Peer evaluations can range from simple suggestions based on casual observations to formal written evaluations based on visits to the classroom. *Principals* can evaluate. Teachers can invite principals to visit the class and to suggest solutions to problems that they are having. *Children* can give teachers valuable pointers on their teaching effectiveness through open-ended discussions initiated by the teacher through simple teacher evaluation checklists that students mark or by responses students make in the classroom. *Parents* can offer evaluative information. Teachers need to keep the line of communication open with parents and ask for suggestions for improvement. Parents can offer helpful information from a unique point of view. *Teachers* can also evaluate themselves. They might use simple evaluative instruments to get an objective view of different aspects of their teaching effectiveness.

What types of evaluations might be used? Teachers can develop a variety of evaluation techniques. They might develop simple *checklists*. These checklists could be used by the teachers themselves or by principals or colleagues. *Questionnaires* also can provide helpful information. Even very young children can answer simple questionnaires if the teacher reads the questions to the children. A questionnaire might look like the one in Figure 3.8.

Teachers have access to many other evaluative techniques. *Observations* can be very helpful for self-evaluation. For objective observations teachers might use audiocassettes or videotapes. These suggestions are just a few of the methods that teachers can use to find out about their teaching behaviors. Teachers might use their ideas in different combinations to create teacher evaluations to fit their own needs.

Figure 3.8
Evaluation of my teacher.

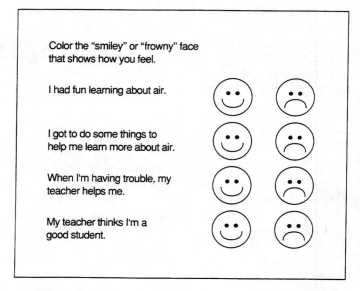

What items might teachers include in their evaluations? The answers to this question can be quite varied. What does the teacher need to know? Does the teacher need to know how well the goals were accomplished? Does the teacher want to know if the lesson flowed in a logical progression? Does the teacher need to gain insight into specific classroom problems? The questions asked in the evaluation instrument should fit the questions that concern the teacher. These questions can be anything related to improving the effectiveness of classroom learning. In the following section, we offer some suggestions of the types of questions that teachers might ask in their evaluation instruments. These questions can be used just as they are. They could be used to initiate thinking about different aspects of teaching. They could also be reorganized into new combinations.

- What is the focus of my science program—acquisition of facts, development of concepts, development of process skills, or a combination? What affective goals are included?
  - What do I do to emphasize the focus?
  - From day to day, how do I work toward the focus?
- How smoothly do my science lessons flow?
  - Do I have interesting ways to introduce topics? How do I motivate the children in the very beginning? Do I give my students a reason for wanting to know?
  - Do I build on past experiences?
  - Do I move from simple to complex—from known to unknown?
  - Do I give clear directions?
  - Do I build in questions that get students involved?
  - How do I draw closure to my lessons?

- How do children react to class activities?
  - What proportion of students are typically actively involved?
  - What proportion of students are typically seemingly bored?
  - What proportion of students volunteer in discussions? In hands-on work?
- How do I handle lab work or hands-on experiences?
  - How often do I actually involve students in hands-on experiences?
  - Do I plan prelab (motivation and directions), lab (actually doing the work), and postlab (sharing results) phases?
  - How do these phases generally work? Are students interested? Do they work constructively and without disruptions? If noise and activity levels are excessive, how can I bring them to an acceptable level?
  - What group sizes do I use for hands-on work?
  - What factors limit the lab work I can have children do? How do/could I work to overcome these factors?
- How do I try to meet the individual needs of the children?
  - How have I accommodated my lessons to the different learning styles among the students?
  - How have I adjusted my lessons to fit the different rates of learning?
  - Have I prepared different activities for those children who need extra help?
  - Have I planned enrichment for those children who would be challenged by it?
  - How do I accommodate children's interests?
  - How have I adjusted my lesson to fit the different cultural needs of children in my class?
- What choices of assignments or ways of working on assignments do I offer children?
- Do I provide a variety of resource materials?
  - Do I use books and magazines on different reading levels?
  - Do I use realia?
  - Do students share reading materials or realia?
  - What additional resources could I add?
- Are my classroom and science materials safe?
  - Can children handle materials that are on display without injuring themselves?
  - Is the equipment that children use independently safe?
  - When I use potentially harmful materials such as candles, extension cords, or hot plates, do I supervise the children and control the materials carefully?
  - Do I discuss safety rules in appropriate situations with children and enforce those rules as children work?
- What are some different ways I have students study science content?
  - What sort of balance do I provide between hands-on and book work?

Evaluation doesn't stop with children. Teachers must constantly try to look objectively at themselves, find areas for improvement, and work toward enhancing the

Working together, teachers explore an exciting hands-on activity to bring to the classroom.

quality of teaching and learning in the classroom. Questions such as the ones presented in this section may help teachers gain insights into their classroom behaviors, goals, and values.

FINAL THOUGHTS

In this chapter, we have discussed questioning strategies and evaluation techniques. As we discussed questioning strategies, we presented various purposes for asking questions. We discussed two different types of questions: divergent and convergent. We introduced Bloom's taxonomy, a framework for asking questions to encourage different levels of thinking. We also reviewed Rowe's wait time strategy for asking questions. Finally, we suggested some guides for improving questioning techniques.

In the section on evaluation, we suggested that evaluations should measure process, content, and attitudes. Not only should children be evaluated, but teachers also need to plan ways to evaluate their effectiveness. We suggested various techniques for evaluation of children's and teachers' progress.

Questions, a typical and natural part of classroom life, do much to influence the quality of science learning in young children. Well-planned questions can guide children's thinking. Questions can enhance the classroom environment and help to make it an atmosphere conducive for investigating. Exploring carefully thought-out questions also helps teachers evaluate children's progress in science.

Evaluation is an important part of teaching science. Trends for accountability and educational improvement make the need for effective evaluation procedures a reality in schools today. For teachers of young children, multifaceted approaches to evaluation are necessary; such approaches provide educators with a wider range of feedback than do single measures. The overall aim of evaluation should be toward progress and growth. Evaluation should not be punitive; rather, it should lead to improvement of children's work and of teachers' performances in the classroom.

NOW IT'S YOUR TURN

Now it's your turn to put into practice some of the evaluation and questioning techniques you have read about. Remember that practical application makes learning more meaningful, so try out some of the ideas you've just learned.

1. One of the many purposes for asking questions is to get children to interact with other children. Plan some specific, science-related topics that would encourage children to interact with one another. If you are teaching, try out your plan in class. Note the amount and quality of classroom interaction you get from your topic.

2. Educators feel that they have made a breakthrough when they move from teacher-oriented questions to the point where children begin to ask the questions. Plan a classroom strategy that will motivate children to ask questions. Try out your plan if you have a class. Evaluate your plan.

3. Analyze your own use of convergent or divergent thinking questions. Count the number of questions you ask. Of the total, how many were convergent? How many were divergent? Convert those numbers to percentages. Divergent thinking questions are typically used by teachers a small percentage of the time. Was your percentage of divergent thinking questions smaller than your percentage of convergent thinking questions? Find ways to raise your percentage of divergent thinking questions the next time you work with children.

4. Focus on the types of divergent thinking questions you ask. There are many ways to ask divergent questions. For example, you might ask children to think of many ways to _____. Alternately, you may ask them to create a new product, express a range of opinions, propose a range of options, or propose various solutions to problems. Observe what you ask the children to do each time you ask a divergent thinking question. Are your questions similar in nature, or do you ask them to think divergently in a variety of ways? Based upon your findings, decide on some ways to improve the variety of your divergent thinking questions.

5. Record the questions you ask in one day. Use a tape recorder if it would be helpful. Note the types of questions you ask according to Bloom's levels of thinking. Look back at the discussion on Bloom's levels of thinking. What questioning levels are you weak in? Plan to use questions in your next science lesson from those question levels you did not previously use.

6. Think back on our discussion of the different means of evaluating children. Do you use a wide variety of evaluative techniques? As you read the section on evaluation, did you find any different evaluation methods that might be applicable for your class? If so, plan to use a new method of evaluation in your class within the nex

week. If you have no class of your own, develop a hypothetical evaluation plan based on a science topic.

7. Think of the diverse learning situations that exist in your class. Plan a specific way to adapt your evaluation to a child who has a different learning characteristic. If you do not have a classroom, create a hypothetical child and plan an evaluation that best suits that child.

8. Suppose your administrator stressed the importance of pencil and paper tests for first- and second-grade science students. How could you convince that person that there are other valid means of evaluation? Plan your strategy.

9. Teacher evaluation is an important part of the evaluative process. If you evaluated your own techniques in teaching science, what qualities would you focus on? How could your children, colleagues, or principal help you evaluate your own effectiveness? Plan and carry out some measure to evaluate yourself as a teacher. Note some changes you could make as a result of this evaluation.

REFERENCES

Bloom, B. S. (Ed.). (1956). *Taxonomy of educational objectives.* New York: Longmans, Green.

Rowe, M. B. (1973). *Teaching science as continuous inquiry.* New York: McGraw-Hill.

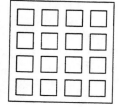

Chapter 4

Organizing and Managing the Classroom

YOUNG children learn science best through active involvement with concrete objects. Yet a hands-on approach can become unproductive and chaotic unless teachers develop management skills that address the unique problems inherent in an active classroom. Careful planning and implementation of management skills is important for many reasons. With good management skills teachers can ensure a smooth flow of activity in the classroom. When a classroom is well organized, both teachers and children work best and accomplish more. Learning is heightened, and children become more productive. They, in turn, develop positive attitudes toward learning and toward school.

In this chapter we will discuss ways to organize children to work in different-size groups—large, small, and individual settings. We will suggest techniques for establishing learning centers, for managing learners in an active classroom, for managing learning materials, and for using a variety of media to help children learn science. Finally, we will give some guides for soliciting help from the home and the community.

ORGANIZING CHILDREN TO WORK IN DIFFERENT-SIZE GROUPS

For the past two weeks, the children in Mr. Weams's class have been studying dinosaurs. This morning, all of the children are gathered on the rug reviewing basic facts they have learned about *Tyrannosaurus rex*. At the end of the large group discussion, Mr. Weams announces the choices available in small group learning centers. In the block center, Mr. Weams has placed paper footprints of different dinosaurs. Children are to estimate how many small blocks will be needed to fit in the area of each footprint and then fill each area with blocks. Mr. Weams chooses one footprint and demonstrates to the entire group how to estimate and fill in the area. Mr. Weams goes to the math center and holds up a 2-by-0.5-m (6-by-1.5-foot) picture of *Tyrannosaurus rex's* footprint. He shows the children how to work in pairs, to trace around their own footprints, and to compare their footprints to that of *Tyrannosaurus rex.* Mr. Weams moves to the language arts center and suggests that the children continue to work on their classroom book, *If I Had a Dinosaur for a Pet.* The sand table has many dinosaur models for the children to use. In the library are a variety of dinosaur books for children to read. After carefully explaining each center, Mr. Weams opens one center at a time. The children each choose the center in which they would like to work, moving to the centers with a minimum of noise. Some work in small groups. Others work independently.

This classroom is reflective of situations in real life. Sometimes we work in large group settings. Often we work in small groups. At times tasks dictate the need for individual work. A classroom that utilizes work in different-size groups prepares children to work flexibly with others. This is a skill they will need the rest of their lives. Making transitions from one group size to another isn't always easy, but with planning and practice teachers can learn how to organize children in such a way as to create a smooth flow from large groups to small settings to individual learning projects. Teachers need to know how to choose the appropriate group sizes to maximize learning. Each group size has its advantages and its limitations. Being aware of the potentials and liabilities, teachers can choose wisely the appropriate group size for each situation.

Children need opportunities to work in large groups, small groups, or individually.

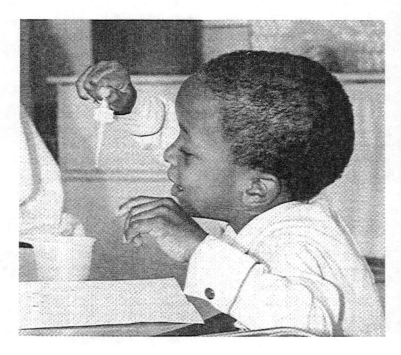

Advantages and Limitations of Large Groups

Many adults are more comfortable with large group work because they are more familiar with teaching in this group configuration. It is often easier and quicker to communicate information in a large group. In a large group setting the teacher has direct control.

However, with all its advantages, large group teaching definitely has its drawbacks. Even though teachers can dispense information facilely, they might find it harder to check just how well that information has been assimilated. Adjusting mistakes made by individual children in a large group can become a nightmare. Large group settings limit children's opportunities for involvement and result in fewer turns for responses per child. When children have to wait long periods of time for their turn, they often lose interest and become restless or "tune out." Let's face the facts. Large groups are not perfectly suited to young children's developmental levels.

Advantages and Limitations of Small Groups

Small groups free the teacher to move among the various groups and interact with individual children. When children work in small groups, they become maximally involved, making learning situations very meaningful. Small group settings provide many opportunities for cooperative learning. Children working together in small groups develop social skills. They learn new ideas from one another. Often children are confronted with ideas different from their own; this exposure helps young children move from egocentric points of view to more socially oriented outlooks. Small group settings can enhance creativity. The skills and interests of different group members can contribute to group productivity. Small groups help children learn to work together—a behavior necessary for competent social living.

Small group work can be fun and motivating, but many teachers are aware of the disadvantages. Nobody enjoys a noisy, chaotic room. Children working in small groups can often generate a great deal of noise. Without good classroom management, a teacher may find small groups to be rather unproductive. Small groups often dictate a need for more planned activities. The teacher may need more materials. Teachers will have to spend more time gathering supplies and deciding what to do with them. Some schools may lack sufficient funds for the extra supplies needed.

Advantages and Limitations of Individual Work

Many times children will need to work independently to maximize the learning situation. Children working on their own can pursue individual interests and develop their own creative ideas. They can move at their individual paces. However, children who lack self-discipline can move in circles when left to work on their own. Children working independently can create overwhelming problems to a teacher who must serve as a resource person for many individual projects.

We see that large, small, and individual work settings all have their assets and their limitations. The keys to successful grouping are to vary your settings and to match your group setting to your purposes. The following sections will present ideas for smooth work in different settings.

Guides for Directing Large Group Work

- Work with your children to *establish basic rules* for large group meetings. Be consistent to carry out those rules.

- Before you start, *make sure that all children are comfortable* and that they can see and hear. If your room has a strong light source, you face the glare, placing the children's backs to it. The light will then shine on your specimens or pictures and not directly in the children's eyes.

- *Select specimens or pictures that are large enough* to be easily seen by the entire group. If your examples must be smaller, walk around the group to show them.

- *Plan ways to get maximum responses.* Be sure to call on different children. Remember that signaling lets everybody respond. After introducing an idea, allow children to discuss it in groups of twos and threes and then to share their most important ideas with the whole group. You can manage this quick transition without moving the children. Allow children to be actively involved at tables sometimes. You can direct the entire group from one point in the room, or you can move throughout the room as you speak to the entire group.

- *Plan motivating introductions and endings* to your lessons.

- *Limit large group sitting time.* Remember, young children do not have long attention spans for most adult-initiated activities. Be sensitive to your children. Cut off your large group time before you lose them.

Guides for Directing Small Group Work

- *Be sure that materials and instructions are out in each center* and ready to go ahead of time.

- *Give directions for small group work to the entire group* during large group time. Go through each small group activity, explaining clearly what the children are to do. If necessary, demonstrate what to do. Time spent giving clear directions in a large group setting will save time and hassle in the long run.

- *Have something definite for the children to do* when they come to work in a center, but allow for deviations. Children need the freedom to work through problems in their own ways and to experiment with the materials.

- *Establish ground rules* for small group work. Rules you might wish to consider are: "Use low voices. Clean up your own mess. Complete your work before moving on to another center. Put your finished work in the box before you leave the center." Establish some system for moving from one center to the next.

- *Make children responsible* for the activity in which they are involved. Children can demonstrate responsibility by filling out a checklist, completing a worksheet, or making a product. Sometimes they may be required to raise their hand and check out their work with the teacher.

- *Expect children to demonstrate good, responsible work habits* such as keeping on task, letting others work, or sharing quietly.
- *Devise a system for handling children's products.* You may wish to hang artwork for display. Collect other finished products and place them in folders or boxes.
- Allow some time where you are not directly instructing any group. Use this time to *circulate among the groups* in order to extend, direct, redirect, and assess the children's work.

Guides for Directing Individual Work

- In setting up your room, *provide a quiet, attractive place in which children can come to work independently.* Be sure supplies and materials are readily available to your independent workers.
- *Provide ample time and motivation* for children to work alone.
- *Make your independent work center self-explanatory or simple enough* so that children can easily work alone.
- *Allow for flexibility* so children can pursue their own interests, solve problems in their unique ways, and move at their individual paces.
- *Give thoughtful responses* to children's individual work. Always begin by making a positive comment to encourage children. Follow up with responses that make children look at their work in greater depth. Ask questions to make children think in more detail. Make responses that help children see their work in another way. For instance, if Susan is working on a rocket model, the teacher might say, "Susan, you've worked hard on your model. Tell me about some of its parts. What else could you add to it? You're having trouble making the rudder stay in place. What's another way we could attach it?"
- *Think big.* Remember, individual work does not have to be finished in one setting. Some projects require a great deal of time and effort if children are to do high-quality work. Allow children to continue projects over a period of time when necessary.
- *Plan a special time and place for children to share* their individual work with others. Individual products may take such forms as homemade books, paintings, or oral presentations. Train children to honor and appreciate each others' efforts. Be sure to model this accepting attitude yourself.

SCIENCE LEARNING CENTERS

A teacher who considers the needs and characteristics of young children will make learning centers an integral part of the classroom. Learning centers, places where children can work and learn, motivate children and promote active learning. Typically, children work in small groups or side by side. Learning centers often feature independent work for students, though at times educators may work with small groups in learning centers.

Using learning centers has many advantages. As they work in learning centers, children are actively engaged. They assume responsibility for their own learning. Learning centers allow for creativity on the part of both children and adults. Learning centers often include work that can be completed in many different ways; children may use a variety of expressive forms as they work with materials and ideas. Adults can use their creative abilities as they plan and implement learning centers. Learning centers help educators carry out unit themes in integrated ways that are meaningful to children. As children work at learning centers, they develop science skills, acquire knowledge, and often learn to work together cooperatively.

Physical Arrangements for Learning Centers

What might a science learning center look like? Where might it be located? How can teachers best plan work for learning centers? Though the answers to these questions depend to a large degree on individual preferences and situations, we offer the following guides for physical arrangements of centers.

- *Think creatively about how centers might be arranged* and placed in the classroom. Centers might be arranged on tabletops, but they might also be placed on a rug, moved outdoors, or neatly tucked on a windowsill. A learning center might be found in a hallway or classroom foyer. Consider the varied ways to arrange centers. For example, a sturdy plastic storage box might be fitted with a cushion and pockets; a learner can sit on the cushion and use materials from the pockets. A "minicenter" on rocks might be contained in a shoebox to be carried to any convenient area by learners. The shoebox need contain only a few rocks and some simple instructions written on the shoebox lid. The instructions might use words and pictures to tell the children to order, classify, or examine the rocks.

Figure 4.1 illustrates more ideas for arranging learning centers. The following are tips for successful learning centers.

- *Keep centers safe and inviting.* Most centers should be designed for independent work by groups of children. Therefore they must contain materials that are safe and easy to use. Hot plates, candles, and metal knives do have a place in science experiences for young children, but these materials should not be placed in centers. Centers need not be fancy, but if they contain intriguing pictures, objects, and things to do, young children will be motivated to work in centers. Educators should guard against science centers becoming overcrowded and cluttered.

- *Plan room arrangements* to facilitate work in centers. Quieter centers of activity might be placed together—away from noisier areas such as the block center or the music center. It is often convenient to place a science center near a restroom or sink so that water is readily available and cleanup is facilitated. If a center is to accommodate plants, consider placing it near a window to take advantage of natural light.

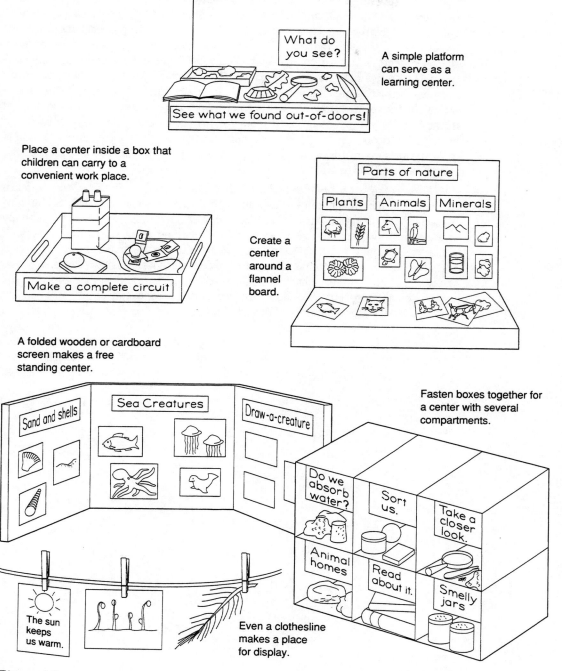

A simple platform can serve as a learning center.

What do you see?

See what we found out-of-doors!

Place a center inside a box that children can carry to a convenient work place.

Make a complete circuit

Create a center around a flannel board.

Parts of nature

Plants Animals Minerals

A folded wooden or cardboard screen makes a free standing center.

Sand and shells Sea Creatures Draw-a-creature

Fasten boxes together for a center with several compartments.

Do we absorb water? Sort us. Take a closer look.

Animal homes Read about it. Smelly jars

The sun keeps us warm.

Even a clothesline makes a place for display.

Figure 4.1
Learning centers.

- Start centers with goals and objectives in mind, but *leave room for suggestions and contributions from children*. Work in centers should complement and supplement goals and objectives educators have established for children. Teachers will want to set up centers with these aims in mind; however, teachers need to make their plans for centers flexible enough to accommodate suggestions and materials contributed by students. For example, Ms. Rabat might want children to see that magnets attract some but not all metal materials. She could set up a center in which children test various materials to see if they are attracted to a magnet. Sam might bring a variety of metal objects for his classmates to test. Amelia might enlarge the scope of the activity by suggesting that pairs of children list things from the classroom that are attracted to the magnet. Thus, the basic idea of the center was expanded and enriched.

- *Emphasize centers for involvement and also plan centers for display.* Children learn through active involvement and by talking to their peers and to adults. So be sure to plan many centers where children can work together and become actively engaged in solving problems, working with tools, and using science processes. A center for learning about autumn might include this open-ended question: "What are some of the many things that you can do with nuts?" Using acorns, pecans, and walnuts in the shell, children might discover that nuts float in water and roll along the tabletop, but the shells are not easy to bend and break. The center might include a large container of assorted nuts, tongs, and small plastic containers with labels or rubber bands marking levels of "full," "half full," and "almost empty" (Figure 4.2). Children can use the tongs to transfer the nuts and fill the smaller containers to the appropriate levels. A label on a jar of nuts might pose the question: "How many do you think are inside?" Children could record their guesses

Figure 4.2
Materials for an autumn learning center.

on scraps of paper and place the papers in a box. A small group of children could arrange the papers in numerical order. They could count the nuts and decide which children made "good" guesses. The center might also include a display of a branch with a cocoon. Children could examine the cocoon without disturbing it, then draw a picture of it or write a story about what might happen to it.

Centers are also wonderful places for displays. To initiate a unit of study, a teacher might set up a center featuring pictures that interest and motivate the children. Children can display finished work in a center; others can observe and admire their work. Children might bring things to place on a display. For the center theme "Tools We Use at Home," each child might bring a safe tool to place on display for a few days.

Displays should feature materials placed at or below children's eye level or have facilities for children to sit down and examine materials. A neat, uncluttered, attractive appearance enhances a display center and invites learners to browse—and learn.

MANAGING LEARNERS IN AN ACTIVE CLASSROOM

A classroom of young children actively engaged in exploring science can be a joy to watch and work in. It can easily become a noisy, chaotic, even dangerous place where little learning takes place, tempers flare, and accidents occur. What makes the difference? The answer is not simple; a combination of high expectations, good planning, and appropriate behavior management are parts of the answer. Let's examine some guides for managing learners and learning experiences in a hands-on classroom.

- *Expect good behavior* from children. Every child *can* learn to speak in a low voice and walk rather than run in the classroom. If experiences are on the appropriate level of interest, every child *can* be expected to stay on task and allow others to do the same. Young children *can* learn to work together sharing materials; they *can* grow in their acceptance of each others' point of view. High expectations must be balanced by judicious planning based on children's developmental levels. Child development literature tells us that youngsters need to talk, move about, and manipulate objects for themselves. It is unrealistic to expect young children to be quiet and listen all day, to sit in one spot for a long period of time, or to learn solely from seeing the teacher demonstrate what to do with objects.

- *Be consistent in expectations for children's behaviors.* Effective teachers often work with their students to establish sensible rules for behavior in the classroom. When children have input into the rules or procedures, they often understand and appreciate them more than with adult-imposed "mandates" for controlling behavior. Once rules are established, educators will need to help children follow them routinely. Consistent expectations for appropriate behavior helps children feel secure.

- *Clearly demonstrate and explain* how to follow classroom rules and use materials appropriately. Showing *and* telling young children what to do is imperative. A teacher can show a child how to cup her hand and hold an earthworm gently. She can wash her hands alongside the child while saying, "We wash our hands after we handle a pet." A teacher can show a large or small group of children how to carefully place objects in the pans of a balance scale, then let a child or two demonstrate the procedure. Children want to behave and cooperate. Adults can help children by making procedures and techniques clear.

- *Use cooperative learning groups to benefit each child.* When children work together, everyone benefits. Feelings of cooperation are developed. Points of view are exchanged. Group thinking is often more productive and diverse than the thinking of one person. In some cases, one child can help another. In other cases, children will assume equal responsibility rather than roles as leaders and followers. Often the teacher should make decisions about which children will work together. He may want to rotate leadership responsibility with the group. He may want to pair shy children with more outgoing peers. At other times, children may form groups on the basis of interest or personal preference.

- *Be alert for potential problem situations.* Address them directly, firmly, and positively before behaviors accelerate to a distracting level. When children are engaged in learning groups or learning centers, the teacher should be aware of potential problems. If the teacher moves about the room, often she prevents problems by her mere proximity. Where inappropriate behaviors such as the banging of classroom instruments are occurring, the teacher will want to approach the group and say, "That's too noisy. Use it softly so you won't disturb others." If a child is furtively reaching into the aquarium, the teacher will want to say, "Stop that. You will harm the fish. Just watch them instead." When interpersonal problems occur, the teacher may want to calm the children, then get them to describe what happened. Children should acknowledge their parts in an offense. The teacher should help the children make a plan to improve their behavior. "What happened here? What can you do to keep this from happening again?" or "What can we do to change this?" are questions that are often effective in helping children to assume responsibility for improving a situation. As necessary, the teacher will have to do some prompting and renegotiating so that children can carry out or revise a plan to change behavior.

- *Plan smooth transitions* from one activity to another. Transitions help children move from one activity to another or one place to another. Transitions help children prepare for the next activity. They also can help relieve stress or help children gain control. For example, if children have listened to a long story, but are becoming restless, the teacher might use a brief stretching exercise or fingerplay before she gives directions for them to move to the next activity. Teachers can encourage children to follow directions in many ways. Good planning is essential. Clear, concise directions help children understand what to do next. Advance notice—"You have five more minutes to work before cleanup time"—will help children get ready for closing an activity. Variety adds spice to transitions. Perhaps the teacher can dismiss children from a large group by the pattern of their shirts or by the length of their hair. Perhaps the teacher can initiate cleanup time with a song or a special challenge, "Let's see if we can clean up before the record finishes."

- *If problems consistently occur, carefully evaluate and change the situation.* Perhaps children experience frustration because an activity is too difficult; the teacher may want to revise it or eliminate it. Perhaps an experience is overstimulating; the teacher may want to "tone down" the activity or not repeat it. Perhaps science time drags when it is conducted late in the day; the educator will want to consider ways to have more active involvement or reschedule science to a time that is more conducive to learning.

No set of guides for managing a science classroom is foolproof. Teachers will want to adapt and add to this list to meet their own needs and styles. Educators should remember that when children are busy and happy, they feel productive and successful; problems are minimized.

MANAGING LEARNING MATERIALS

Learning materials are essential as children explore science. Obtaining and storing a variety of supplies and equipment takes planning and organization. Maintaining a balance of materials is also a challenge. In this section, we will discuss various aspects of managing learning materials.

Educators will want to gather and purchase a variety of simple materials. Some materials—leaves, dirt, or earthworms—are readily available in most settings. Other materials such as rubber bands, straws, and paper towels may be available as ordinary school supplies. Still other supplies, such as magnets, batteries, lenses, and balloons will cost money. Whatever materials are used in the science classroom should be safe for children to handle and kept in good repair. In collecting and purchasing supplies, educators will want to obtain a variety of materials to provide a curriculum balanced with hands-on experiences in life sciences, environmental sciences, and physical sciences. They will also want a variety of materials to appeal to children's different senses and learning styles.

A long-term plan for obtaining and purchasing supplies and equipment is essential. Educators could make a general plan for the year and see what is needed for each topic or unit. Some supplies might be provided by parents, while others will need to be purchased at a variety store, school supply company, or science supplier. Where budgetary constraints are a problem, teachers of young children might need to make a plan to purchase needed equipment over a period of several years. Sometimes talking to administrators about the reasons for the request of certain materials will yield positive results. When administrators understand how materials will be used to benefit children, often they can find ways to provide needed money. Educators will also want to think about their plans and see what simple, inexpensive materials they can substitute for more costly ones and save their money for things that must be purchased.

Following is a list of purchased materials that may be used many ways in science work with young children. Each kind of material has potential dangers, so each should be used under adult supervision and after safety concerns have been discussed with children.

Hot plate
Plastic mirrors
Rope
Magnets
Seeds
Medicine droppers
Funnels

Balloons
Thermometer (inexpensive with large numerals)
Dry cells (No. 6 or flashlight batteries)
Wire
Small sockets and light bulbs
Hand lenses

Educators will want to see what supplies may be shared within a school. Several kindergarten teachers can easily share a set of magnets if they plan to use them at different times. A single battery and light bulb setup could be shared among five or six second-grade classrooms. In a school system, often upper-grade science teachers or science coordinators have materials that they will share with teachers of young children.

Most families will be glad to help with gathering or donating supplies to use in science experiences. Some educators compile a list of needed supplies and send it home at the beginning of the school year; others send written requests for materials at one- or two-month intervals. Most family members are willing to help children gather specimens such as leaves or rocks to share at school. Others are willing to donate household supplies such as flour, salt, vinegar, soda, wax paper, foil, plastic bags, or straws.

Educators will store some supplies; other materials should be readily available. Simple measuring equipment, hand lenses, cleanup supplies, and plastic bags might be available to be used as they are needed. Supplies that are needed only occasionally may be stored on high shelves, closets, or other less accessible spots. Many teachers have developed workable systems for storing materials. Putting things in clear, labeled containers facilitates their retrieval. Many educators organize supplies and store them according to teaching units/topics. Efficient educators put materials away in good order—clean and organized. A list near a storage area makes it easy to note things that need to be replaced or refurbished before they are used again. A list might be placed inside a document protector. It might look like the list in Figure 4.3.

Figure 4.3
Storage area list.

Locker #1 Contents	
10 bottles of Elmer's glue	
5 boxes of paper clips	
15 packs of construction paper	
2 packages of clothespins	

With several blank lines between categories of items, the list is easy to update with new items. A checkmark made with an erasable marker or a grease pencil when that item reaches the minimum number gives the next shopping list of items that should be on the next order. Where can materials be stored? Locations might include closets, lockers, stackable plastic bins, or file cabinets. Many educators benefit from helping each other brainstorm about solutions to storage problems.

USING MEDIA TO HELP CHILDREN LEARN SCIENCE

In today's media-oriented society, a variety of media exist to enrich children's science experiences in the classroom. To supplement science lessons, teachers can choose from pictures, magazines, books, films and filmstrips, videotapes, computer programs, and other audiovisual sources.

Children's books are an excellent source for enriching almost any science topic. Many children's books today display high-quality workmanship presenting accurate information on a young child's level. Some books have realistic photos; others use graphic, colorful drawings.

With the help of a librarian, teachers should be able to choose appropriate books to fit their children's levels of understanding and to enhance the science topics that children are studying. Teachers will also be able to gain helpful suggestions in selecting young children's science books from book reviews in the journals *Science and Children* and *Young Children.* The American Library Association publishes *The Museum of Science and Industry Basic List of Children's Science Books.* This helpful book groups science books into eighteen subject categories and provides information such as annotation, evaluation, and reading level of each science book reviewed. The Museum of Science and Industry updates its basic list periodically. The Association for Childhood Education International publishes a *Bibliography of Books for Children* that is updated periodically. This publication reviews children's books on physical science, earth science, biology, botany, the animal kingdom, and technology. For information on the aforementioned literature and additional sources for children's science books, see the lists at the end of this chapter.

Children's magazines also offer opportunities for learning about many topics. Teachers can add zest to their science curriculum by becoming familiar with and using these science-oriented magazines. The National Wildlife Federation publishes two excellent children's magazines, *Your Big Backyard* and *Ranger Rick.* Both magazines are beautifully illustrated with photographs and realistic drawings and provide interesting information. *Your Big Backyard* is appropriate for three- to five-year-olds, while *Ranger Rick* would appeal to children from six to twelve years old. *World* is an attractive magazine written on a K–6 reading level, published by the National Geographic Society. Like *National Geographic,* the illustrations are excellent in quality and the coverage includes a wide range of topics such as science, different cultures, and countries. *Zoobooks* is a magazine about different topics such as big cats, spiders, and dinosaurs. Each issue provides detailed information about featured animals, their habits, and habitats. Although the reading level extends to the fifth grade, even very young children will learn much from studying the realistic illustrations. Children will also be intrigued by using such magazines as *Science Weekly,* which provides information related to science, math, and technology. *Scienceland,* for kindergarten through third grade, presents one science topic per issue, ranging from space adventures to human hands. The magazine, *Electric Company,* also features one topic in each issue and is appropriate for grades one through four. (Addresses for these magazines can be found at the end of this chapter.)

Adult books and magazines can also be excellent resources for a wide variety of science topics. While adults can gain much background information from these sources, children also will have fun looking at the pictures. They can learn about animals they've never seen and other science phenomena they might never have an opportunity to experience firsthand. Teachers might start with such magazines as *National Wildlife, International Wildlife,* and *National Geographic.* Magazines such as *Ad Astra* provide excellent information on space, while publications such as *Omni* provide broader ranges of topics such as space, earth, the human body, and stars. *Odyssey* is another magazine that adults might consider when gathering information related to space exploration and astronomy. Although this magazine is written for older students, teachers will be able to simplify information and use illustrations with children. Teachers might wish to consider *Connect,* a newsletter that presents current information, research, and activities related to science and math. A librarian can help adults find other books and magazines to meet special needs. Addresses for adult magazines mentioned here and for many other magazines carrying potential science information are included in the lists at the end of this chapter.

In choosing films and filmstrips related to science, teachers will find librarians to be quite helpful. Another source that might prove valuable is *Science Books and Films,* a magazine published five times a year that reviews 16-mm films, filmstrips, and videos in science. Teachers will also want to preview their television guides to find interesting science programs to videotape for later use in the classroom.

For information regarding using computers in the classroom, adults might check such magazines as *Classroom Computer Learning* and *Teaching and Computers,* both of which include articles about practical ways to use computers to improve the educational process. *Teaching and Computers* addresses specifically the needs of elementary-age children. For addresses, see the list at the end of this chapter.

Guides for Choosing and Using Media

In selecting and using media, teachers need to remember that different media forms have their assets and limitations. For instance, films provide active demonstrations whereas pictures, magazines, and books do not; pictures, magazines, and books invite active and varied participation from the children. Computer programs are excellent for inviting active participation and for motivating children, but children probably have limited access to a computer. Only one or two children can work on a computer at one time. Our guidelines to choosing and using media follow.

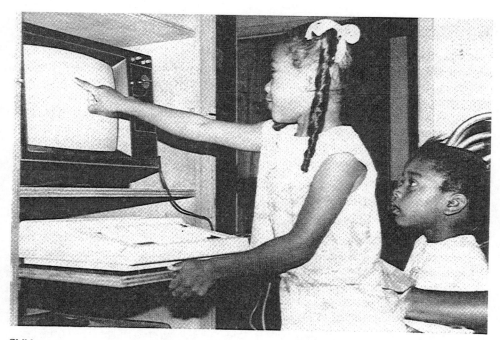

Children can use computers to learn science in many meaningful ways.

- *Become familiar with a wide variety of media.* Make use of many different kinds of media to extend children's learning experiences.

- In choosing media, *plan to appeal to different learning styles* and to expose children to the idea that we learn from many kinds of materials.

- *Check the school library and public library for appropriate media* such as books, films, and computer programs. Build a relationship with librarians and other professionals so they can alert you about new media. Plan with your librarian to order a variety of audiovisual materials. Organize your plan in a prioritized way. Make notes of how you can work various kinds of media into units and themes during the year.

- *Go through magazines before you discard them.* Tear out appropriate pictures and articles. Ask parents to collect pictures from their old magazines. Be sure to laminate those pictures that you plan to use on a long-term basis.

- *Set up a filing system* to coordinate with your themes and units.

- *Give clear directions* to your students on how to use any media available in your room. Show children how to use and care for all kinds of media such as books, records and record players, audiotapes and players, and computers and software. Let children practice caring for media as you observe. Help children establish a responsible attitude for putting away materials.

SOLICITING HELP FROM THE HOME AND COMMUNITY

Teachers become more effective when they use people and places outside the class-room for resources than when they rely only on themselves as the source of knowledge. People in the community can provide many areas of expertise to which teachers themselves would not have access. Thus, use of parents, other community helpers, and places within the community extends the learning environment for children beyond the classroom and broadens children's horizons. A natural extension of learning experiences from home to school to the community helps children develop the disposition that there are many interesting things to learn in our world—wherever we go.

Guides for Getting the Maximum Benefit from Home and Community Resources

- Early in the school year *send out a questionnaire* to find out what resorces parents have to offer. You might be surprised at the wealth of knowledge available from your own students' parents. Think in terms of a wide range of possibilities. You will have parents who can share from their occupational expertise, parents with interesting hobbies and special skills, and parents with collections to share. Some parents might be willing to bring gentle pets to school. (If they do so, plan ways to keep both the pet and the children safe.) Other parents might have traveled to interesting places and collected slides, photos, or memorabilia to show. Parents from other cultures might be willing to share experiences from their different backgrounds. A carefully worded questionnaire that taps these different resources will serve as a starting point from which you may plan for the school year.

- *Realize that people need not be scientists or even experts in their fields to share information.* A parent who enjoys cooking bread can teach children many valuable concepts as they cook bread together. Older people can share about the change

This father shares his skills and expertise with a child.

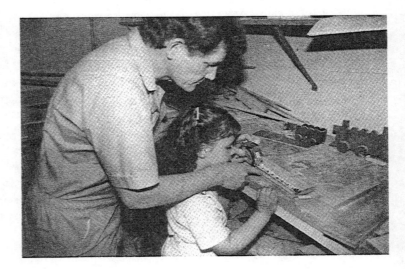

process that comes with aging. A mother can bring a baby. A handicapped person can demonstrate special equipment. Health care workers, maintenance people, mechanics, and farm workers all have something interesting to share to enrich young children's lives.

- *Investigate the community for areas of interest.* Look beyond the obvious to find out what might be enlightening to children. For instance, a catfish farmer might show children how he blows the food from the truck to feed the fish or how he uses his seine to harvest the catfish. It would also be interesting for children to see aspects of fish reproduction and growth: how the fish spawn, robbing the eggs from the spawning containers and taking them to the hatchery, hatching the eggs, and vaccinating the fingerlings and stocking them in a rearing pond.

- When community resource people agree to work with your class, *help them plan* what they will share. *They* know their areas of expertise, but *you* know what children are like. Most resource people will be grateful to get some helpful hints. Help them make their presentations short and simple. Suggest that they bring real objects to share. Encourage them, if at all possible, to let children become actively involved in the learning experience. Make suggestions as to what they might do to get children to interact.

- After a resource person visits or children go out into the community, help your children *develop the habit of being gracious by writing a thank-you note.* Sometimes you might let your children write a group thank-you note. At other times, you might give them individual assignments in which they draw pictures related to their experience and write about that experience—using dictation, invented spelling, or regular writing.

FINAL THOUGHTS

In this chapter we have dealt with many aspects of management. We have discussed ways to maximize learning and productivity by using different-size groups. We have presented practical suggestions for setting up and using learning centers in the classroom. To help teachers manage active learners effectively, we have presented a variety of tips for behavior management. We have also made suggestions for gathering, caring for, and storing learning materials necessary for a hands-on approach to science. Because media enhance the learning experience, we have shared a variety of resources that the teacher might use in the classroom. To help educators extend learning beyond the classroom, we have provided some hints for organizing and utilizing community resources.

NOW IT'S YOUR TURN

By studying this chapter you have learned a variety of guides for management of hands-on science with young children. Now it's your turn to apply and extend these management ideas. Choose a variety of items from this list for further study and work.

1. Monitor your own use of different group sizes (or observe a teacher working with large and small groups and individual learners). Evaluate your time allotments in terms of appropriate practice for enhancing young children's learning. Suggest needed changes. If you should find, for instance, that in a given week you spent about 90 percent of your science time in discussion in large group settings and about 10 percent with individual "seatwork," you might want to plan for several more small group sessions to give children a chance for hands-on work and more informal conversation.

2. Think about your management of large and small groups and individual work. Use our guides for management of groups to find ways to improve. Add and apply your own guides, if necessary.

3. If management of children's behavior in small groups is a problem for you, plan ways to make children responsible for their own behavior. For example, are you having problems with children staying on task? Find some way to resolve the problem. Do you think you have so many "special problem" children that small group activity would be inviting disaster? Videotape your children in action. Study your videotape and use it to help you plan some strategies for making small group participation work for your class.

4. Plan a new science learning center for your present or future classroom. Perhaps you will want to choose a topic or theme for the center in an area where you currently feel less secure. Planning the center may help you learn about the topic and feel more confident. Plan and sketch a background for the center. Write down suggestions for several things you could display or at least four things children could do in your center. You might want to implement the center, and solicit suggestions about it from children.

5. Choose a child with a special need—for extra help, for an unusual challenge, or for an improvement in behavior. Plan a science experience that you think will help to meet the child's need or capture her interest. Implement your plan if you can.

6. Select an item from our guide for managing children's behavior. Apply the guide to improve children's behavior in your classroom or write about why the guide is important. You might also observe a teacher who has good involvement yet has well-behaved learners. See what techniques that teacher uses and write about some specific ways you could also use those techniques.

7. Review the section of this chapter on using media. Plan a lessson using a kind of educational medium that is new or less familiar to you. Write a lesson plan making media an integral part of the children's learning experience.

8. Obtain a computer supply catalog. Based on the program descriptions, select one or two programs that would be among your top priorities for purchasing. Defend your choices.

9. Choose a science topic or theme. Select at least three children's books or magazines related to the topic or theme. Also, gather at least one adult reference on your topic or theme. Use the materials to supplement your teaching.

10. *Science and Children* and other journals regularly include reviews of children's

books. Use these reviews to select at least three books that you think would be valuable to use in your classroom. Share your selections with a colleague.

11. Plan a field trip or invite a resource person for a unit. Help the visitor fit his or her presentation to the level, interest, and needs of the class. Plan a meaningful follow-up assignment for your children.

12. Do you ever find yourself saying, "If only I had this piece of equipment, I could be a more effective teacher?" Develop a "wish list" of supplies, materials, and equipment you would like to have. Prioritize your list. Plan a way to present your needs to your administrator or to a potential funding source. Parents might be willing to supply some of the items on your list. Design a letter soliciting parent contributions.

SCIENCE MAGAZINES FOR CHILDREN

Electric Company, Children's Television Workshop, One Lincoln Plaza, New York, NY 10023.

Infant Projects, Scholastic Publications, Marlborough House, Holly Walk, Leamington Spa, Warwickshire, England.

Ranger Rick and *Your Big Backyard,* National Wildlife Federation, 1400 Sixteenth Street NW, Washington, DC 20036–2266.

Scienceland, Inc., 501 Fifth Avenue, New York, NY 10017–4145.

Science Weekly, P.O. Box 70154, Washington, DC 20088–0154.

World, National Geographic Society, P.O. Box 2895, Washington, DC 20013.

Zoobooks, P.O. Box 18870, San Diego, CA 92128.

SOURCES FOR SCIENCE MATERIALS AND MEDIA

Science Supplies Companies

Carolina Biological Supply Co., 2700 York Road, Burlington, NC 27215.

Central Scientific Co., 2600 South Kostner Avenue, Chicago, IL 60623.

Chaus Scale Corp., 29 Hanover Road, Florham Park, NJ 07932.

Cuisenaire Company of America, 12 Church Street, Box D, New Rochelle, NY 10802.

Delta Education Inc., P.O. Box M, Nashua, NH 03061.

Fisher Scientific Co., Educational Materials Division, 1259 N. Wood Street, Chicago, IL 60622.

LaPine Scientific Co., 6001 South Knox Avenue, Chicago, IL 60629.

National Aeronautics and Space Administration (NASA), NASA Headquarters, Washington, DC 20546.

A. J. Nystrom and Co., 3333 North Elston Avenue, Chicago, IL 60618.

Sargent-Welch Scientific Co., 7300 North Linder Avenue, Skokie, IL 60076.

Science Kit, Inc., 777 East Park Drive, Tonowanda, NY 14150.

Computer Programs and Activities

Computer Programs, Classroom Computer Learning, 2451 East River Road, Dayton, OH 45439.

Teaching and Computers, 730 Broadway, New York, NY 10003–9538.

SCIENCE MAGAZINES FOR ADULTS

Ad Astra, National Space Society, 922 Pennsylvania Avenue SE, Washington, DC 20036–2140.

Animal Kingdom, New York Zoological Society, Bronx, NY 10460.

Astronomy, Kalmbach Publishing Co., 21027 Crossroads Circle, P.O. Box 1612, Waukesha, WI 53187.

Audubon, National Audubon Society, 950 Third Avenue, New York, NY 10022.

Bibliography of Books for Children, Association on Childhood Education International, 11141 Georgia Avenue, Suite 200, Wheaton, MD 20902.

Connect, Teachers' Laboratory, Inc., P.O. Box 6480, Brattleboro, VT 05301–6480.

Field and Stream, P.O. Box 55652, Boulder, CO 80322–5652.

International Wildlife, National Wildlife Federation, 1400 Sixteenth Street NW, Washington, DC 20036–2266.

National Geographic, National Geographic Society, P.O. Box 2895, Washington, DC 20013.

National Parks, 1015 Thirty-first Street NW, Washington, DC 20007.

National Wildlife, National Wildlife Federation, 1400 Sixteenth Street NW, Washington, DC 20036–2266.

Odyssey, Kalmbach Publishing Co., 1027 North Seventh Street, Milwaukee, WI 53233.

Omni, Omni Publications Int., Ltd., 1965 Broadway, New York, NY 11023–5965.

Sea Frontiers, 3970 Rickenbacker Causeway, Virginia Key, Miami, FL 33149.

Science and Children, National Science Teachers Association, 1742 Connecticut Avenue NW, Washington, DC 20009.

Science Books and Films, American Association for the Advancement of Science, 1333 H Street NW, Washington, DC 20005.

Southern Outdoors, Number 1 Bell Road, Montgomery, AL 36117.

Sports Afield, P.O. Box 10069, Des Moines, IA 50301.

The Museum of Science and Industry's Basic List of Children's Science Books, American Library Association, Publishing Services, 50 East Huron Street, Chicago, IL 60611.

Wilderness Quarterly, The Wilderness Society, 1400 Eye Street NW, Washington, DC 20005.

Young Children, National Association for Education of Young Children, 1834 Connecticut Avenue NW, Washington, DC 20009–5786.

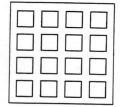

Chapter 5

The Human Body

A N important part of science for young children is study of the human body. This study is natural and intriguing to most egocentric young children. Children love activities that focus on them, their uniquenesses, and their capabilities. Children show an interest in their bodies at an early age. Babies examine their own hands and toes and touch and look at the faces and bodies of their caregivers. Very young children learn to move their bodies in purposeful, controlled ways. All through their lives people refine their muscle skills and extend things they can do with their bodies.

Study of the human body includes exploration of characteristics of people as living things and examinations of likenesses and uniquenesses in people. It extends to the study of the ways body parts function and to care of the body through healthy habits. Study of the body is rich in potential for learning. Cognitive learning and appreciation of the body and desire to care for it can be built together. As children work together and focus on each other's uniquenesses, social and emotional learning are enhanced. Study of the body, like other topics in science, also provides opportunities for children's growth in language and creativity.

This chapter includes the following concepts related to the human body:

- People are living things.
- Our bodies are alike and different in many ways.
- Our body parts have different functions.
- We must take care of our bodies.

PEOPLE ARE LIVING THINGS

People, like plants and animals, exhibit similar characteristics. They move and respond to stimuli. Their bodies grow and repair small injuries. People use air, food, and water and give off wastes such as exhaled air, urine, feces, and sweat. People, like other living things, reproduce their own species.

Educators, by using concrete experiences, can introduce children to the idea that they are living things. Children can demonstrate their learning through expressive forms such as talking, drawing, role playing and gesturing, and writing. To begin study of the human body, you can use the following activities.

☐ ☐ ☐ People as Living Things

Science Processes.   Observing, communicating, using time and space relationships, and measuring.

Help children focus on the characteristics of living things through a series of "listen and do" activities such as these. Depending on the children's attention spans, you may wish to do all the activities at one time or over a period of several days.

Seat the children in a group and, after they have settled down, "accidentally" drop a book. The children will probably react in some way. Let them tell what they did and why. Make a funny face at the children and again ask them to describe their reactions. Discuss the fact that living things react to other things. Let the children describe some events and their reactions to those events.

Reactions often involve large and small movements. Living things move in various ways. Ask the children to demonstrate some ways they can move a finger, a leg, then an arm and a leg. Ask the children to sit as still as possible and see what, if any, body parts still move. After several seconds, let some children describe some body parts that they could not stop from moving (breathing, eyes blinking, and hearts beating). Discuss some ways that people move for fun, to work, or to get from one place to another. Let children take turns demonstrating some of their suggestions.

People, as living things, grow and change. Their bodies can repair many injuries, especially with proper care and medical attention. Ask the children how they know that their bodies are growing. Ask them what happens to their hair and fingernails after they are cut. Encourage children to tell things they can do now that babies cannot do. Let them describe things they will be able to do when they are older. Show the children a drawing of a life-size baby about 55 cm (22 inches) long. Have them compare the drawing to their bodies: How does the baby's size compare to the length of their legs? To their arms? Are they as tall as two babies?

Discuss injuries with the children and how the body repairs many injuries. Scratches and sores heal. Broken limbs mend after several weeks or months. Colds and stomachaches go away. Stress that medical workers work very hard to find ways to combat and prevent diseases.

As living things, people need food and water. Their bodies need food for growth and for maintenance. Ask the children to tell about some foods they like that are good for their bodies. Discuss the fact that water is needed for the cells—very small parts

The children compare their bodies to those of the younger children. They tell what they can do that the younger children cannot do.

of the body—to function properly. People would die if they did not get water, or foods with water in them, for four or five days.

Living things reproduce. Discuss the fact that each person has a mother and father (even though not all people live with both of their parents). Ask the children to tell some ways that parents and other family members care for their babies. Stress that being a parent or caregiving family member is an important role that has great responsibility.

Living things breathe and respire. Ask the children to describe ways their bodies work night and day. If they do not mention it, discuss breathing. Most of the time people are hardly aware of breathing, but we breathe several times a minute throughout our entire lives. Use a watch with a second hand and have the children count the breaths they take in one minute. Have the children take deep breaths, shallow breaths, and fast and slow breaths.

Have the children review with you some of the characteristics of people as living things. Make a list as the children recall items.

Questions. Help the children focus on the characteristics of living things as you discuss these questions. "What are some ways you are like this doll? What are some ways you are different? What are some ways you are like an older person (name a particular person)? How are you different?"

Evaluation. Note the children's interest, attention, and willingness to participate. Assess the number and quality of the examples they offer.

"I'm Alive!" Booklets

☐ ☐ ☐

Science Processes. Observing, communicating, measuring, and using time and space relationships.

Help children complete "I'm Alive!" booklets. They might work on the booklets over a period of several days. Prepare pages for the booklet. Paper folded in half makes a nice size. You might prepare captions or "starters" for most pages, or you might let the children create their own pages. Have the children complete the inside pages first, then design covers that show something about themselves as living things. A booklet made from two sheets of paper folded will look like the one in Figure 5.1.

For the "I can move" page, children can draw themselves moving about. They might select magazine pictures of foods and beverages for the "I eat and drink" page. The children can picture some aspect of growth on the "My body grows" page. They can show a baby with its family on the "People have families" page. On the "I can breathe" page, children might picture a situation in which they are conscious of breathing. For instance, a child might be conscious of breathing while running.

For the book's final page, help children write in their ages and make a fingerprint. Prints can be easily made by scribbling with pencil onto scratch paper, rubbing a fingertip in the scribble, then printing onto the sticky side of transparent tape. The children can then attach the tape to their booklet pages. Set up a place to work with the children in small groups and measure each child's height and weight. Children can compare and discuss their measurements after they record them on the last page of their books.

Children will enjoy reading all others' "I'm Alive!" booklets before taking them home. The booklets are also favorites to present to family members at an open house.

Questions.   "Tell me more about your pictures. What are some other ways you might have shown people moving?" (Or use parallel questions about the other pages.) "How does your height compare to that of a classmate?"

Evaluation.   Note on a checklist the children's abilities to accurately convey ideas in their pictures and their abilities to describe their pictures. Make anecdotal records of any work that is especially creative.

Figure 5.1
Booklet made from two folded
sheets of paper.

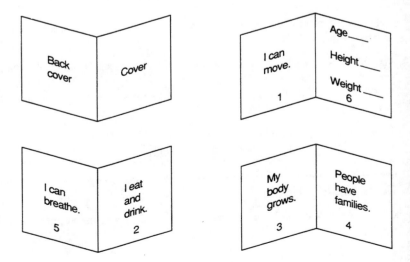

OUR BODIES ARE ALIKE AND DIFFERENT IN MANY WAYS

Conchita's hair is dark and glossy. Her dark brown eyes are fringed with heavy lashes. Conchita's skin is a dark red brown. Vicki's thin hair is almost white and her blue eyes are surrounded by short, sparse lashes. Vicki's pale skin sunburns and flushes easily. As the girls play together, their teacher notices how healthy and attractive each girl is.

A close look at children or adults reveals many obvious differences in features such as height, weight, skin tone, eye color, and body proportion. An even closer look shows more similarities than differences. Most people have hair, two eyes, a mouth, and two feet. Unless they are severely handicapped, all people move and react to stimuli. People also grow and change at different rates.

To draw children's attention to the many similarities and differences in their bodies, use activities such as the ones that follow.

Alike and Different Graphs

Science Processes. Observing, communicating, classifying, ordering, measuring, and using time and space relationships.

Over a period of several days, help the children make a variety of graphs to show some of the likenesses and differences in their bodies. You might use some of these topics and formats.

Boys and Girls Clothespin Graph
Mark on a cardboard strip the categories "boy" and "girl" and the question, "Are you a boy or a girl?" Have children use clothespins to mark their gender (Figure 5.2).

Hair Type Glue-on Graph
Help children look in a mirror and describe their hair. Is it curly, straight, permed, or relaxed? Let children decide and then draw their hair type on a square piece of paper. Have children glue their squares in the appropriate category on a "What Is Your Hair Like?" graph (Figure 5.3).

Real People Height Graph
Choose children in groups of six to eight at a time and let their classmates compare their heights to a designated child's height. Have the children stand in categories on a graph form made from plastic shelf paper. The children could be separated into three categories—taller than the designated child, about the same height as the designated child, and shorter than the designated child (Figure 5.4).

Real People Lineup
Choose a characteristic and have three to five children line up on a plastic shelf paper strip. Their classmates can decide how to arrange them in order based on the chosen characteristic. You might arrange children from longest to shortest hair or from widest arm span to narrowest. Once the children are in position, their classmates might decide where to "insert" another child or two in the order.

Figure 5.2
Clothespin graph.

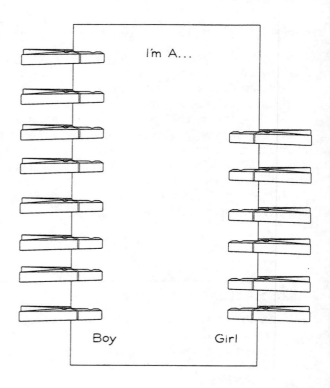

Eye Color Felt Face Graph

Have children look at their faces in a mirror and decorate felt circles to represent their features—eye color, hair color, skin color, and so on. Have them arrange the felt faces on a flannel board to show categories of eye color (Figure 5.5). Save the children's markers and use them for other felt board graphs depicting hair color and skin tone.

Magnet "Handedness" Graph

Have children show their preferred hand for drawing or eating. Let their classmates tell whether it is their right or left hand. Have children affix name tags to a magnetic board using small pieces of magnet to show their preferred hand. You may also wish to check for "footedness" by letting children kick a ball and noticing which foot each child prefers to use (Figure 5.6). You could display "handedness" and "footedness" graphs next to each other and compare them.

As you complete the graphs, help children discuss them. Encourage the children to suggest more topics for graphs that relate to body likenesses and differences.

Questions. "What does this graph show us? Which category has the least number? The most? Do any categories have zero? How many people in all are shown on the graph?"

Evaluation. Note each child's ability to decide on and represent his own body characteristics. Note the children's interest and their abilities to discuss the graphs.

What Is Your Hair Like?

Straight

Curly

Permed

Relaxed

Figure 5.3
Glue-on graph.

Reactions and Preferences   □ □ □

Science Processes.   Communicating and using numbers.

Just as people have both similar and different outward appearances, their reactions and preferences vary. Draw children's attention to their range of feelings and preferences by having discussions and making graphs.

Talk with children about emotions such as feeling happy, sad, excited, peaceful, angry, scared, and confused. Have the children tell about situations in which they felt emotions. Describe situations such as the following and have children tell how they would feel.

- School is closed because of a bad storm.
- The sky is very dark. It looks like a tornado is coming.
- You are at the circus and see many clowns and animals.
- You hear the sound of sirens coming closer and closer.

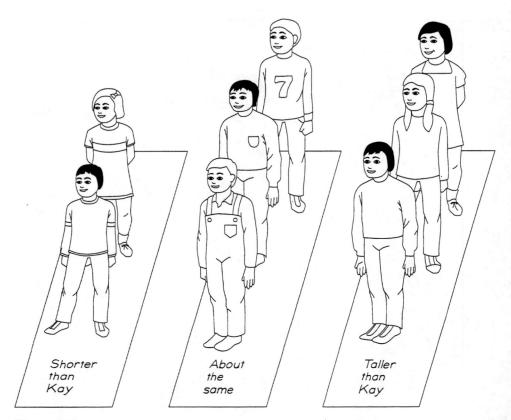

Figure 5.4
Real people graph.

As the children describe their feelings, help them fill in a space on a laminated graph form that names the feelings (Figure 5.7). Let children express their views on a wide range of topics. You might let children pick favorites such as ice cream, kinds of pizza, after-school activities, and books. You can have children choose blocks to show their preferences or draw their choices on square pieces of paper. They can pile their blocks up to form a bar graph or pin their papers on a bulletin board to show their preferences (Figure 5.8).

Questions.   "How many people preferred _____? How many more preferred _____ than _____? What else does our graph show us?"

Evaluation.   Let teams of two or three students poll their classmates to find out about their preferences or reactions. Guide each group to select a topic and decide on categories. Have them walk around with a "pollster's" clipboard and seek their class-mates' opinions (Figure 5.9). Have them report their results to the class. Judge the children's independence and cooperation as they complete their polls.

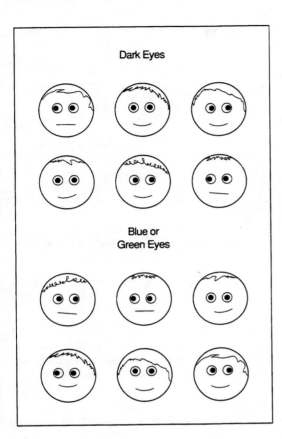

Figure 5.5
Felt face graph.

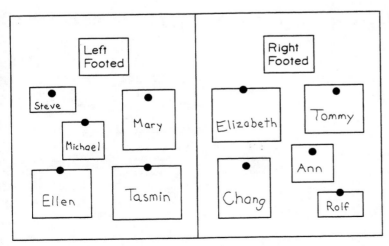

Figure 5.6
Magnet graph.

Figure 5.7
Laminated graph form.

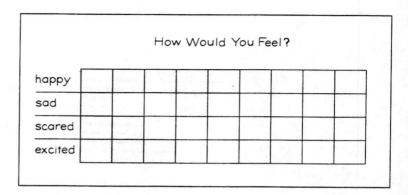

☐ ☐ ☐ Growth Rates

Science Processes. Observing, communicating, measuring, using time and space relationships, and ordering.

Each person grows, but people grow at different rates. Help children focus on this idea by charting aspects of their growth. Toward the beginning of the school year, work with children in groups of three and four and measure their heights. For each group, decide who is tallest and shortest and whose height is in between. Record the children's heights again and compare the measurements to those made earlier in the year. Discuss any differences.

To make a height graph, you can help each child measure and cut a piece of yarn or adding machine tape to represent his height. The lengths can be taped or pinned to a bulletin board for life-size picture of the children's heights (Figure 5.10). The children can identify classmates' heights and compare them.

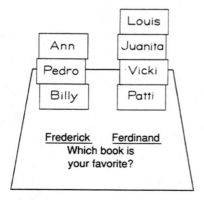

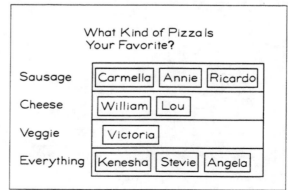

Figure 5.8
Graphs showing preference.

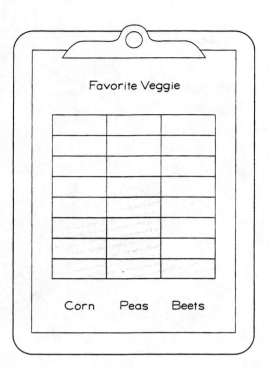

Favorite Veggie

Corn   Peas   Beets

Figure 5.9
Pollster's clipboard.

How Tall Are You?

Ben   Kelly   LaToya   Jorge   Shirley

Figure 5.10
Height graph.

These children are simulating different handicaps to develop a sensitivity to the way handicapped people move from place to place.

You might also weigh the children two or three times during the school year and compare their weights. Children could trace around their feet and compare their foot lengths.

Questions. "Show me about how big or tall a baby is. Compare your height to that of a baby. Besides growing taller, how else does your body grow and change?"

Evaluation. Note the children's interest and abilities to compare their body measurements to those of others.

□ □ □ Simulating Handicaps

Science Processes. Observing, communicating, and inferring.

When children "put themselves" in another person's place, they can begin to understand that person's condition better. Set up classroom situations to allow the children to simulate different handicapping conditions.

Let children make blindfolds with scrap fabric and elastic. Plan a short lesson during which the children participate while wearing their blindfolds to simulate working with impaired sight.

To simulate a broken arm, let children work in pairs and use a scarf to tie one hand to the body. (Tie up each child's dominant hand.) Present a task that requires the children to use their hands.

Perhaps you could borrow a child's wheelchair and/or small crutches and place these devices in the science center. Let children practice moving about with the aid of crutches or a wheelchair.

A loss of hearing can often result in people feeling quite isolated from their friends. Provide several pairs of earmuffs or earphones from your language arts center. Have children use these "ear insulators" outside during recess. Encourage them to try to play an entire recess period without taking off their earmuffs or the headpieces of their earphones. This experience might help them build empathy for others with hearing impairment. (See "Now It's Your Turn" for more on handicaps.)

Questions. "How did you feel working/playing without your eyes? Ears? Hand? Legs? What was hardest for you? Did your friends treat you differently? How? Did you find that you used another part of your body more to help you? Which body part did you use? How could we be more helpful to someone with this handicap?"

Evaluation. Observe children's abilities to accurately simulate these handicaps and describe their responses to the handicapped experiences. Which children seem to develop more empathy as a result of these expereinces? Which simulations appear to be most effective?

OUR BODY PARTS HAVE DIFFERENT FUNCTIONS

From the moment we awaken each day, our body parts help us react to and receive stimuli. Even before we open our eyes, we hear sounds. A quick glance tells us what the weather is like. A stretch before leaving the bed helps us get our muscles moving and prepares us for a busy day. Our muscles and skeletons work together to support and move our bodies. As we eat breakfast, few of us consider how our digestive systems process the foods that our bodies metabolize and how the circulatory, respiratory, and excretory systems work to circulate blood and oxygen to all our body parts and remove wastes.

All during the day and night our digestive, respiratory, excretory, and circulatory systems continue to work. Our endocrine and nervous systems regulate and control our bodies. Cells in our bodies are constantly replaced. Indeed, the human body is a fascinating and intricate composition of interrelated parts and functions.

Part of our work with young children is to help them learn more about the makeup of their bodies. From simple naming of body parts to examination of body symmetry, to learning about organs and systems of the body, our study can be concrete and exciting. Study of the senses is appropriate and important. Young children can explore some aspects of the skin, circulatory, skeletal, digestive, and muscular systems. Study of the excretory, nervous, reproductive, and endocrine systems are best conducted with older children.

This section offers a variety of activities to deepen children's understanding of the idea that our bodies have many different parts with different functions.

Body Symmetry

Science Processes.   Observing, communicating, and using time and space relationships.

Start this science activity with an art activity. Let children blot paint by putting blobs of tempera paint on one side of a piece of paper, folding the paper in half vertically, and smoothing the paint between the paper by rubbing the back side. When the paper is opened, the children will find a good example of vertical symmetry. Talk to the children about how one side is a reflection of the other side.

To help children become aware of symmetry found in plants, animals, and in their own bodies, bring in leaves that show clear examples of symmetry. Talk about how one side of a leaf looks very much like the other side, and if you fold the leaf in half, you have something that looks like a mirror image.

Bring a pet to school. As you discuss the way the pet looks, point out the symmetry found in its body—its eyes, ears, front legs, back legs, and so on.

Ask children to look at a partner or at themselves using a mirror. Have them tell about body parts on one side of their bodies that are similar to parts on the other side of their bodies.

At the science table, give children individual felt boards made from file folders and felt body pieces. Have children make felt dolls demonstrating the symmetry found in one's body.

Questions.   "Put your hands together. Can you make one hand fit exactly to the other hand? How are your hands alike? What differences do you notice? Can you think of any body parts that are covered by your clothes that you have two of and that look alike?"

Evaluation.   As you question children and as you watch them make felt board dolls, notice how well they understand the concept related to the symmetry found in our bodies.

Body Tags

Science Processes.   Observing, communicating, and using time and space relationships.

Prepare several lightweight cardboard tags and insert a yarn tie in each. Write names of body parts or simple clues for body parts on the tags (Figure 5.11). You might prepare tags that say things like the following: ankle, elbow, ear, neck, waist, calf, forearm, you stand in tiptoes on these (toes), your hair is on this (head), its nickname is pinkie (little finger), it's between your waist and neck (chest or torso).

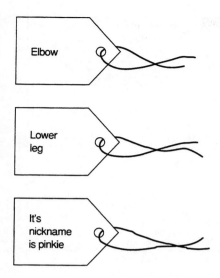

Figure 5.11
Body tags.

Read the tags to the children and let them take turns hanging the tags on the appropriate body parts of volunteers. Have each volunteer describe or move the body part as it is identified.

Have children work in small groups to make more tags and hang or pin them on large body shapes drawn on paper or on dolls. Children can also draw their own body pictures and label at least ten parts on each.

Questions.   Choose two body parts and have children compare them. For example, focus on the elbow and knee—"How are they alike? How are they different?"

Evaluation.   Seat the children and have them wiggle or move body parts as you name them. As you notice children who are hesitant or incorrect, schedule extra activities for them to give them more practice.

Sensory Bingo   ☐ ☐ ☐

Science Processes.   Observing, communicating, and classifying.

Have first through third graders fold a square of paper in halves, then quarters to make sixteen sections. List words and symbols on the chalkboard and have children fill in a bingo-like card as in Figure 5.12. The children's columns and rows may be in any order; encourage each child to fill in the card to make it different from her classmates.

Let children take their bingo cards outdoors and lay them on the ground. The children should then collect small specimens to fit the characteristics and lay them on the bingo card squares. You might play until each child calls bingo, or until each child

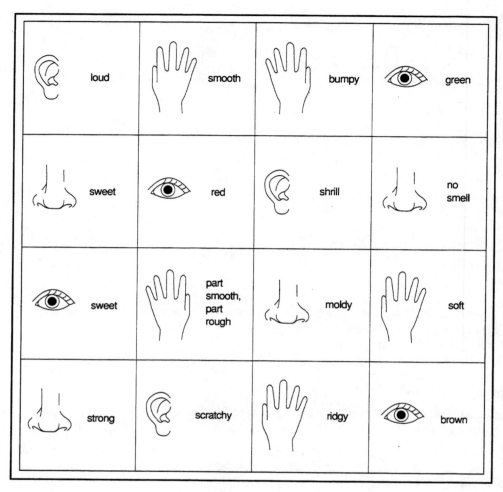

Figure 5.12
Bingo-like card for the senses.

fills her card. Have children check each others' cards and show each other why they picked the objects they did.

Have children choose and describe to small group members their most interesting objects. Specify what the children are to do with their objects—return them to the locations where they found them, discard them, or keep any objects they wish in a small bag. If children can take objects back into the classroom, they might fix a display table with labels such as "We saw that these objects were red," "These objects make shrill noises," or "These things smell moldy."

Questions. Which objects were easy to find? Which objects could fit into more than one classification?"

Evaluation. Observe the children's abilities to follow directions and to choose objects to fit each classification.

Sensory Books

Science Processes. Observing and communicating.

Help the children make sensory books. They can show on the pages things they observed with their senses. The children might make the books a page at a time after completing experiences like the following.

"I Can See" Page

Set up a "looking center" at a table or on a rug. Provide hand lenses, a microscope, a mirror, and perhaps binoculars or a simple telescope. Encourge children to examine their skin, clothing, faces, and faraway objects using the tools that enhance sight. Have the children draw an eye on their "I can see" page and depict some favorite part of their experiences.

"I Can Hear" Page

Provide musical instruments or tape recordings for the children to use. On their book page, ask them to draw an ear as well as something that their ears let them hear.

"I Can Touch" Page

Have children trace a handprint, then collage onto each finger something of a different texture. Provide cloth, various papers and cardboards, sandpaper, and other materials for the children to choose.

"I Can Taste" Page

Have children draw a big mouth and tongue. Provide little samples of food—chocolate chips, lemon slices, apple slices, raw and cooked carrot rounds, cubes of bread, and so on—for the children to sample. Talk about the foods' tastes and textures, then have the children draw or cut from magazines pictures of food to paste on and near their tongue pictures.

"I Can Smell" Page

Have a small group of children help you prepare some "smelly jars." Use plastic film cans or baby food jars covered with contact paper. Place samples of things with strong odors inside. Some examples are perfume, rubbing alcohol, or furniture polish on a cotton ball; garlic, onion, cinnamon, lemon, or orange; wet sawdust; hand lotion; or shaving cream. Supervise as children lift the lids, smell the jars without peeking inside, and talk about the smells. For the "I can smell" page, have children draw a nose and pictures of things with distinctive odors.

"I Can Use All My Senses" Pages

Have children draw two pages to depict situations in which they use all their senses. They should add one more blank page. Children can make and decorate covers for their books. After trading and reading each other's books, the children can take their books home to complete the last page, "Using My Senses At Home."

Questions. "How do your senses work together when you eat pizza? When you walk down the street?"

Evaluation. Note the care and thoroughness with which children complete their books. You might want to write a complimentary note inside each book for the children's parents to read as they finish the books at home.

□ □ □ Teacher's Sensory Bingo Chart

Science Processes. Observing, communicating, ordering, and classifying.

Children need a variety of sensory experiences. They can practice various skills and use a variety of processes as they participate in these experiences. To help you maintain variety and balance in the activities you offer, you might use the sensory bingo chart for ideas (Figure 5.13).

As you can see, the chart uses five different skills. To practice the describing skill, have children tell about the experience. Encourage them to use a wide variety of descriptive words and to tell how the experience made them feel. Use the drawing and writing skills to follow up an experience with each child recording what has happened. In comparing, children go beyond describing and examine similarities and differences among two or more objects. As they order, children arrange objects along a continuum on the basis of some observable characteristic. For example, children could feel fabric squares and arrange them in order from smoothest to roughest texture. Finally, children can use classification to make two or more groups of objects.

The chart briefly mentions materials to use for experiences. You will be able to think of many more readily available materials to use as you provide a variety of sensory experiences for children.

Questions. For any experience, ask questions about using the skill with a different sense or with different materials. For example, after looking at things and describing them, you might ask, "How do these things feel? What other senses could we use? What other materials could we look at and talk about?"

Evaluation. Note on a checklist the children's interest and attention as they participate. Note those children who are able to use language skills and ordering and classifying skills as they work with the sensory experiences.

□ □ □ Skin Studies

Science Processes. Observing, classifying, using time and space relationships, communicating, and inferring.

Talk about how the skin is a protective covering over the body. It prevents bacteria from getting inside the body and keeps fluids from escaping. One of the best ways to make young children aware of the functions of the skin is to introduce the subject casually when occasions arise. When a child comes in with a cut or a scrape, let children examine the cut. Have children observe the skin wound on the child each day

Skill/Sense	Sight	Hearing	Touch	Smell	Taste
Describing	Look through hand lenses at hands, small objects.	Listen to tape recording of familiar voices.	Tell about the feel of a classroom object. Have someone identify it.	Break or scratch fresh leaves and tell about odors.	Tell about tastes of popcorn: plain, buttered, salted, sprinkled with sugar and cinnamon.
Drawing or writing about	Draw a picture of things you can see on the ground, at eye level.	Use classroom instruments. List high sounds, low sounds.	Trace around hand. On each finger, make a different texture rub.	Write the word "smell" with glue. Sprinkle on "smelly" spices.	Write and draw about a vegetable tasting party.
Comparing	Compare appearance of seashells.	Say the same sentence loudly, softly, smoothly, roughly. Compare the sounds.	Compare textures of shoe soles.	Compare odors of fresh oranges, canned orange juice, orange candy.	Compare tastes of slivers of apples, raw potatoes, turnips, radishes.
Ordering	Order fabric scraps from lightest to darkest shades.	Listen for 60 seconds. Name loudest to softest sounds.	Lift rocks. Put in order from heaviest to lightest.	Smell wildflowers. Order from very strong odor to little odor.	After tasting samples, put lemonade in order from most sour to sweetest.
Classifying	Group crayons by color, used or "new," or primary colors or not.	Play samples of fast tempo and slow music. Sort selections into groups.	Examine shapes inside a "feely" bag. Group by holes or no holes in shapes.	Group foods by "good smells," "not-so-good" odors.	Classify food pictures by "I like" and "I don't like."

Figure 5.13
Teacher's sensory bingo chart.

and discuss the changes they notice. As the wound heals, talk about how the skin is able to repair itself.

Another function of the skin may be observed on a hot day when the children have returned from the playground all hot and sweaty. Ask, "Why are your faces so red and damp?" Help the children understand that when it is warm, we sweat. Our skin has millions of sweat glands that give off salt, water, and other waste products when we get warm. Give children hand lenses and let them observe the tiny pores that lead to the sweat glands. Have them take a stiff piece of paper and fan themselves. As children describe the cooling effect of the fanning process, explain that the skin begins to cool as the water evaporates from their skin. This process of sweating is one of the ways the skin cools the body.

Our skin has nerve endings that help us feel. With the nerve endings near the surface of the skin, we can feel hot or cold temperatures, pressure, or pain. Have children experiment with these sensations. Give children ice cubes to press on different parts of their bodies—elbows, knees, toes, fingers, ears, and calves. Encourage them to tell where they feel the coldness the most. Have them work in pairs. One child in each pair keeps his eyes shut while the teacher directs the partners to use the eraser of a pencil to write a numeral on their partner's backs, on the back of the hands, on the palms, on the top of the foot, or on the sole. The partner whose eyes are shut should try to identify the numeral written each time.

Questions. When children see cuts on a child's skin, ask questions such as these: "What do you notice about Robert's cut? Why is it bleeding? Why is the rest of his body not bleeding, but this cut place is bleeding? Why did we have to wash and put disinfectant spray on Robert's cut?"

When the children investigate the sweat glands in the skin, ask questions such as: "How did you feel before you started fanning yourself? What happened when you began to fan? How was it different? Where do you think the water came from? Lick the top of your hand. How does it taste?" Reinforce the fact that when we sweat, the sweat glands in our skin give off waste products such as water and salt. Ask children: "What are other ways our bodies give off waste products?"

As children investigate the nerve endings below the skin's surface, have them think of other ways to test the sense of feeling found in the nerve endings of our skin.

Be sure to follow up with culminating questions such as: "Why do we need our skin? How does our skin help? What would it be like if we didn't have skin?"

Evaluation. Notice children's comments as they observe the way their skin reacts in different situations. As you draw a closure on your skin studies, observe children's abilities to give brief summaries of the functions of the skin.

☐ ☐ ☐ Muscle Manipulations

Science Processes.   Observing and communicating.

Our bodies have many muscles, both voluntary and involuntary. We can control our voluntary muscles. To help children become aware of the voluntary muscles in their bodies, play the following little game. Construct a spinner by cutting out of a magazine pictures of different body parts. Glue these pictures to a cardboard circle. Place a spinner in the center of the circle, as shown in Figure 5.14.

Select one child to be the "muscle manipulator." Spin the spinner. Whichever body part the spinner stops on, the "muscle manipulator" must move a muscle of that body part. For instance, if the spinner stops on a picture of the head, the child may move a muscle around the lips and smile or grimace; she may move muscles around the eyebrows, or eyelid muscles. The rest of the group has to name specifically where the muscle is located. Then the children must copy the "muscle manipulator" and move that particular muscle on their own bodies. They should put their hands on the muscle and feel as it is flexed and feel it again as it relaxes.

Mention to the children that some muscles in our bodies move beyond our control. See if children can suggest any involuntary muscles in their bodies such as the heart and circulatory muscles, digestive muscles, and muscles related to breathing. Challenge your students to try to stop using an involuntary muscle. For instance, ask them to see how long they can stop breathing. Let them feel their heart beating. Tell them that the heart is a strong muscle about the size of a fist. Remind them that the heart keeps beating without any effort on their part.

Questions.   As the spinner stops on a body part, challenge children to think of other muscles in that particular area. Ask: "Why is this muscle so important to our bodies? What would happen if we couldn't use this muscle?" Challenge your students to suggest what might happen if our hearts stopped beating or if we stopped breathing.

Evaluation.   Notice children's abilities to think of a variety of different muscles to flex for each body part. Observe their actions as they flex and relax each muscle. Do they give an indication of understanding that they can control some muscles? Note the understanding they show as they make inferences about the importance of different muscles.

Figure 5.14
Spinner for muscle manipulation.

☐ ☐ ☐ Build a Skeleton

Science Processes.   Observing, communicating, using numbers, using time and space relationships, and ordering.

Seat the children and have them feel their legs and describe what they feel. Point out that the skin covers our bodies, and inside are muscles, blood, bones, and other substances our bodies need to function. Have the children feel their shin bones and hard kneecaps. Have them feel their bumpy spines and curl their spines to get an indication that the spine has many small bones that make it flexible. Have children gently feel the skin, muscles, and bones of their faces. Instruct them to move their jaws and describe how the lower jaw (mandible) is a bone that is separate from the other facial bones. Show the children how to gently feel around their eyes; they will feel their eye sockets. People's noses and ears are made of cartilage and feel softer and perhaps more flexible than bony areas of the body. Invite children to discuss other bones they can see and feel.

Organize children into groups of three or four. Give each group a paper skeleton with its bones cut apart. The National Science Teachers Association (1742 Connecticut

One child points to a part of the skeleton while the others find that part on their bodies.

Avenue NW, Washington, DC 20009) offers a wonderful, child-size paper skeleton for three dollars, or you may purchase several Halloween skeletons and cut the bones apart. Let the children lay out their bone pictures and talk about and compare them.

Now lead the groups in putting their skeletons together. Describe different bones and groups of bones, and have the children pick out the bones and lay them on the floor. You might expose the children to the scientific names of some of the bones as you go along. Your discussion might sound like this:

- Let's find the part that protects our brains. It's made of several bones that are joined together. It has "holes" for the eyes and nose. It's the skull.
- Now let's find the lower jawbone. This is the hardest bone in the body. It holds half or our teeth. It's the mandible.
- Find seven small bones that make up our necks. Most mammals—even giraffes—have just seven neck bones. Attach them to the skull.
- Now find the ribs and backbone. We have ribs on each side of a breastbone. Feel your own breastbone and ribs. Let's count the ribs. The rib cage helps protect the lungs and heart.
- Now find some bones from the lower back. They're called vertebrae. Attach them to the rib cage and upper backbones.
- Now find some oddly shaped bones—the pelvis. This gives a shape to our hips and gives our legs a place to attach.
- Let's decide which are the arm bones and leg bones (the arm bones are shorter). The lower leg and lower arm each have two bones in them. Can you find the kneecaps? They're in the middle of the leg bones. The kneecap's scientific name is the patella.
- Now decide how to attach the hands and feet. How many bones do you notice in the hands and feet? The many bones in our hands and feet make them very flexible.

After the groups have put their skeleton models together, have them compare their results. Allow time for interested children to reshuffle their bones and put them together again. They could lay the bones out on the floor or pin them to a bulletin board.

Questions. "Find the longest bone in the body (the upper leg or femur). Find other long bones. Show me some curvy bones and bones with holes in them. Describe some of these bones. What are some things you can tell about the bones in your body by feeling them from the outside?"

Evaluation. Observe the children's interest and abilities to following directions.

Skeleton Dances

Science Processes. Observing, communicating, classifying, and using time and space relationships.

Conduct a "talk and do" session to establish some background for your skeleton dance. Ask the children to feel their hands and describe what they feel. Have them wiggle their fingers and watch carefully, then wiggle and feel. Discuss the fact that each finger has three bones and two joints—except the thumb, which has two bones and one joint. Have the children locate some joints in their hands and other parts of the body.

Talk about these facts: Bones are hard, bones support our bodies, muscles attached to bones move our bodies, and strong bones are built with good food and exercise. Have children feel the bones in their forearms, ribs, knees, and toes and describe what they feel. Have any child who is willing let a classmate gently feel some of the bones in his spine and watch his shoulder blades as he moves his arms.

Work some more with joints. The joints in the fingers are known as hinge joints. They move in just one direction. Help children locate and move other hinge joints—in toes, elbows, and knees. Some joints let body parts move in several directions or rotate about. These are called ball-and-socket joints. People have ball-and-socket joints in their ankles, hips, wrists, shoulders, and necks. Have the children feel and rotate their ball-and-socket joints.

Now for the skeleton dance. Play some lively music. Ask the children to choose a space where each can move about but not disturb others. Have the children follow instructions such as the following as they "dance."

- Let one hinge joint move and dance to the music. Now add another hinge joint.
- Move some parts of your skeleton above your waist. Dance with many bones.
- Suppose you had no knee joints. Show how you would dance.
- Dance with one ball-and-socket joint. Add another. Now move as many ball and socket joints as you can to the music.
- Suppose you had no skeleton. Show how you would dance.

Invite children to suggest and perform other skeleton dances.

Questions. "How can you tell you have hard bones inside your body? Some bones help to protect other body parts because they enclose them. Show me some examples."

Evaluation. Observe the children's willingness and abilities to follow directions and describe bones they see and feel. Note the children's enjoyment of the skeleton dance exercises.

Breathe and Beat

Science Processes. Observing, using numbers, communicating, using time and space relationships, and inferring.

Encourage children to put their ears against another's chest and listen to hear the heartbeat. Be sure each child gets his partner's permission to listen. To magnify the heartbeat sound, let children make a "stethoscope," by tightly stretching a balloon over one end of a toilet tissue tube. The child may listen by pressing the end with the balloon on it against the other child's chest and by holding the open end to her ear.

Another type of "stethoscope" can be made by removing the bottom from a Styrofoam or plastic cup. The two open ends allow sound to travel from the child's heart to the ear. Inexpensive classroom stethoscopes can be purchased for less than ten dollars.

As children listen to heartbeats, encourage them to tap their fingers in rhythm with the heartbeats. Have partners listen to each other's heartbeat while the "examinee" is relatively quiet. Then have each "examinee" exercise vigorously. Compare the heartbeat while resting with that after exercise. If you have a clock with a second hand, let children count the number of heartbeats in 15 seconds. Have them take a count before their partner exercises and then again after exercise. Encourage children also to count the number of breaths a child takes while relatively quiet and compare that to the number of breaths taken after a child has exercised.

During the course of the children's experiments, talk about the circulatory system and how the heart pumps blood through the blood vessels all over the body. Have children locate a few blood vessels in their bodies. Introduce them to the fact that our circulatory system carries digested food and oxygen throughout the body and takes away waste materials. Remind the children that our lungs help us breathe in oxygen and exhale waste material called carbon dioxide.

Questions.   "When do you breathe the fastest—when you are sitting very quietly or after you have exercised? Which time do you think your heart beats the fastest? When you are asleep, do you think you breathe? Does your heart beat then?"

Evaluation.   Notice children's abilities to test their partners and to observe accurately breathing rates and heartbeats before and after exercise.

Body "Maps" of the Digestive System   □ □ □

Science Processes.   Observing, communicating, using time and space relationships, measuring, and using numbers.

Present to second and third graders some basic information on the digestive system. This system helps us take in food and processes food so our bodies can use it. We chew food and it mixes with saliva in our mouths. Our tongues help us swallow food. Food goes down a long tube, the esophagus, to the stomach. Here food remains for 2 to 4 hours and is mixed with digestive juices and broken down to small pieces and liquids. The food then passes a little bit at a time to the small intestine. Here it is broken down further, and nutrients pass through to the bloodstream and then to all parts of the body. Parts of food that cannot be digested pass to the large intestine and leave the body as feces.

Have children work in groups of three. They should have one group member lie down on a large sheet of paper and trace around her outline. Help them discuss parts of the digestive system and draw the organs on the outline. Help children with the proportions and locations of organs. They should draw the mouth and perhaps add teeth and a tongue. The esophagus goes straight down the neck area and should be drawn about as wide as two fingers. The stomach is on the left side in the lower rib cage area. It can be drawn as a pear-shaped organ about as big as a child's outstretched hand. The children might add a "liver" drawn on the right side a little larger than the stomach.

Help the children cut newspaper or computer paper to make "intestines." The small intestine (which is narrow but long) should be about 5–6 m (5–6 yards) and 2 cm (less than 1 inch) wide. The large intestine (which is shorter but wider than the small intestine) can be cut about 1–1½ m (1–1½ yards) long and 5 cm (2 inches) wide. The children should coil the small intestine in the abdomen area. They can glue it in place as shown in Figure 5.15 or place it in a plastic bag stapled to the abdomen area.

Let children display their drawings and describe the passage of food through parts of the digestive system. Encourage the children to discuss the fact that our bodies are complex and wonderfully "designed" even though we often take their functioning for granted.

Questions.   "What part do the teeth (or tongue, stomach, or small intestine) play in digesting food? How do you think the small intestine got its name? Why do we chew our food before we eat it?"

Evaluation.   Observe the children's abilities to work together cooperatively. From their products and descriptions, evaluate the children's understanding of the interrelated parts of the digestive system.

Figure 5.15
Body map of the digestive system.

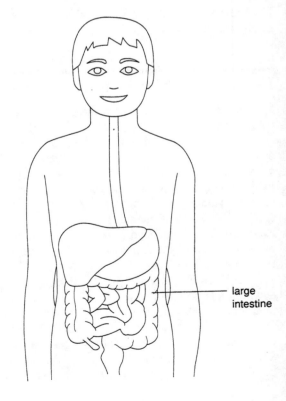

large
intestine

WE MUST TAKE CARE OF OUR BODIES

Healthy living pays big dividends. Healthy people feel good and are full of energy for work and play. Their hair and eyes have a sparkle and their walk has a bounce. They are ready to learn and contribute.

Maintaining good health requires consistent attention. Even young children can begin to learn about the need for good diet, exercise, rest, and cleanliness. Teachers can help children maintain good health habits at school. They can also reinforce children's understanding of the need for health care—visiting the doctor and dentist— and the need for avoiding dangerous situations.

The activities in this section present a variety of ways educators can help children learn to care for their bodies. Together with positive support from home, these activities can help to build healthy young learners who respect their own bodies and are committed to caring for them.

Healthy Living in the Classroom

Science Processes. Communicating and inferring.

If you really care about children developing healthy living habits, help children establish a few of these habits in the classroom.

Talk about the importance of keeping clean. Lead children into a Socratic-type discussion in which you talk about the importance of keeping our bodies clean, why we don't put our fingers in our mouths, why we must wash our hands before meals and after we use the toilet, the reasons we cover our mouths when we cough or sneeze, and the importance of brushing our teeth.

As follow-up activities, encourage children to bring a toothbrush and toothpaste to school to brush their teeth after each meal. Invite a dental hygienist to come and demonstrate the proper way to care for teeth. Perhaps the dental hygienist could provide free toothbrushes and toothpaste for the children.

To encourage washing one's hands at appropriate times, make a hand-washing chart in the restroom. Let children check off as they wash their hands. Discuss conservative use of liquid soap and water during hand washing, but be sure children use enough to do a thorough job.

Praise children who remember to cover their mouths when they sneeze or cough. Pause from time to time with appropriate comments stating the reasons for covering our mouths.

Discuss with the children the importance of getting plenty of exercise every day. Remind children that exercise keeps our muscles strong; it keeps the blood circulating through the body so that food and oxygen can get to all parts of our bodies and waste products can be removed. Good exercise also builds our lungs and helps us breathe better, bringing fresh air and oxygen into our bodies and getting rid of waste products or carbon dioxide. To reinforce the need for daily exercise, plan daily periods when children exercise in class. Perhaps you might introduce some aerobic exercises in your classroom right before lunch or before dismissal time. Some teachers might take the first 10 minutes of recess for organized exercise. On a daily routine, you might look for certain periods in the day when children seem restless or fatigued. Interrupt your schedule with some strenuous movement to help children relax and to build up breathing and heartbeat rates.

Rest is also important and can be emphasized in the classroom. Notice the time of day the energy in your classroom seems to lag. Plan a 5 to 10 minute rest period with lights out when children *and teacher* take a break and just rest.

Teachers can also reinforce in the classroom healthy eating habits. Discuss the need for a balanced diet and the importance of eating healthy snacks rather than junk food. Over a period of time, plan snacks that include foods from each of the food groups. Be sure to direct your snacktime conversation to the foods that belong in each food group.

Questions. "How did you feel before you exercised? Rested? How do you feel now? What do you notice that is different about your body now? How does exercise help our bodies? What foods are good for you? Which of those foods do you like the best? What junk foods do you eat that are not good for you? What could you substitute?"

Evaluation. Notice how consistent and willing the children are to adapt healthy classroom habits.

Healthy Habits Home Chart

Science Processes. Observing, communicating, using time and space relationships, ordering, using numbers, and inferring.

If children truly are to develop healthy living habits, they must practice these habits at home daily. To help children extend the practice of healthy living, make charts for children to mark in order to keep up with their own health practices at home. The chart might look similar to the one in Figure 5.16. Adapt your chart to fit the health practices you are emphasizing in your classroom.

Questions. "What are some other good health habits you practiced this week? Which did you do most each day—watch TV or play outdoors? What nights did you not get enough sleep? How did you feel the next day? How could you change your habits in the evening so you could get more sleep?"

Evaluation. Study children's charts. Note those children who need special help with specific health practices. Plan a strategy for helping them. This strategy might include soliciting parental help.

Health Habits Mural

Science Processes. Observing, communicating, and classifying.

Lead a discussion of staying healthy and safe. Write down things the children say on sentence strip papers. Encourage many answers. Help children reread their suggestions. Have the children decide how to arrange their suggestions under six (or more) headings: good diet, exercise, rest, cleanliness, health care (visiting a doctor

Healthy Habits	Monday	Tuesday	Wednesday	Thursday	Friday	Saturday	Sunday
I bathed							
I brushed my teeth							
I got this many hours of sleep							
I played out-doors and ex-ercised							
These are some healthy foods I ate							
Other health habits I prac-ticed were . . .							

Figure 5.16
Healthy habits chart.

or dentist), and avoiding dangerous situations (poisons, dangerous appliances, sharp tools, strangers, or unwanted advances from people). If the children have not offered suggestions in some of these areas (or others you wish to use), help them discuss these ideas.

Supply a large piece of paper for a background. Organize the children into six groups and let each group draw and cut out figures to go on the mural to illustrate each area of staying healthy. When children finish with their assigned area, encourage them to make pictures to illustrate any other ideas that they wish.

Display your mural, perhaps along with your sentence strips, in the hall for others to see.

Questions. "What are some of your healthy habits? What could you do to stay healthier?"

Evaluation. Record on a checklist the children's willingness and abilities to contribute. Note the care and details evident in their artwork. Ask children who can write to list at least three healthy habits. Check their papers for accuracy and clarity of expression.

Healthy Habits Posters

Science Processes. Communicating.

Help children work with partners and make small posters to depict some of the healthy habits and ways of staying safe that they have learned. You might assign topics to the pairs of children, or they might choose their own topics. You might use a poster design in which one half shows what to do to stay healthy and the other half shows things to avoid. For example, on a poster that focuses on exercise, the children could cut out pictures of children running and playing. They could depict children watching television as an activity to limit.

Let the children use any technique they wish to create their posters—drawings, paintings, or collages are all appropriate. Have children show their posters to the class and tell about them. You might also arrange for children to show their posters to children in another classroom. You could also display the children's posters in an area outside your classroom.

Questions. Encourage the children to add details to what they have shown on their posters by asking: "How could you carry this out? How can you encourage others to have healthy habits?" Also ask: "Besides posters, how can we show others what we have learned about staying healthy?" Plan to follow up on some of the children's ideas.

Evaluation. Judge the children's understanding of ideas by looking at their products and listening to their explanations. Mark on a checklist your judgment of the children's interest and enthusiasm.

What Should We Do?

Science Processes.   Communicating and inferring.

Children should have many opportunities to discuss dangerous and questionable situations in order to know how to respond to them. With preplanning they should be better prepared to respond should the situation arise.

Set up role-playing situations for children to act out. Follow up each situation with discussions on "why" or "why not." Let children talk about their own experiences if they wish.

Let your students role-play some of these situations. Adjust them to fit your classroom needs.

- You are walking home. A man you do not know stops the car and offers to drive you home. (Have one student act as the child, and another as the strange man.)

- Someone stops you as you are getting ready to go into the school building. She offers you free candy.

- Your father goes to the drugstore and buys pills for you to take.

- Someone you know wants to touch you in a place that makes you feel embarrassed or uncomfortable. This person says, "It's okay, but don't tell." (Just talk about this situation or act it out without really touching.)

- You go to the doctor's office, and the doctor touches you in a place that makes you feel uncomfortable or embarrassed. (Just discuss this situation.)

- Your parents have tools on the workbench—a hammer, nails, saw, electric drill, and so on. You want to repair the birdhouse.

- You are walking over to a friend's house. You discover a new dog in the neighborhood. It begins to run toward you.
- Your pet has been hit by a car and is thrashing in pain near your driveway.
- You are home alone. The phone rings, and the person on the phone asks, "May I speak to your mother or father?"
- You are home alone, and someone knocks on the front door.
- You are home alone, and someone tries to get in the house.
- You are home alone, and you smell smoke in the apartment or house.
- You are home alone, and your head begins to ache.
- Your baby brother finds some matches and is playing with them.
- Your little sister is playing with a bottle of cleaning fluid.

Questions.   Direct your questions to each mock situation. Adjust your questions using the Socratic method if you detect that some children lack an adequate understanding of appropriate responses in some of these situations.

Evaluation.   Observe children's role-playing and their responses to determine whether or not they have a clear understanding of the proper way to respond in each situation.

NOW IT'S YOUR TURN

Participating in activities that focus on the human body "turns on" most children. Now, as usual, here's your opportunity to turn on your mind and body and extend some of the ideas we have presented in the chapter.

1. Carry out a row, column, or diagonal of activities from our "Teacher's sensory bingo chart" (see Figure 5.13). Reflect on the experiences you provided and evaluate your "performance" in terms of questions such as these: "How did I try to involve each child? What could I do to get more involvement? What higher-level thinking questions did I raise? Could I do more to stimulate children's thinking? How did I introduce and summarize the activities? Could I make the beginnings and endings to activities more interesting?"

2. Work with a colleague and add at least ten items to the "Teacher's sensory bingo chart." Plan items that feature easily obtainable materials or items that provide unusual and memorable experiences for your students.

3. In this chapter, we have described several child-made books or booklets. Brainstorm ideas for more child-made books or booklets you could make during or after an experience. Perhaps you can also think of ideas for a teacher-made book to use as you teach a concept related to the human body. Select your best idea and carry it out with children.

4. Nutrition is a pertinent topic. Children should begin learning to eat foods that build healthy bodies when they are very young. Plan one good activity to help your students learn this concept.

5. Get your own body moving. Try a new exercise or creative movement activity. Focus on your muscles and bones and the ways they work. Be aware of your heartbeat, breathing, and perspiration. Think about some ways your body systems work together as you move. Plan to share your experiences with children.

6. Children in most classrooms look very different, yet each is appealing and attractive in many ways. Consider ways to recognize each child's appearance and ways to make individual children proud of their appearance and body types. Share some of your ideas with colleagues.

7. As a busy professional in an occupation that is often stressful, you may need to develop or extend some ways of relaxing. Using your senses is a good way to unwind. After the children have left your classroom, sit down for a few minutes. Close your eyes and listen to all the sounds around you. Stretch your legs, then your arms and neck. Feel your muscles tighten and relax. Find an area of your classroom that pleases you. Look carefully at it, noting details and complimenting yourself on the work that you or students do in this area. Now leave your seat and have a beverage or snack. Smell your food carefully, then eat or drink it. After using all your senses, it's time to resume your busy schedule.

8. Survey your community for people with various handicaps. Find out how some of these people feel about their handicaps and how willing they might be to share some of their conditions with your class. Invite several of these people to visit your class. Plan ahead of time what they might say and do.

9. Research your community environment to determine the problems that might have the greatest effect on the children in your classroom. For instance, what is the drug situation in your community? What ages are being affected? How high is the incidence of child abuse? Check out these problems or any others that might be appropriate. Contact the police department, the school nurse, health care workers in the emergency room, and other helpful resources. Share your information with the teachers in your school and with the parents of your children. Plan a strategy for attacking at least one problem.

SELECTED CHILDREN'S BOOKS

Ball, J. A., & Hardy, A. D. (1989). *What can it be?: Riddles about our bodies.* Morristown, NJ: Silver Burdett.

Ball, J. A., & Hardy, A. D. (1989). *What can it be?: Riddles about the senses.* Morristown, NJ: Silver Burdett.

Berger, G. (1989). *The human body.* New York: Doubleday.

Burstein, J. (1977). *Slim Goodbody: The inside story.* New York: McGraw-Hill.

Cobb, V. (1989). *Getting dressed.* Philadelphia: Lippincott Junior.

Cobb, V. (1989). *Keeping clean.* Philadelphia: Lippincott Junior.

Emmert, M. (1989). *I'm the big sister now.* Niles, IL: Albert Whitman.

Greenfield, E. (1988). *Grandpa's face.* New York: Philomel Books.

Human body. (1983). Tokyo: Froebel-Kan Co., Ltd.

Lemaster, L. (1984). *Your brain and nervous system.* Chicago: Children's Press.

Rius, M., Parramon, J., & Puig, J. (1985). *The five senses: Sight.* Woodbury, NY: Barron's.

Rius, M., Parramon, J., & Puig, J. (1985). *The five senses: Smell.* Woodbury, NY: Barron's.

Rius, M., Parramon, J., & Puig, J. (1985). *The five senses: Taste.* Woodbury, NY: Barron's.

Rius, M., Parramon, J., & Puig, J. (1985). *The five senses: Touch.* Woodbury, NY: Barron's.

Showers, P. (1982). *You can't make a move without your muscles.* New York: Thomas Y. Crowell.

Turner, D. (1989). *Foods we eat: Bread.* Minneapolis: Carolrhoda.

Turner, D. (1989). *Foods we eat: Eggs.* Minneapolis: Carolrhoda.

Turner, D. (1989). *Foods we eat: Milk.* Minneapolis: Carolrhoda.

Turner, D. (1989). *Foods we eat: Potatoes.* Minneapolis: Carolrhoda.

Van der Meer, R., & van der Meer, A. (1987). *Your amazing senses: 36 games, puzzles, and tricks that show how your senses work.* New York: Aladdin Books.

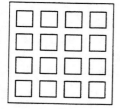

Chapter 6

Animals

ALTHOUGH human beings are a special kind of animal, the focus of this chapter is on the non-human members of the animal kingdom. These creatures range from tiny ants and mosquitoes to huge whales and elephants. Most children have a natural curiosity about animals and an affinity for them. Educators can capitalize on this interest and help children learn many different kinds of things about animals. The study of animals especially enhances children's use of the science processes of observing, communicating, and classifying. Increasing children's knowledge of animals through meaningful experiences also develops positive attitudes toward animals. Appropriate study of animals fosters appreciation and wonder as well as responsibility in caring for animals. To make children's study of animals meaningful, adults should include as many experiences as possible with real animals.

This chapter includes the following five concepts about animals:

- Animals are living things.
- The animal kingdom includes a wide variety of creatures.
- Animals live in a variety of places.
- People benefit from animals.
- Animals benefit from people's care.

A discussion of each concept is followed by descriptions of several learning activities.

ANIMALS ARE LIVING THINGS

From the slow-moving sloth to the tiny hummingbird to the seagoing octopus, animals exhibit characteristics common to all living things. The study of animals should help children to see the commonalities (and differences, too) among animals, people, plants, and protists such as molds, mushrooms, and yeast.

☐ ☐ ☐ An Animal Visitor

Science Processes.   Observing and communicating.

Arrange for an animal visitor such as a calm, gentle dog or cat, or a goldfish. Make the necessary arrangements to keep the animal safe and comfortable in your classroom. Obtain a stuffed animal that looks like the live animal or make a picture of the animal that will visit your classroom. Seat the children where they all can see the animal visitor and toy. Establish the fact that they should watch the visitor closely, but touch it only under supervision.

Ask the children to tell some things they notice about the animal visitor and the stuffed toy. Have them notice the animal's movements and describe how it moves. Ask: "Is the stuffed toy moving?" Talk about the fact that the animal has grown from a small puppy (or cat or fish). If your animal has toenails, show them. Perhaps you can cut a toenail and discuss how it will grow back. If the animal is cut or scratched, discuss the fact that it will heal. If the animal is furry, brush it and show some loose hair. Explain that the animal will grow more hair (people do this, too) to replace lost hair. Let children talk about other ways the animal grows or repairs itself. Ask: "What will happen if you cut or scratch the toy? Could it repair itself? Does it grow?"

Offer the animal some food and water. Watch it eat. Offer some food to the toy and ask the children what happens. Tell them that living things respire or use air. Draw the children's attention to the animal's breathing. A child or two could gently touch the animal's sides as it breathes. Have the children observe the toy to see if it breathes. Clap your hands and ask the children to notice how the animal and toy react. (You could tap on the fishbowl if you are using a fish.) Have a child call the animal's name and see how the animal reacts. Have another child pet the animal and toy to see if they show signs of enjoyment. Let the children offer other suggestions of things to do; try them, and have the children watch for reactions from the animal and toy.

Finally, talk about reproduction, emphasizing that each living thing reproduces its own kind: dogs have puppies, fish have baby fish; cats have kittens. If possible, tell about the animal when it was a baby or show a photograph of a similar baby animal. Mention that the toy was not a baby, and it cannot reproduce.

Ask the children to tell some things they have learned. Help them draw some conclusions about the animal and the toy. The children should have noticed that the animal has exhibited many of the characteristics of living things, whereas the toy has not. Have each child write or draw about what happened with the animal and the toy.

Compliment the children on their behavior around the animal visitor. Caution them about approaching or touching stray or wild animals. Otherwise, the children may assume that every animal is friendly, gentle, and safe.

The children compare a live pet and a stuffed animal.

Questions. "What foods are good for our animal visitor? What baby animals have you seen? Tell about them. What are the ways we knew our animal visitor was alive?"

Evaluation. Look at the children's writing or drawing to see what characteristics of living things they have included.

Earthworm Investigations

Science Processes. Observing, communicating, predicting, inferring, and using time and space relationships.

Earthworms are simple but amazing animals. This activity will draw the children's attention to worms' body features, movements, and reactions. A close look at earthworms may help children appreciate them more.

Divide the children into small groups. One or two groups can use a piece of glass, a mirror, and two blocks set up as shown in Figure 6.1. This device will let them watch the earthworm from the top; it will also let them see the reflection of the earthworm's underside. Have groups take turns using the device.

Tell the children that they will be observing and handling earthworms. Explain that they should handle them gently to show respect for living things. Encourage children who are hesitant, but do not force them to touch the worms.

Figure 6.1
Earthworm viewing setup.

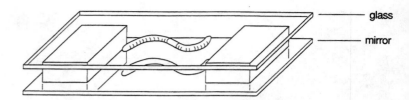

glass

mirror

Provide two or three worms in a cup for each group. Let group members describe the worms. Have the children take turns holding the worms and observing them using their senses of sight, smell, touch, and hearing. (The worms won't make many sounds that can be heard.)

Have the children use hand lenses and try to locate these parts of their earthworms: .

- *Segments*—cylindrical body sections. Ask: "About how many segments are there?"
- *Head*—consider the front part as the worm moves forward to be its head.
- *Mouth*—an opening in the head. Ask: "What shape is the mouth?"
- *Clitellum*—an enlarged glandular area about 1/4 of the way from the head to the tail; a segment or "saddle" that looks different from the other segments.
- *Setae*—four tiny spines or bristles on each segment. Ask: "Where are setae located?"
- *Other features.*

Have each group place a worm gently on a damp paper towel. They should turn the earthworm gently on its back and see how it reacts. The children can also place a worm between a damp and dry paper towel and see where the worm moves. Have the children predict how the worm will react. Ask: "Does it seem to prefer moving or staying on the damp or dry towel?"

Next, the children could place a worm between dark- and light-colored papers, predict where the worm prefers to move, and then observe the worm's reactions. Have the groups share some things they observed and learned about earthworms. Collect the earthworms. Release them in a spot where they can live, or have a child take them home and release them.

Questions. "How did your senses help you find out more about the earthworms? What are some ways that worms help people? How do we know that worms are living things?"

Evaluation. Note the children's skill in observing, describing, and inferring. Note their interest and respect for the worms.

☐ ☐ ☐ Animals Move!

Science Processes. Observing, communicating, and using time and space relationships.

After observing several live animals and the way they move, use video or film to show the children other animals in motion. Before viewing, suggest some things the children could look for. Ask: "Do the animals move slowly or fast? Do they move with legs, wings, or other means? Do they move on land, in air, or in water? Is their movement smooth, jerky, or bounding?"

After viewing the film, let the children talk about it and discuss what they saw. If there are questions or disagreements, perhaps you can look at parts of the film again. Have the children act out some of the animal movements they observed. They might also write a group composition or make a chart about their observations. A chart might look like this.

Animal	Speed	Where It Moves	Kind of Movement
rabbit	fast	land	jumps
snake	slowly	land	slithers
shark	very fast or motionless	water	smooth—tail moves it

Questions. "How are these animals' movements like the movements of people? How are they different? What are some words that describe the animals' movements?"

Evaluation. Make note of the children's attention and communication skills as they describe and act out animal movements.

Speedy Animals

Science Processes. Observing, measuring, communicating, and using time and space relationships.

Some animals, including humans, move slowly and some move quickly. You can help 2nd- and 3rd-graders compare their top speeds to those of animals. Have a group of children help you lay out a "race course" of 50 meters. Perhaps the children could use a trundle wheel to measure the course. If not, they could measure and cut a 10-meter length of clothesline and use this length to lay off the 50-meter course.

Discuss with the children the fact that animals move slowly or quickly depending on the circumstances. Let the children discuss when an animal might be inclined to move slowly or quickly. Let the children name animals they think of as slow or fast.

Show Table 6.1 to the children. Ask them to use the data in the table to point out the slower and faster animals.

Take the children to your 50-meter race course. Explain that if they run down the course and back, they will have run 100 meters. Have children volunteer to run—at top speed—over the course for 1 minute. Have others help time their classmates and count the number of times the runner completes the 100-meter course. Record how many times each child can run the 100-meter course in 1 minute. Help children interpret the data on the chart. Ask: "How did your speeds compare to those of the various animals? How long do you think you could run at "top speed"?

Questions. "What are some things we learned from this activity? What characteristics do the faster animals have in common? Do the slower animals have anything in common?"

Table 6.1
Animal Speeds

Animal	Approximate Number of Times Animal Can Run 100 Meters in 1-Minute
Antelope	16
Cheetah	19
Chicken	2–3
Elephant	7
Human adult	7–8
Human child	(to be determined by class members)
Pig	3
Snail	Very small part—perhaps 1/2 meter in a minute

Adapted from *World Almanac*.

Evaluation. Assess the children's interest in the activity and their abilities to use the measuring tools and make comparisons. Record observations of children's abilities on a checklist.

☐ ☐ ☐ Animal Reproduction

Science Processes. Observing, communicating, and using time and space relationships.

Many animals will reproduce in the classroom. In this activity we suggest three small animals appropriate for study by young children.

Snails belong to the mollusk family. They have soft muscular bodies protected by spiral shells. Snails are invertebrates; they have no skeletons. Land snails breathe air and move on a flat "foot" that is kept moist by a slimy secretion that the snail makes. Children can often see a slimy "trail" left by land snails. Children can note four tentacles on the heads of land snails: two tentacles are sensors, and the two hind tentacles have eyes on the ends.

Aquatic snails usually have only two tentacles on their heads. Some have gills for breathing; others have breathing pores. Aquatic snails may be kept in a medium- or large-size fish bowl or in an aquarium. Aquatic snails reproduce readily. After mating, snails lay small round eggs, usually in clusters. After several days tiny snails emerge from the eggs. Aquarium snails may be fed *small* amounts of lettuce or fish food.

Guppies, which are small fish, also reproduce readily. They may be kept in a large fish bowl or balanced aquarium, allowing 1–2 liters (1/4–1/2 gallon) of water per fish. The water should be kept at a temperature of 18–23° C (65–75° F). Guppies may be fed a small pinch of dry fish food each day—adults will need medium size-food; babies require fine-size food. Children can notice that male guppies are smaller but have fancier tails than the larger, heavier females. After guppies mate, their young are born alive.

Another interesting animal for children to observe is the spider. Spiders have eight legs and two body parts. In contrast to most insects, they have no feelers, antennae, or wings. Spiders eat soft foods, sucking the food with their fangs. Try to find a spider's web outdoors or in an undisturbed part of the classroom. Look for an egg sac attached to the web. The young spiderlings stay in the web for several days after they hatch. Some mother spiders care for their young; other spiderlings can survive independently soon after they hatch.

You may find other classroom animals that will enable the children to observe reproduction and growth. Mice, gerbils, or hamsters are relatively easy to keep in the classroom. No matter what the animal is, children will be able to watch it move, react, and eat. Be sure to point out that these are characteristics common to living things. Encourage children to keep records of phenomena they observe. Since the children will probably observe animals over a period of time, have them date their records.

After the study of live animals, you might have children work with pictures of animals and their offspring. The children could discuss the pictures and describe all the details they notice. The children might act out the movements of the animal mothers caring for their babies. For example, children could dramatize birds setting on eggs, feeding their babies, and then pushing them out of the nest and protecting them as they learn to fly. The children could also match pictures of animals and their offspring. The children might review pictures of butterfly metamorphosis and act out being tiny motionless eggs, voracious caterpillars, cocoons, and then becoming beautiful butterflies.

Questions. "What do you think the young of these animals will look like? How are the adults like their young? How are they different?"

Evaluation. Note children's curiosity and sustained interest. Note the skill with which they communicate about their animals and keep records. In listening to the children's comments and answers, judge whether they are focusing on the characteristics of living things.

A WIDE VARIETY OF CREATURES EXISTS IN THE ANIMAL KINGDOM

Some animals are so small that we cannot see them without microscopes; others are many times larger and heavier than people. Animals exist virtually everywhere on our globe and have adapted to survive. Animals vary dramatically in their appearances, abilities, and habits. As young children study animals, they can begin to learn about and appreciate the variety of life in the animal kingdom.

Huge Animals, Real Sizes

Science Processes. Observing, measuring, ordering, communicating, and using time and space relationships.

Help children gain an idea of the enormous size of a large animal such as a giraffe, whale, or dinosaur. Choose two animals. Show the children pictures of each and let them tell what they know about each animal's size. Encourage the children to verbally compare the animal's size with the size of other things and, have them show with body language how big they think the animal is.

Using measurements from a reference book, help children make a "model" of the two large animals you have discussed. You might "lay out" a model of the animal in the hallway or schoolyard. For example, to represent a giraffe that is about 5 to 6 meters (15 to 19 feet) tall, you might help children use a meter stick or trundle wheel and place masking tape in the hallway to represent the actual height. After the initial tape is in place, teams of children can use more tape to outline the giraffe's head, neck, body, and legs in approximately correct proportions. For a giraffe-size animal, you could also let the children make a newspaper or butcher paper picture of the actual size.

To represent a Tyrannosaurus rex, about 15 to 16 meters (50 feet) tall, you might move to the schoolyard. Have children use a heavy yarn to mark the dinosaur's height on the ground. They can then finish the figure with yarn. Tongue depressors or small sticks can be used to anchor the yarn. Tyrannosaurus rex's teeth were approximately 15 cm (6 inches) long. You could help the children add paper teeth of that length to the model.

These children are comparing the size of this dinosaur with their own size.

After your two figures are completed, have the children compare the figures to their own bodies. The children could guess about how many of their own body lengths it would take to be as tall as each huge animal figure. Children might volunteer to lie down directly on the model to verify their guesses. They might use a long pole to measure the height of the door or classroom ceiling to see if the animals could fit in the classroom. Ask the children to make other comparisons between their own sizes and the sizes of the animal models. If you can leave your models in place for a few days, help the children make signs to explain to others what the measurements and the model represent. Display the signs near the models.

Questions.   "How might your life be different if you were as large as the giraffe (or other model)? What do you and a giraffe (or other model) have in common? How are you different?"

Evaluation.   Note the children's cooperation and willingness to participate as you complete the animal models. Make note of children's abilities to work with lengths and proportions, and to make predictions and comparisons.

Observing Animal Bones   □ □ □

Science Processes.   Observing, classifying, communicating, and using time and space relationships.

Collect some chicken bones. Clean them by boiling, scrubbing, and drying them. (They can also be washed in the silverware tray of the dishwasher). Use the diagram of the chicken skeleton at the end of this chapter. Let children match the chicken bones to the diagram of the chicken skeleton, placing the bones in the correct positions. Encourage the children to compare the various bones of the chicken with the bones in their bodies. For instance, ask: "How do the wing bones compare to the bones in our arms? How is the wishbone like and different from a human's collar bone and breast bone?"

Bring in other animal bones to compare. Use beef and pork bones or a backbone from a cooked fish. Label the bones. Display them on bone mobiles.

Questions.   "How do our bones help us? What makes strong bones?" Observe a cross section of a beef bone and a chicken bone with a hand lens. "How are they different? How are they alike?"

Evaluation.   Note children's abilities to match chicken bones to the diagram. Observe their answers as they compare and contrast bones.

Classifying Animal Pictures   □ □ □

Science Processes.   Observing, communicating, and classifying.

Collect pictures of a variety of animals. Pictures of mammals are easy to find, but be sure to include other vertebrates such as birds, reptiles, amphibians, and fish.

Collect pictures of invertebrates such as insects, spiders, sponges, snails, octopi, and crabs. The children can help collect pictures.

For a small group activity, have children look through and talk about a collection of 20 to 30 pictures. Use sorting mats and encourage the children to classify the pictured animals (Figure 6.2). Have them specify what categories they are using and use one mat for each category. They can write the names of the categories on the mats with crayon or washable marker.

For instance, the children could classify the animals by size—"animals smaller than I am," "animals about my size," "animals larger than I am." Encourage the children to discuss their decisions and check each other's work to see that the animals are in the appropriate categories.

After the pictures are classified one way, have the children think of another way to classify them. Some possible ways to classify pictures follow:

- *Body coverings*—furry, scaly, smooth, bumpy, or other. (An "other" category is often handy.)
- *Eating habits*—meat eaters (carnivores), plant eaters (herbivores), meat and plant eaters (omnivores).
- *Number of legs*—0, 2, 4, 6, 8, or "other."
- *Movement*—walk, run, crawl, swim, fly, other, or more than one way to move.
- *Where animals live*—habitats such as deserts, oceans, forests, plains; or farm, zoo, and homes (pets).

Questions.   "What other ways could you group, or classify, the animal pictures? Which animal is your favorite? Why did you choose it?"

Evaluation.   Observe and note the children's abilities to classify. Can they classify animals appropriately once categories are set up? Can they suggest other ways to classify animals? Can they identify the categories?

 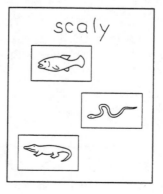 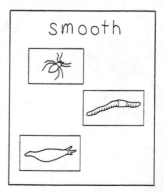

Figure 6.2
Sorting mats.

Animal Observations

☐ ☐ ☐

Science Processes. Observing, using time and space relationships, and communicating.

Take your class on a field trip to observe the wide variety of creatures in the animal kingdom. You may take a walk in the neighborhood or visit a farm, pet shop, or zoo. Encourage the children to observe the various characteristics of different animals such as body coverings, sizes, sounds they make, habits, or tendencies to live alone or together. Ask children questions to encourage them to observe beyond the superficial level.

After the animal observation field trip, let the children work in pairs or independently and observe a particular animal. Encourage them to consider animals such as insects, birds, or fish for their observations. Have them carefully watch the animal of their choice and answer the questions on the observation sheet, "Animal Watch" (Figure 6.3). After children have collected their data, let them share their findings in small groups.

Questions. "What was the biggest animal we observed? The smallest? Which animals moved the fastest? Which ones took up very little space? Which ones seemed to like to be with other animals? Which ones lived alone? What else did you observe that was interesting?"

Evaluation. Note children's responses as they comment on their animal observations. Evaluate the answers recorded on their "Animal Watch" sheet. Note the detail and accuracy of their map in question 6 on the "Animal Watch" sheet.

ANIMALS LIVE IN A VARIETY OF PLACES

Animals live almost everywhere on earth. Forests are homes to animals such as deer, chipmunks, owls, and toads. Meadows and grasslands provide habitats for giraffes, antelope, kangaroos, wild dogs, and dozens of other animals. Swamps and marsh lands are home for creatures such as snakes, alligators, and clams. Even frozen tundra and ice floes are homes to animals such as polar bears, seals, and penguins. Most areas of the ocean and many lakes and ponds team with life. Water creatures are as diverse as frogs, fish, shellfish, crustaceans, sponges, and whales. Birds, insects, and worms live virtually everywhere on land.

Animals live in wild and sparsely populated areas of the earth, but they also live in densely populated cities. City children can observe wild birds, insects, people's pets, and zoo animals. Many rural children are familiar with farm animals and wild animals that live near their homes.

To live in the world's different habitats, animals have adapted to their surroundings. For example, a polar bear's thick coat and white color protect it from its cold northern habitat. A coyote's fur protects it from temperature extremes in its desert environment, and its long legs enable it to wander over a large territory in search of prey.

---

1. My animal is _____.

2. The body covering is _____.

3. Its size is _____.

4. How does it move? _____. Does it move fast

   or slowly? _____.

5. When it moves, does it cover a lot of space or very little space?

   _____

6. Draw a map on the back of this sheet of the places your animal went while you observed it.

7. Does your animal live alone or with other animals? _____

   _____

8. Did you see your animal eat? _____? What did it eat?

   _____. How did it eat its food?

   _____

9. Did it make sounds? _____.

   What did it sound like? _____.

10. Write something else you learned about your animal.

11. Draw a picture of your animal.

Figure 6.3
Animal Watch.

Migrating birds are equipped with wonderful senses that guide them in their journeys to find proper habitats for breeding and eating.

In this section we provide activities to help broaden children's understanding of the variety of places in which animals live. Educators will want to add activities that will stimulate children's observations of animals in their immediate environment. They can also draw the children's attention to animals' habitats that are shown in pictures, films, and videos.

☐ ☐ ☐   Familiar Animal Habitats

Science Processes.   Observing, communicating, predicting, and inferring.

Help children notice animals in your immediate surroundings. Ask children to predict what animals they might see if they walk around the neighborhood or yard.

Make a list of their predictions. Now take the children for a walk. Draw their attention to birds, insects, spiders, people's pets, and other animals.

Perhaps you can find a suitable area and have the children sit down and listen for the buzzing of insects or the calls of birds and squirrels. If the children do not see all the animals they hear, help them make inferences about what animals may have made those sounds. Write a group composition about their observations.

Local naturalists or forest service workers may be willing to share their expertise with your class. They may come to your classroom to show specimens or pictures to the children. You may also be able to arrange for a hobbyist or expert to meet you in a park, empty lot, or other natural area to talk to the children. Don't overlook the possibility of taking the children to a zoo or aquarium to see animals and to notice how the habitats for the animals meet their needs for protection, food, and exercise. Be sure to write a thank-you letter to any resource person who has helped you.

Questions.   "What do (specific) animals need to live? How do they meet their needs in this environment? What are some animals we would expect to see here? Why do you think we will see them?"

Evaluation.   Note on a checklist the children's interest and cooperation. Note the quality of children's observations as evidenced by their comments and contributions to the group composition.

Animal Habitat Books

Science Processes.   Observing and communicating.

Supplement children's direct observations of animal habitats with published books and child-made books. Choose books with photos or realistic pictures that show animals in their natural habitats. You might use *Animal Homes* (Entwistle, 1986) or *America: Land of Wildlife* (Jensen, 1984).

Read the animal books to the children and encourage them to browse and "read" the text and pictures on their own. Ask: "What is it like where this animal lives? Does the animal need much water? How does it get water? How does the animal protect itself from the weather?" These questions will direct the children's attention to how animals have adapted to their habitats.

Let groups of children make their own animal habitat booklets using information from their direct experience and from books. You might let children draw pictures, then dictate or write information about their pictures. You might let children use cutout animal pictures and draw each animals' habitat. You might also let each group make a booklet of animals in one habitat. For example, one group could do a "Desert Animals" book while other groups work on "Water Animals," "Forest Animals," and "Grassland Animals." Groups might also work on booklets on different "Dinosaur Habitats" such as swamps, oceans, or grasslands.

Questions.   Show the children a clear picture of an animal and its habitat and ask "Could this animal live in our area? How are the animal's surroundings like ours? How are they different?"

Evaluation.   Note each child's ability to relate to pictures in books and to describe or draw what she reads or sees.

☐ ☐ ☐   Animal Habitat Boxes

Science Processes.   Observing, communicating, and inferring.

Have individuals or groups of children select an interesting animal or group of animals. Provide books and pictures so they can learn more about the animals' habits and habitats.

Help the children make little scenes in shallow boxes to show their animals in their habitats. They can draw "scenery" and place dirt, sand, rocks, grass clippings, and twigs in the box to simulate appropriate environments for their animals. The children can clip pictures of their animals from magazines, draw their own animals, model clay animals, or use plastic animal models in their boxes.

Have the children show and tell each other about their boxes. They might display their boxes in a "museum" for another class to see.

Questions.   "What did you learn about your animal's habitat? What problems did you solve or investigate as you made your box? How is your animal's living place like your own? How is it different?"

Evaluation.   Note each child's ability to apply information as he makes the animal habitat box. Record evidence of each child's ability to tell about his box.

☐ ☐ ☐   Animal "Home" Specimens

Science Processes.   Observing, communicating, and inferring.

Collect examples of animal homes. Add to your collection by purchasing inexpensive samples at museum shops or from science supply companies. Enlist help from the children's families in collecting specimens for the children to examine.

Your collection might include birds' nests, empty cocoons, honeycombs, sea shells, coral, shells of dead turtles, vacant wasps' nests, and other specimens.

Let the children examine the specimens and speculate how the animals "made" the specimens. You might let children dictate a list of descriptive words for each specimen. Display the lists near the specimens.

Questions.   "How did this animal's "home" protect the animal? How are these two specimens of animal homes alike and different? What size might the animal from this home have been?"

Evaluation.   Observe the children's interest in and sense of wonder at the animal homes. Note on a checklist the children's ability to describe and compare the specimens and to make inferences.

PEOPLE BENEFIT FROM ANIMALS

People derive many benefits from animals. Animals provide food, clothing, and transportation for people. Animals also provide fun and companionship for people; they are often a source of wonder, excitement, and pleasure.

An Animal Sharing Table

Science Processes.   Communicating and classifying.

Furnish a few items to start a "sharing table" to display things that show how people benefit from animals. You might start with an item to represent foods from animals (tuna, an egg, or a picture of meat); clothing that comes from animals (a small item made of silk or wool); and animal transportation (a plastic figure or picture of a horse and rider). Also, provide a picture to represent animal-human companionship (a person playing with a pet).

Talk to the children about your display. Encourage them to draw pictures of items to add to the categories on display. Children can also made clay models and bring items from home. As your display grows, let the children tell their classmates about the items they have contributed.

Questions.   "Animals help us in many ways. Which way do you think is most valuable? Why do you think so? How do people in other lands benefit from animals?"

Evaluation.   Observe the children to note if they correctly classify the examples of animal benefits they contribute. Note also the skill with which children draw, model, and discuss their contributions.

How Animals Help Us

Science Processes.   Classifying and communicating.

To help the children organize their thinking about ways animals help us, make a chart for the children to use. It might look like this one.

Animals Help Us

Food	Clothing	Transportation	Friends	
pig	sheep	horse	dog	goat
cow	goat	husky (dog sled)	cat	fish
fish	rabbit	elephant	gerbil	rabbit
chicken	worm (silk worm)	camel	hamster	parrot
rabbit		goat (goat cart)	parakeet	guinea pig
goat			horse	snake

Encourage children to discuss which animals fit in more than one column. For instance, a horse can be a means of transportation and a friend. The children might decide that goats are used for food and clothing and can be friends. As they discuss goats, the children might decide to add goats to the transportation list because goats can pull a cart.

Questions. "Which column has the most animals in it? The fewest? Which animal would you choose as a friend? Which animals would you like to use as your means of transportation?"

Evaluation. Observe children as they add to the chart. Which children answer freely? Which ones rarely contribute ideas? Which children elaborate on the ideas they contribute? Who has the most unique contributions?

ANIMALS BENEFIT FROM PEOPLE'S CARE

Animals and people coexist in our crowded modern world. Many animals thrive without special care, but others could not survive without people's attention. People need to be sensitive to the needs of animals in our environment. They may provide habitat, protection, food, and water for animals.

We can begin nurturing young children's sensitivity to animals' needs as we talk about and observe different animals in various settings. This sensitivity should lead children to assume responsibility in caring for animals.

☐ ☐ ☐ Animal Letters

Science Processes. Communicating.

Collect pictures of a wide variety of animals that benefit from people's care. Use your pictures to generate a group discussion on how people care for the animals in

Helping children to care for a classroom pet builds feelings of responsibility and helpfulness.

the pictures. After the discussion, encourage each child to select an animal, pretend to be that animal, and write a letter thanking the person who takes care of it. For instance, a lion might write a letter of thanks to the zoo-keeper for providing fresh meat, water, and a clean display area. A horse could write a letter to the farmer. A dog could write a letter to its master. After letters are written and illustrated, let children work in small groups reading their letters to each other.

Questions. Encourage children to compare likenesses and differences in the needs of their animals.

Evaluation. Observe the letters to see if children show a clear understanding of the needs of the animal they chose.

What Makes a Good Pet?

Science Processes. Communicating and classifying.

Encourage evaluative thinking through the following activity. Ask: "What makes a good pet?" The children should be led to make up criteria such as "A good pet must be safe. A good pet must be easy to care for. You must be able to get its food cheaply and easily. You must have good shelter for it." After children have established criteria for judging what makes a good pet, record the criteria on a chart. Let each child choose an animal and use the criteria to determine whether that animal would really be a good pet. Give the children a big collection of animal pictures. Let them sort the pictures into two categories: those that would make good pets and those that would not make good pets.

Questions. The major question in this activity is the evaluation question in which the children set criteria and make judgments based on those criteria. As they make and use criteria for "good" pets, ask supportive questions to extend their thinking. For example, ask: "Where would you get the food? How would you pay for it? If your parents wouldn't let you keep that animal indoors, where would you keep it?"

Evaluation. Observe the logic in children's answers as they formulate criteria and judge whether their animal choice would be appropriate. Note those children who participate and those who are more hesitant.

Endangered Species

Science Processes. Communicating and inferring.

Collect pictures of animals that are endangered. (The journals *National Wildlife* and *International Wildlife* are a wonderful source of pictures.) Have a class discussion about what those animals need for survival. Talk about their environment and how it has changed. Ask children to think about why those animals are endangered. Encourage them to talk about things that might be done to improve the environment to heighten the animal's chances of survival.

Questions.   Ask each child to talk to an older person to learn how animal populations have changed in their lifetime. Ask: "What changes have occurred? How do the changes make the older person feel?"

Evaluation.   Observe children's participation and depth of understanding as they discuss possible reasons for and solutions to the problems of endangered species.

NOW IT'S YOUR TURN

Extend the ideas we have presented for teaching animals. Choose one or more of the following options to enhance your knowledge of animals and to add to your repertoire of activities for teaching about animals.

1. Read more about an animal you don't know much about. Study pictures of the animal. Decide on a way to share what you have learned about the animal with the children.

2. Suppose you worked in an inner-city school. Suggest some meaningful ways you could help children develop concepts about animals.

3. Browse through some issues of *Science and Children*. Find the "Classroom Animal" column that appears in several issues each year. Read one or two columns to find a new animal that would be suitable for your classroom. Acquire the animal and prepare a place to keep it. Secure the food you need for your animal. Use the information in the "Classroom Animal" column to keep the animal safely in your classroom for at least several days. Plan several activities to acquaint the children with the new animal.

4. Invite a parent to bring a gentle animal to your classroom and conduct a show and tell session for the children. Think about rules to make and enforce to help your human and animal guests feel safe and comfortable. After your guest leaves, have the children follow up with illustrated thank-you letters.

5. Animals, their body characteristics, and their habits are amazingly diverse. Plan a creative science activity for your classroom teaching the concept—a wide variety of creatures exist in the animal kingdom. Focus on some animals that are new to you.

6. When the real animal is unavailable, pictures and books are useful in helping children develop understandings of the animal kingdom. Supplement your science materials by adding more colorful pictures of animals to your collection and a few new, interesting books about animals to your book corner.

7. Examine an issue of *National Wildlife, International Wildlife, Ranger Rick,* or *Big Back Yard.* All are published by the National Wildlife Association. Pick some interesting pictures or topics. Plan how you could use this information with the children.

SELECTED CHILDREN'S BOOKS

Arnosky, J. (1987). *Raccoons and ripe corn.* New York: Lothrop, Lee & Shephard.

Back, C., & Olesen, J. (1986). *Chicken and egg.* Morristown, NJ: Silver Burdett.

Ball, J. A., & Hardy, A. D. (1989). *What can it be? Riddles about baby animals.* Morristown, NJ: Silver Burdett.

Berger, G. (1987). *Sharks.* New York: Doubleday.

Brennan, J., & Keaney, L. (1987). *Zoo day.* Minneapolis: Carolrhoda.

Burton, J. (1988). *How your pet grows! Caper; Dabble; Gipper.* New York: Random House.

Burton, J. (1989). *How your pet grows! Pacer; Hoppy.* New York: Random House.

Burton, M. (1987). *Insects and their relatives.* New York: Facts on File, Inc.

Cohn, D. (1987). *Dinosaurs.* New York: Doubleday.

Coldrey, J., & Goldie-Morrison, K. (1986). *Hide and seek.* New York: Putnam.

Dixon, D. (1988). *Be a dinosaur detective.* Minneapolis: Lerner.

Drew, D. (1989). *The life of the butterfly* (big book). Crystal Lake, IL: Rigby.

Dunn, P. (1985). *Animal friends.* New York: Random House.

Entwistle, T. R. (1986). *Animal Houses.* New York: Random House.

Fischer-Nagel, H. & A. (1986). *Life of the honeybee.* Minneapolis: Carolrhoda.

Fitzsimons, C. (1987). *My first insects.* New York: Harper & Row.

George, W. T. (1989). *Box turtle at Long Pond.* New York: Greenwillow.

George, W. T., & George, L. B. (1988). *Beaver at Long Pond.* New York: Greenwillow.

Gibbons, G. (1987). *Dinosaurs.* New York: Holiday House.

Gregory, O. B. (1982). *Fishermen.* Windermere, FL: Rourke.

Heller, R. (1982). *Animals born alive and well.* New York: Grosset & Dunlap.

Hurd, T. (1987). *A night in the swamp.* New York: Harper & Row.

Jensen, K. (1984). *America: Land of Wildlife.* National Wildlife Federation, NWF Books.

Kalas, S. (1986). *The goose family book.* Framingham, MA: Picture Book Studio Ltd.

Lane, M. (1985). *The chimpanzee, the elephant, the giraffe, the lion.* New York: Random House.

McGovern, A. (1989). *Down under, down under: Diving adventures on the Great Barrier Reef.* Riverside, NJ: Macmillan.

Miller, S. S. (1982). *Whales and sharks and other creatures of the deep.* New York: Simon & Schuster.

Parker, S. (1989). *Mammal.* New York: Alfred A. Knopf.

Roe, R. (1985). *Baby animals.* New York: Random House.

Sabin, F. (1982). *Amazing world of ants.* Mahwah, NJ: Troll Associates.

Selsam, M. E. (1970). *Egg to chick.* New York: Harper & Row.

Smith, E. S. (1987). *Guide dog goes to school.* New York: Greenwillow.

Stewart, F. T., & Stewart, C. P. (1988). *Fishes.* New York: Harper & Row.

Stokes, D., & Stokes, L. (1987). *The bird feeder book: An easy guide to attracting, identifying, and understanding your feeder birds.* Boston: Little, Brown.

Thornhill, J. (1989). *The wildlife 1, 2, 3: A nature counting book*. New York: Simon and Schuster.

Weiss, E. (1988). *A visit to the Sesame Street Zoo*. New York: Random House.

Wolff, A. (1986). *A year of beasts*. New York: Dutton.

Zapun, S. (1989). *Wonderful wild animals*. New York: Grosset & Dunlap.

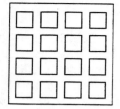

Chapter 7

Plants

THE study of plants offers children many inexpensive opportunities for active involvement with concrete materials. Children gain great satisfaction from growing their own plants. With proper guidance from a well-informed adult, children can become highly motivated as they study the wide variety of plants and learn about their interesting characteristics and functions. As they observe and collect data about plants, children can use science processes in meaningful ways.

Plants are familiar parts of each child's environment. People and animals eat a wide variety of plants. However, before starting work on plants, educators will want to discuss plant safety with children: children should not eat or taste plants or seeds without an adult's permission; some plants are poisonous to eat; others are poisonous to touch. Educators should also ascertain whether any children are allergic to specific plants or pollen. If so, teachers will need to find ways to prevent these children from having contact with these substances.

This chapter introduces four basic concepts related to plants:

- Plants are living things.
- A great variety of plants exists.
- Plants have different parts with different functions.
- People use plants in many ways.

PLANTS ARE LIVING THINGS

We know that animals are living things because they respond to stimuli, they need food, they respire, they give off wastes, they grow and repair, and they reproduce. Plants are living things also. They have these same characteristics, but they manifest them in different ways. Even though plants don't move from place to place, their parts do move in subtle and dramatic ways; they respond to stimuli such as light, water, heat, gravity, and touch. Just as animals need food and water, plants need minerals and water from the soil and carbon dioxide from the air. Plants, like animals, respire. They need energy to live. They get this energy by taking in oxygen to burn their food and giving off carbon dioxide and water as their waste products. Plants make food or glucose, and use that food to repair old, worn-out cells and to grow new ones. Plants also reproduce.

The following activities are samples of experiences teachers can use to help children explore some of the characteristics that demonstrate that plants, like animals, are living things.

☐ ☐ ☐ Plant Diary

Science Processes.   Observing, communicating, measuring, using numbers, using time and space relationships, and predicting.

Children need many opportunities to grow plants and record their observations. However, start this activity before you begin working with the children: plant some seeds in advance in order to have samples of plants at various stages of growth. You might use Table 7.1 to find some seeds that are easy and reliable to grow.

Before children begin to plant, pull up a few of your plants that you have started. Show the children the root systems and differences in the size of the plants. Have them compare two of the plants. Discuss the growth and change of the more mature plants over the younger plants. Discuss things that plants need to grow—light, water, air. Have seeds, dirt, water, and enough cut-down milk cartons for each child. Following Figure 7.1, help children plant seeds in their milk cartons.

Table 7.1
Seeds.

Kind of Seed	Approximate Sprouting Time	Special Notes
Mung beans	3–4 days	Buy seeds at health food store; these are "bean sprout beans."
Radishes	5–7 days	Plant in sandy soil.
Beans	7–14 days	Grow beans to eat fresh with dip.
Marigolds	7–14 days	Flowers are hardy.
Zinnias	7–14 days	These are pretty, sturdy flowers.

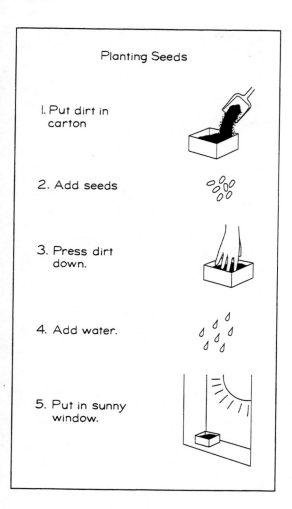

Planting Seeds

1. Put dirt in carton

2. Add seeds

3. Press dirt down.

4. Add water.

5. Put in sunny window.

Figure 7.1
Planting directions.

Provide time for children to water their seeds each day. Once a week have children measure their plant growth using a centimeter ruler. Give each child individual charts on which to record plant data (Figures 7.2 and 7.3).

Questions.   Before children plant their own seeds, show your plants that have been planted at different stages. Ask: "How are these two plants alike? Different? This plant was planted two weeks ago and this one was planted three weeks ago. How tall do you think your plant will be in one week?"

Evaluation.   Observe children's data chart to determine their abilities to record data accurately, to make predictions, and to communicate clearly.

Plant Diary

My name _____

My plant's name _____

When I planted my plant _____

How I planted my plant _____

_____

_____

My prediction about my plant is _____

_____

Was my prediction right? _____

_____

Figure 7.2
Plant diary.

Mar. 5	**Mar. 12**	**Mar. 19**	**Mar. 26**	**Apr. 2**	**Apr. 9**	**Apr. 16**

Figure 7.3
Plant growth in centimeters.

☐ ☐ ☐ I Want To Know: Plant Investigations

Science Processes. Observing, communicating, using time and space relationships, predicting, and inferring.

The following questions are just a few examples that might lead children to experiment to find answers. "What happens to plants that don't get water? Do plants need light to grow? What makes leaves green? Do plants grow toward the light or away from it? Which way do roots grow? What happens to plants put in front of a strong heat source?" Experiments that help answer these questions will help children begin to understand that plants are living things like us that respond to different stimuli and have needs like we do. Let children work in small groups or individually to make some of these plant investigations following the directions given on the next few pages. Have the children set up plant samples and observe them over a period of time. Have the children draw pictures and record what happens to their plants. Help the children come to some conclusions about their plants.

Do Plants Need Water To Grow?

Help children grow two plants using the following controlled experiment. Raise the plants side by side. Give one plant sufficient water, but give the other plant no water.

Do Plants Need Light to Grow?

Children can grow two plants making sure to give each plant the same amount of water and the same care with one exception: place one plant where it receives sufficient sunlight, but place the other plant in a dark closet.

What Makes Leaves Green?

Provide a healthy plant with plenty of green leaves. Show children how to make little "envelopes" for a few of the leaves by folding and taping construction paper. Slide the envelopes on a few of the leaves (Figure 7.4). Cover one leaf partially and one leaf completely. Cut a little shape out of one leaf envelope before sliding it on a leaf. Place the plant in a sunny window for several days. Have the children observe what happens.

Do Plants Grow Toward or Away from Light?

Place a plant in a sunny window for a few days. Notice which way the plant leans. Mark with an arrow indicating the direction in which the plant and leaves are tilting.

Figure 7.4
Plant with leaf "envelopes."

Probably the plant will lean toward the sun. Now turn the plant in the opposite direction with the arrow pointing away from the sun. Observe the plant again in a few days. Which way are the leaves and stem pointing now—in the same direction as the arrow or away from it?

Which Way Do Roots Grow—Up or Down?
Soak a few bean seeds in water. Place beans on a moist paper towel in an airtight plastic bag. Tape the bag to a windowpane and watch the beans sprout. Notice the root system. The roots will grow down in response to gravity and the stems will grow up pulling against gravity. Let children mark with an arrow on the plastic bag indicating the direction in which the roots are growing. Turn the bag on its side; in a few days notice the direction in which the roots are growing now. Mark root growth direction again with an arrow.

Does Moisture Affect the Direction in Which Roots Grow?
Let children grow plants in two different pots. One plant should be watered carefully only on one side. The other plant should be watered frequently in the normal way. After the root system has had a chance to become established, remove the plants from both pots and carefully pull away the dirt. The plant that has been watered in a normal way should have an evenly distributed root system. The other plant will probably have its root system growing toward the area where the water was applied.

What Happens When Plants Are Placed in Front of Strong Heat?
Have the children predict what might happen if a healthy plant is placed on a radiator or in front of a heater. Let children place a plant near a strong heat source and observe the plant several times a day. Help the children note changes in the leaves or stem of the plant. Ask: "Does the color or texture change? Does the plant change in other ways because of the heat?"

Do Some Plants Respond to Touch?
At different seasons large supermarkets or nurseries stock novelty plants such as Venus's flytraps. The lobes of the leaves have reddish centers and secrete a sweet-smelling liquid to attract flies, crickets, beetles, and other small insects. Once the insect lands on a leaf and touches one of the tiny trigger hairs, the leaf snaps shut and holds its prey. Take a tiny piece of hamburger meat and place it on a leaf. Watch the leaf close. Other wild plants such as jewel weed and pepper weed respond to touch in different ways such as popping out their seeds or closing their petals. Potteridge pea will close slowly when touched. Find plants in your area that respond to touch, and let children observe them.

Questions.   As children experiment with plants, encourage them to make predictions about what they think will happen in each situation. For example, ask: "What might happen if we water some of our seedlings, but not others?" After each experiment ask the children to describe the results and to tell why they think they got those results. For example, ask: "What caused the plant to grow bigger and greener than the other one?"

Evaluation. Observe children's abilities to carry out controlled experiments. What do they observe in their experiments? How accurately do they record data and communicate their findings? Are their predictions and inferences logical?

PLANTS HAVE DIFFERENT PARTS THAT PERFORM DIFFERENT FUNCTIONS

Even a quick glance at plants shows that they have several parts. We don't ordinarily see plants' roots, but they are important. Roots support plants, anchor them to the ground, absorb water and nutrients from the soil, and send these to the rest of the plant. They also store food for plants.

Stems are easy to see. Ordinarily long and thin, stems carry water and nutrients from the roots to the leaves and support the leaves and flowers of a plant.

Leaves vary greatly in appearance. They may be large or small, wide or narrow, and have lobed, straight, or sawtooth edges. The main functions of leaves are to make food for the plant. Green leaves have a green substance called chlorophyll in them. Chlorophyll makes it possible for plants to use water and carbon dioxide to carry on the process of photosynthesis in which the leaf makes food—glucose—for the plant. The food is then carried by the stem to the roots for use and storage.

Flowers are beautiful, but they also perform a special and important role in plants— they produce new plants of the same kind. The male parts of flowers produce pollen. The pollen fertilizes the female parts of other flowers to help them produce seeds that will grow into new plants.

Seeds come in many sizes and shapes. Each has a seed coat, stored food on the inside, and a tiny new plant—the plant embryo. Under the proper conditions, seeds grow into new plants.

Children can observe and identify the many parts of plants. They can learn about the functions of different parts by using activities such as the ones in this section.

Plant Farming

Science Processes. Observing, communicating, and classifying.

Just as animals reproduce, so do plants. Their methods of reproduction are quite varied. New plants can be grown from many parts of plants—from roots, seeds, stems, or leaves. Let your "young farmers" grow new plants from different plant parts. Use the following chart for ideas. Add new ideas of your own.

Plants That Grow From

- *Roots*—sweet potato, dahlias
- *Seeds*—rye, corn, bean, avocado
- *Stems*—coleus, philodendron, strawberry, Swedish ivy
- *Leaves*—African violet, sedum, Christmas cactus

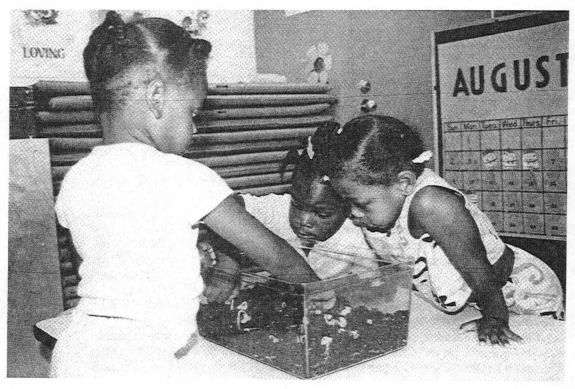

These "young farmers" are observing the bean plants they have grown from seeds.

Questions. "From what parts of a plant can we grow new plants?" Have children compare the likenesses and differences in growing plants from roots, seeds, and stems.

Evaluation. Notice children's observations and their interest as they grow their plants.

☐ ☐ ☐ Grow Like a Plant: Pantomime

Science Process. Communication.

After children have had opportunities to grow plants, to observe different characteristics of plants, and to talk about their observations, plan a classroom drama. Let some of the children pretend to be seeds. One child may be the farmer, and other children can be the sun and the rain. Let the farmer take each of the "seeds," dig a hole, and pretend to plant the seeds in the ground. The "seeds" should be nestled close to the floor in a tight ball pretending to be covered with dirt. Make up a story about the seeds growing roots and a stem and then poking out of the dirt one little leaf at a time. Your story might continue with "The rain comes and waters the little seedlings and the sun shines and makes them grow. The plants grow and grow and get larger. Each day the sun rises and moves across the sky and sets. The plants face the sun." Make your story simple or elaborate depending on the interest and maturity of your children. You might want to let a group of children help you select some music to play as you simulate plant growth.

Questions. "What made the plants grow? What kind of plant were you? How did you feel when you were planted in the ground? When it rained on you? When the sun grew hot?"

Evaluation. Notice children's abilities to follow the directions in the story and to accurately portray the story.

A GREAT VARIETY OF PLANTS EXISTS

Take a look at the children in your classroom. They represent many families, each of which is related in some way to hundreds of other families and thousands of other people, each with unique characteristics.

So it is with plants. There are many classes, orders, and families of plants, and among these groups infinite varieties exist. For example, you might mention to the children that there are mosses and liverworts, ferns and horsetails, as well as a variety of trees, shrubs, vines, flowers, weeds, vegetables, and grains. If they look out their window, they will probably be able to see quite a variety of plants.

The purpose of the activities in this section is to help you begin to stretch children's horizons to notice and appreciate the wide variety of plants that live in their environment. These activities are intended as introductory experiences to get you started. Supplement them with activities from Chapter 8, and add your own ideas.

Neighborhood Nature Walk

Science Processes. Observing and communicating.

Take the children for a nature walk around the block or to a park. Help them become familiar with the plants in your area. You might need to preview the area ahead of time. As you take your walk with the children, point out the different colors around you. In fall you will have a wide array of colors. In spring the different shades of green can be quite interesting. Each season has its own color tones.

Ask children to count how many different kinds of plants they can find. Help them notice the variety around them. Look for mosses, conifers, and other trees, flowers, shrubs, and vines. Help them identify some of the plants. Point out interesting features. Discuss whether it is appropriate to gather specimens and why; in many neighborhoods or in wildlife preserves, people must leave growing things intact for others to enjoy. Take magnifying lenses along so children can make detailed observations.

When you return to the classroom enumerate the things you saw. Encourage children to "write" about their walk in some way—by dictating an experience chart, by coloring pictures, by painting a mural, or by compiling a nature walk book.

Questions. On your walk ask questions suited to the environment. Ask: "Point out your favorite plant. What do you like about it? What is the tallest tree around? Does anyone know its name? How many different mosses have we found? Where were they?"

When you return to the room, play a guessing game with clues such as "I'm thinking of a tree we saw. It had cones on it—and long needles instead of leaves. A squirrel was sitting in it." Children can make up their own riddles and clues for the others to guess.

Evaluation. Notice children's interest and their observations as they walk. When they return to the classroom, observe their abilities to solve the riddles in the guessing game.

☐ ☐ ☐ Plant Surveys

Science Processes. Observing, communicating, and classifying.

Let your children work in small groups to survey the different plants in your areas. For instance, one group may survey trees to see how many different kinds they can find. They may focus on the various bark formations or the different types of leaves. Other groups may choose flowers, shrubs, weeds, or grasses to observe and research. If possible, each group should collect samples and display them in a unique way. Perhaps they may choose to display them in an arrangement in a bowl, on a strip of contact paper, in a book pressed between wax paper leaves, or attached to a clothesline with clothespins. Each group should report their findings to the class and explain their displays of nature samples.

Questions. Ask questions that guide your survey groups to keep moving, to remain motivated, to obtain pertinent information, and to keep on track. For example, ask: "Why do you think we found dandelion and plantain weeds growing close together in the yard? How would you compare the bark of the pine trees to the bark of the oak trees? What is different about the shapes of the trees?" As children report their findings, encourage others in the classroom to ask relevant questions.

Evaluation. Observe each group's research, report, and display for quality and organization. Notice how well children work together in groups.

☐ ☐ ☐ The Gift of Spring

Science Processes. Observing, communicating, inferring, and using time and space relationships.

The cold winter months make us long for the first signs of spring. Cut twigs from forsythia, flowering quince, pussy willow, spirea, or fruit trees that have tiny closed

A small group of children give this "gift of spring" to a senior citizen in a nursing home.

buds on them. Show the children how to put the twigs in warm water to force the buds to bloom. Replenish water when needed. Have the children collect and decorate old jars, bottles, and bud vases and arrange the flowering twigs in the containers. Take your children to a nursing home and let them share their "gifts of spring" with the residents.

Questions. "What did those twigs look like when we cut them? How have they changed? What made them change? Which flowers do you like the best? How do you think those people felt when we gave them our flowers?"

Evaluation. Notice children's answers to questions to determine the depth of their observations. Observe their responses and their sensitivity to the people in the nursing home.

Fruit Observations □ □ □

Science Processes. Observing, using numbers, using time and space relationships, communicating, and inferring.

Gather a wide variety of fruit for the children to examine including a few that are unfamiliar to them. Before the children have an opportunity to see the fruit, introduce them one at a time hidden in a bag. Let the children feel the fruit and describe the interesting textures, sizes, and shapes. Encourage the children to smell each fruit in the bag before they see it to determine if they can identify the fruit by smell. Then cut each fruit open and let them describe the smells. Let the children taste each fruit describing the taste and listening for crunch, squish, or other sounds as they chew.

Culminate your fruit observations with an art printing activity. Cut each fruit in half, into interesting shapes, or leave it whole. Let the children roll or dip cut pieces of fruit or the entire fruit in paint and print fruit designs on their papers. You may wish to have fruit task cards, as in Figure 7.5, for children to use in making their designs. They may use any design they like as long as they include the correct number of each fruit in the task card.

Questions. "Which is your favorite fruit? Of all the fruit we tasted, which was the sweetest (softest, crunchiest, largest)? What ways do we have to find out about this fruit? If you couldn't see, could you tell me about this fruit? How? What makes a successful picture (art print)? Is yours a good one? Why?"

Evaluation. Notice children's descriptions of the fruit. Which sense do they rely on the most? Which children are able to summarize or analyze this activity by telling the senses they used to help them observe the fruit? Note their abilities to evaluate their art prints.

☐ ☐ ☐ Creating Plants

Science Processes. Observing, classifying, using time and space relationships, and communicating.

Bring into the classroom various examples of plants. Point out the different parts of the plants: the root systems, stems, leaves, flowers, fruit, and seeds. After children have had opportunities to examine numerous plants and to talk about the variety found among plant parts in different plants, prepare them to create their own plants on a felt board.

Figure 7.5
Fruit task card.

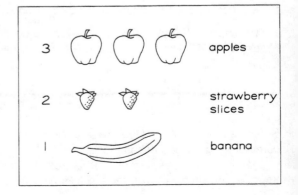

Make several felt boards by gluing felt to the inside of colorful manilla folders. Cut out several examples of stems, roots, leaves, flowers, fruits, and seeds. Provide extra felt for children to create their own plant parts if they wish. Have plant catalogs available to give children ideas. Let children put together the different parts of a plant on their felt boards to create their own plants. Encourage them to describe and identify the different parts they have assembled.

Questions. Have children compare and contrast the different plant parts with those of their peers. Ask: "What makes a complete plant? Is yours complete?" (Encourage children to check to make sure they have all of the necessary parts.)

Evaluation. Notice children's abilities to assemble a plant with all of its necessary parts. Observe the degree to which children elaborate as they create a plant.

Plant Snacks

Science Processes. Observing, classifying, and communicating.

As children observe and discuss the different parts of plants and create their own plants on felt boards, plan a special plant snack week. On one day serve roots for snacks, on another day stems, then leaves, flowers, fruits, and seeds. On this day you serve roots, place other examples of foods that come from roots in the science center. Change your science center focus to fit the snack you are serving. Be prepared each day to lead an appropriate discussion at snack time to accompany your specific examples.

The following list will give you ideas of foods to prepare for each snack time and foods to display in the science center.

- *Roots*—carrots, radishes, beets, turnips, parsnips, sweet potatoes, ginger, licorice, sassafras.
- *Stems*—celery, asparagus, sugar cane, maple, cinnamon bark.
- *Leaves*—lettuce, cabbage, spinach, endive, chard, parsley, kale, thyme, sage, spearmint.
- *Flowers*—cauliflower, broccoli, cloves, saffron.
- *Seeds*—peanuts, coconut, rice, corn, wheat, oats, barley, beans, peas, chocolate, coffee.
- *Fruits*—plums, pears, apples, bananas, kiwi, grapes, peaches, tomatoes, lemons, oranges, grapefruit.

Questions. "How does your snack taste? Is it salty, sweet, or sour? Is it juicy or dry? Is it crunchy or soft? What other words can you think to describe it? What are other roots that we can eat? Where are the roots on a plant? Why does a plant need roots?" Ask similar questions for each plant part.

Evaluation. Observe children's descriptions of their different plant snacks. Notice their comments as they talk about different plant parts. If you have done the previous felt board activity, "Creating Plants," make a felt board plant and see if children can place their snack in the correct place in relation to the felt board plant.

What Did You Eat?

Science Processes. Classifying and communicating.

After talking about the different parts of plants that we eat, give your children a home assignment. Have them record the foods they eat that come from plants and designate which part of the plant each food comes from. Encourage family members to help with this assignment. After children have returned their data to the classroom, compile children's lists in a large class chart, grouping foods according to plant parts.

Questions. "What was your favorite food? What part of the plant does it come from? On our class chart, which did we eat the most of—foods from roots or stems?"

Evaluation. Note children's ability to collect data and to classify their foods with the correct plant part.

Leaf Match

Science Process. Observing, and using time and space relationships.

Collecting an assortment of leaves with different shapes. Laminate each leaf if possible. Draw the outline of each leaf on a poster board. Let children match the leaf shape to the leaf outlines on the poster board.

Questions. "Which is the biggest leaf? The smallest? Find a leaf that has several lobes. How are these leaves alike? Different?"

Evaluation. Notice children's ability to match leaves correctly to the outlines.

Leaf Search

Science Processes. Observing, communicating, classifying, and using time and space relationships.

Let the children help you gather a variety of leaves. In your collection be sure to have representations of leaves with different edges (smooth, lobed, sawtooth, and wavy), surfaces (shiny, dull, hairy), vein configurations, colors, and smells. At group time, be sure to point out various features found in the leaves. Let the children actually feel the leaves and talk about what they observe.

Follow up with a small-group assignment at the science table. Display the leaves, magnifying lenses, and worksheets. The worksheets should be designed so children can place the actual leaves beside each description. On your worksheet have the children locate different features. (See the sample worksheet in Figure 7.6.) Let children work in pairs and check each other's worksheets. After children have completed their worksheets, have them remove their leaves from the worksheets to be used again.

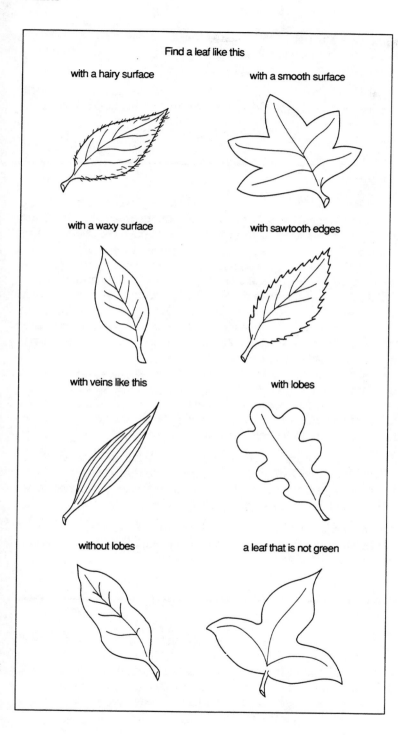

Find a leaf like this

with a hairy surface   with a smooth surface

with a waxy surface   with sawtooth edges

with veins like this   with lobes

without lobes   a leaf that is not green

Figure 7.6
Worksheet for leaf search.

Questions. "Can your group put all of the lobed leaves together? Find another leaf with a hairy surface. Use your magnifying lens to find an interesting feature on a leaf. Draw a picture of what you saw."

Evaluation. Note children's ability to complete their worksheets accurately, to work in small groups and pairs, and to communicate clearly with partners. Observe their interest as they work.

Give a Plant a Drink

Science Processes. Observing, communicating, predicting, and inferring.

Let children pick some weeds or flowers to bring into their classroom. After children have described the plants they have picked, have them place them on the science table out of water. Ask them if they think their plants will look any different in several hours. Later in the day have children observe their plants again. Many of the plants will be wilted and droopy because of lack of moisture. Have children describe the differences they notice in their plants and suggest reasons for the changes. Ask for suggestions of ways to freshen their plants. (Some might suggest pouring water on them. Others might suggest placing plants in a glass of water.) Try out the children's ideas so they can see which plans work best. Help them understand that stems carry the water up the plant to the leaves and flowers.

On the next day, follow up your experiment to reinforce this concept by letting the children place the stem of a white flower such as Queen Anne's Lace, magnolia, or daisy in a glass of water with food coloring. Remind them of their experiment on the previous day. Let them predict what might happen. Observe the flower after several hours and the next day. Let children describe what they notice.

Questions. "Describe your flowers. Do they look fresh? What will happen if we don't put them in water? Why? Why did this plant turn a different color? Do plants need water to live? What else needs water to live? How does water get carried to all parts of your body? How do plants carry water to their leaves?"

Evaluation. Notice the children's descriptions, their abilities to carry out both experiments, their predictions, and the inferences they make explaining how the water is transported in plants.

Seed Estimate

Science Processes. Observing, using numbers, communicating, using time and space relationships, and predicting.

Buy some fresh lima beans or peas from the grocery store. Have children work with the teacher assistant at a center estimating the number of peas found in each pod, recording their estimates on their charts, shelling the peas, and then recording the actual count. The chart may be similar to that in Figure 7.7.

My name _____

How many peas are on each pod?

My guess   The number I found

_____   _____

_____   _____

_____   _____

Figure 7.7
Chart for seed estimating.

Children will probably get closer to the actual count with repeated estimates. After all of the peas have been shelled, let a small group of children cook them and serve them to the class for a snack. Discuss the fact that you are eating seeds.

Questions. "On your chart which of your estimates was closest to the actual number? What was the farthest from the actual number? Did you get better as you estimated? What part of the plant are peas? Could we plant these peas and grow other plants? What kind of peas or beans are your favorite to eat?"

First graders estimate the number of peas in a pod. They record and check their predictions.

Evaluation.   Observe children's abilities to estimate and to interpret their work charts. Note which children actually count before they estimate and those who will venture a guess. Note those children who understand what part of the plant a pea is.

☐☐☐   Seed Race

Science Processes.   Observing, measuring, predicting, communicating, and using time and space relationships.

In the spring you may be able to find many seeds—such as dandelion, milkweed, and maple seeds—that travel by blowing in the wind. Have your children collect some of these seeds and have a seed race on the playground. Set up a start and finish line and let children blow their seeds to see which one can maneuver the seed to the finish line first. If your children take the competition too seriously, remove the competitive element. Just let each child work to try to get his seed across the finish line at his own rate of speed.

As an extension of this activity, give children lengths of colored yarn about 2 meters long. Have them work in groups of three, estimating how far they can blow their seeds. Two children may stretch out the yarn and hold it from start to finish to designate their estimate. The third child may blow the seed. Have them compare the difference in their estimates and the actual distance the seed was blown.

Questions.   "Did your seed blow as far as you thought it would or farther? How do seeds get from place to place? Can you find anything on your seed that helped it travel in the air? Show me with your body how the seed looked as it traveled through the air. What are some other ways seeds travel?"

Evaluation.   Notice children's abilities to work together and solve problems in groups. Observe how close their estimates are to the actual measurement and how accurate they are in measuring. Observe which children seem to have a clear understanding of the different ways seeds travel.

☐☐☐   "Match Me" Book

Science Processes.   Observing, classifying, and communicating.

Locate a four-ring notebook to make a classroom book in which children can match seeds with their fruits. Have the children bring different seeds from home such as apple seeds, cantaloupe seeds, blackberry seeds, beans, corn, rice, and coffee beans. Let the children clip pictures from magazines and seed catalogs showing the fruit or food products that come from each seed. Use sturdy poster board for the pages of your "Match Me" book (Figure 7.8). Let children glue the picture of a fruit on the top half of each poster board page and glue or tape the corresponding seed on the bottom half of the page. On the back of each page let them write the name of the food at the

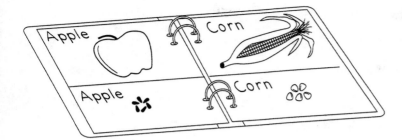

Figure 7.8
"Match Me" book.

top and the bottom of the page. Cut each page in half and add it to your loose-leaf notebook. Move the top halves of all the pages so that they won't be in the same order as the bottom part of the pages. Let children flip through the pages of the book and try to match the seed to the correct food. The duplicate words on the top and bottom of the back of the pages will serve as a self-check.

Questions. "Which foods have tiny seeds? Big seeds? Which seeds look alike? Which is your favorite food that comes from seeds?"

Evaluation. Observe children's abilities to match the seed to the corresponding food in the book.

Art Activities with Plants

Science Processes. Observing, classifying, and communicating.

Children will enjoy collecting different parts of plants and combining them in various ways to create beautiful, satisfying art products. Try some of the following suggestions in your classroom.

- Let children string seeds (popcorn, watermelon, cantaloupe, fresh beans, or peas) with a needle and thread to make a necklace or other jewelry. Encourage them to plan and extend a particular pattern. If seeds are hard, teachers may punch holes in them beforehand.

- Let children make a weed weaving (Figure 7.9). Provide small, forked branches. Show children how to wrap thin string, plastic fish line, or yarn back and forth around the crook of the branch to form the woof of the weaving. Let them collect long leaves, pine needles, and grasses to weave them to form the warp of the weaving.

- Make leaf collages by ironing pretty fall leaves between two sheets of waxed paper. Each child selects and arranges the leaves. The teacher places another sheet of waxed paper on top of the leaves and irons the two sheets of waxed paper together, sealing the leaves between the waxed paper. The final products may be used as placemats or they may be taped on the window to show off the beautiful colors of the leaves.

Figure 7.9
Weed weaving.

- Make other types of collages using the following combinations.
  - Glue different plant parts on colorful construction paper to make an artistic design.
  - Collect different patterns of bark and glue them in a box top to make a "framed" collage.
  - Use crayons and make rubbings of the bark on different trees. Cut out the rubbings in various shapes and arrange and glue them on construction paper in a pleasing design.

Questions. As children work on their art projects, lead them to discuss the variety of plant materials they are using. Encourage them to tell what part of the plant each item comes from. For example, ask: "What materials have you used in your weaving? Tell me about them. What parts of a plant are these pieces of grass? What parts are the pine needles?"

Evaluation. Notice the children's interest level and creativity as they work. Observe their abilities to identify the plant parts.

PEOPLE USE PLANTS IN MANY WAYS

We couldn't exist on our planet Earth if we didn't have plants. Many of the foods we eat come from plants. Plants provide many of the fabrics for our clothing. Some of these fabrics come from natural fibers; others come from synthetic fibers that have plant derivatives. The materials used to build houses often come from plants. Many of the chemicals, which are such a natural part of our daily lives, are derived from plants. Telephone poles, railroad crossties, wooden boxes, baskets, machinery parts, paper, perfumes, soaps, dyes, medicines, and rubber all come from plants. Truly, plants are very versatile in providing many of our needs. The following activities should help children become aware of many of the ways we use plants.

Feed the Doll

☐ ☐ ☐

Science Processes. Observing, classifying, communicating.

Make a doll from corrugated board or poster board (Figure 7.10). Cut a slit for a smiling mouth and a large circle in the abdominal area. Cover the large hole with clear acetate. Cut away one side of a paper sack. Tape the acetate stomach and the remainder of the sack to the back side of the doll. Let children make food cards by cutting out pictures of foods and gluing them to pieces of construction paper. Have them make a self-check code on the back of each card. A smiley face indicates that the food comes from a plant. A frowny face indicates that the food does not come from a plant. Show children how to use their food cards and play the game "Feed the Doll." The object of the game is to feed the doll only foods that come from plants.

Have children insert the food cards in the mouth hole and see the food drop into the abdomen by looking through the acetate covering. (The food cards will actually drop into the paper sack that has been taped to the back side of the doll.) Children can reach into the sack, pull out the food cards, and check to make sure they have fed the doll only plant foods.

Questions. "Can you feed the doll only fruits? Vegetables? Feed the doll two vegetables and one fruit. Feed the doll your favorite fruit. Find a plant where the part that you eat grows underground. Feed it to your doll."

Evaluation. Notice children's ability to make food cards and to designate the self-check on the back of the card correctly. Observe children's accuracy as they play the game.

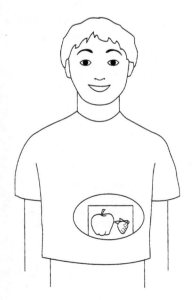

Figure 7.10
Feed the doll.

☐ ☐ ☐ Plant Lotto

Science Processes.   Classifying, communicating and inferring.

Make a lotto game on a big poster board similar to the one in Figure 7.11
Help children collect pictures of things that come from plants. Be sure that you have
a variety of things that fit into each category. Children may wish to add small objects
to their picture collection. Let children play the lotto game by placing their pictures
and objects in the correct category.

Questions.   "I'm thinking of a floor covering that goes on the kitchen floor. It is
made from a plant. Find a picture of it on your lotto board. Find a picture of something
that comes from a plant that you use to tie things together with." Use riddles such as
these to help children solve problems.

Evaluation.   Observe children's abilities to categorize correctly. Note their problem-
solving abilities when you present riddles to them.

☐ ☐ ☐ Making Paper

Science Processes.   Observing and communicating.

The paper we use is made from plant products. Share information with your class
about how paper is made. Then let your children make recycled paper from used paper
and other plant materials. Tear paper into small bits. Mix in bits of grasses, leaves,
or sawdust. Put the mixture in a blender. Fill the blender 3/4 full of the paper mixture
and water and blend. Make a screen frame. Spread a portion of the paper mixture on
the screen to make a thin layer. Pat out as much of the moisture as possible and pack
the paper bits together. Lay sheets of newspaper on top of the paper mixture to
absorb the moisture. Put the paper mixture in a sunny area to dry.

Let each child make his own paper. Use the paper to make a greeting card for a
friend. (See "Now It's Your Turn.")

Plant Lotto People use plants in many ways.		
Clothes	Foods	Houses
Chemicals	Enjoyment	Other

Figure 7.11
Poster for plant lotto.

Questions. "Name some paper products we use at home. If we didn't have any paper, what would we do?"

Evaluation. Observe children's interest as they make paper.

NOW IT'S YOUR TURN

Helping children work with plants is fun and easy. To extend your knowledge of plants and repertoire of teaching activities, now it's your turn to do some more work with plants. Use some of the suggestions that follow or create some of your own.

1. Did any questions arise in your mind while you were conducting plant investigations with children? If so, plan a carefully controlled plant experiment and carry it out to find an answer to your question. Use your finest scientific skills. Plan how you will carry out your experiment and the best way to record your data. Be accurate and consistent in executing your plans. Share your findings with a friend or with your children.

2. Become familiar with the plants in your area. You may wish to focus on one category such as wild flowers, spring shrubs, or trees. Take photographs or press plants for a plant scrapbook for your children to enjoy.

3. Plan an interesting home assignment for your children based on plants.

4. Invite a garden club member, a plant nursery expert, a landscape architect, or a florist to visit your classroom. Together plan what type information might be most relevant to your children.

5. Organize a "plant farm" day when you plan to have your children start plants from different sources (roots, seeds, stems, or leaves). Invite interested parents to come and bring plants or other materials to work with. Set up centers for each type of planting with parents directing each center. You should plan to circulate to keep the organization flowing smoothly. (See "Guides for Directing Small Group Work" and "Guides for Directing Individual Work" in Chapter 4.)

6. Many products are derived from plants. Use the categories food, clothing, housing, chemicals, and enjoyment to make a list of all of the products you can think of in each of these categories. Now do some research. Look through science books, encyclopedias, and other books. Increase your knowledge of plant products. Using your new information, add to your list.

7. Research the history of paper making. Share your findings in an interesting way with your class. Invite a community helper who works with paper to your classroom. Have the visitor tell about what she does with paper. For instance, you might invite someone who is interested in recycling paper. Have the visitor talk about and demonstrate something concerning paper recycling.

8. Choose your favorite learning activity from this chapter. Reread the activity notic-

ing the senses children would use as they participate. Suggest ways to add more sensory experiences to the activity. Also suggest at least one way to adapt the activity for a child who is a slower learner or one who needs an extra challenge.

SELECTED CHILDREN'S BOOKS

Bose, S. (1985). *Know your vegetables*. Tokyo: Froebel-Kan Co., Ltd.

Bose, S. (1985). *Know your flowers*. Tokyo: Froebel-Kan Co., Ltd.

Bose, S. (1985). *Know your fruits*. Tokyo: Froebel-Kan Co., Ltd.

Burnie, D. (1989). *Plant*. New York: Alfred A. Knopf.

Felts, S., & Bailey, J. (1988). *Naturescapes*. New York: Viking Kestrel.

Florian, D. (1986). *Discovering trees*. New York: Scribner.

Heller, R. (1984). *Plants that never ever bloom*. New York: Grosset & Dunlap.

Heller, R. (1985). *The reason for a flower*. New York: Grossett & Dunlap.

Jennings, T. (1989). *Seeds and seedlings*. Chicago: Children's Press.

Mitgutsch, A. (1981). *From seed to pear*. Minneapolis: Carolrhoda.

Seymour, P. (1988). *How things grow*. Berkeley, CA: Lodestar.

Waters, M. (1988). *The victory garden kids book*. Boston: Houghton Mifflin.

Watts, B. (1987). *Potato*. Morristown, NJ: Silver Burdett and Ginn.

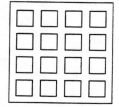

Chapter 8

Nature

WHETHER you live in a large city or a rural setting, helping children to study and appreciate nature is an exciting and important aspect of early childhood science. By exploring nature, educators provide concrete experiences for children. They extend and deepen children's awareness and understanding of living and nonliving things, of care of the environment, of change in the environment, and of the many interesting things found in nature. This variety of fascinating things in nature makes it a perfect vehicle for developing children's abilities to use science processes such as observing, communicating, and using time and space relationships. Attitudes such as interest in nature and responsibility for caring for the environment can also be developed as children investigate nature. In this chapter we will present the following four concepts related to nature:

- Living and nonliving things are found in nature.
- People must take care of the environment.
- Our environment changes.
- We can find many interesting things in our environment.

For each concept you will find descriptions of several activities that will promote the children's understanding of the concept.

LIVING AND NONLIVING THINGS ARE FOUND IN NATURE

As children explore natural settings, they will find a rich variety of living and nonliving specimens. Identifying and classifying examples of living and nonliving things helps children clarify their concepts of these things and their relationships.

☐ ☐ ☐ What's in a Square Meter?

Science Processes.   Observing, communicating, classifying, measuring, and using numbers.

Divide children into groups of three or four. Help each group select an area in which to "stake off" a square meter. Children might work in shady or sunny areas, on hilly or flat terrain or in a heavily traveled or out-of-the-way place. Help the children make a 1-meter square by placing tongue depressors or sticks for corners of the square and stretching yarn around the corners. Ask each group to be seated outside their square and to closely examine the ground within the square. Children will find a wide variety of things in their square meters. Encourage them to talk about what they find and to identify some specimens. Help children classify the things they observe as living or nonliving. Children might make a list of the things they found and count the numbers of living and nonliving specimens.

Call the children together in a large group; walk from one staked-out spot to another. Let the children show each other some interesting living and nonliving things.

Children can find many interesting living and nonliving specimens in a small area when they are taught to observe in depth.

from each spot. Encourage the children to compare their findings. Have them pull out the stakes and remove the yarn to leave the area as they found it.

Questions.   After examining one or two square meters, ask children to predict what they might find in the next square meter. For example, say: "We've seen two square meters now. What do you expect to find in the next square meter? It's in the sun and these two have been in the shade. What different things might we find?"

Evaluation.   Observe the children's cooperation in group work, ability to observe, skill at classifying specimens as living or nonliving, and ability to communicate findings to others. Record your observations of the children's behaviors on a checklist.

Nature Bags and Baskets

Science Processes.   Observing, classifying, communicating, and ordering.

In many natural settings children can collect specimens. Making and using nature bags and baskets (Figure 8.1) creates excitement and also helps children organize their collection.

You can make clear vinyl bags for specimens or help children to make their own bags. Cut a piece of clear vinyl about 40 cm × 20 cm; cut a second piece about 40 cm × 15 cm. Stitch the smaller piece to the larger piece as shown to create two pockets. Most sewing machines will easily stitch through vinyl, or the children can

Figure 8.1
Containers for nature collections.

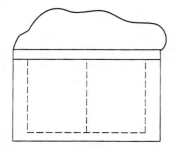

nature bag

nature basket

stitch by hand with some assistance and supervision. If you wish, attach a "handle" (yarn or rickrack) to each nature bag.

Help the children make nature baskets by cutting away part of the top of a clean, gallon milk carton. Leave the handle attached for easy carrying. Children can decorate their nature baskets with crayons or permanent markers.

After the children have completed their bags or baskets, secure permission, if necessary, to gather specimens in an outdoor area. To use the bags, have the children collect examples of living things in one pocket and nonliving things in the other. To use the baskets, pair children and have one collect living things and the other collect nonliving things. After a period of collecting, let the children describe and compare their findings. Have them identify the largest living specimen and the smallest. Choose several other specimens and have the children insert them in order from largest to smallest. You could also order some of the specimens from darkest to lightest in color, or heaviest to lightest in weight. Children could also display their most interesting findings on a science table, grouping their specimens as living things and nonliving things.

Questions.   "What helped you decide if your specimen was living or nonliving? Which is your most interesting specimen? Why did you think it was interesting?"

Evaluation.   Note on a checklist your observations of the children's work. Include aspects such as skill in classifying, ordering, and describing specimens.

☐ ☐ ☐   Sandpaper Rubbings

Science Processes.   Observing, communicating, and classifying.

Help children make attractive rubbings with living and nonliving materials in this unusual art and science activity. Take children outdoors and show them how various materials can be rubbed onto fine-grained sandpaper to leave subtle or dramatic traces of color and texture. Have children gather various living and nonliving specimens to rub with. Give each child a small rectangle of sandpaper to fold in half. Instruct the children to rub a design on one half with living materials and to rub a design on the other half with nonliving materials. Encourage children to show each other some materials that make the best effects on the sandpaper. Occasionally objects will not rub very well onto the sandpaper; these objects can be discarded. Divide the children into groups. Have each child in the group tell what material produced the most interesting results.

Questions.   "How did you decide whether a specimen was a living or nonliving thing? Which rubbing that you made did you like the best? What other things could we bring home to make rubbings?"

Evaluation.   Note the children's abilities to classify materials as living or nonliving. Observe their skills at describing and sharing their results. To assess individual children's understanding of the concept living and nonliving, make a signal check. See

"Different Purposes of Questions" in Chapter 3. Hold up living and nonliving objects one at a time. If the object is living, children must signal with thumbs up. If the object is nonliving, children signal with thumbs down.

PEOPLE MUST TAKE CARE OF THE ENVIRONMENT

People are responsible for care of the environment. People can choose to clean up and beautify the environment, or they can choose to litter and ruin it. Educators can help young children develop the attitude that care of the environment is a natural and pleasant responsibility rather than a chore. Children can learn that through small efforts by many people, the beauty and safety of our environment can be enhanced.

Litter Walk

Science Processes. Observing, communicating, and classifying.

Discuss what litter is with the children. Write their ideas on an experience chart or chalkboard. Pair children and give each pair a plastic garbage bag or grocery bag.

These children are assuming the responsibility of caring for their playground.

Go on a litter walk around your schoolyard or neighborhood. Help the children find litter, pick it up, and carry it in their bags. Caution them to be careful with sharp, rusty, or greasy items.

Before you return to your classroom, help the children lay out and classify some of their litter by the material of which it is made. They will probably have found things made of glass, metal, plastic, and paper. Talk about how some items could be recycled and reused. Help the children gather all of their items, dispose of their litter and bags in a proper container, and wash their hands thoroughly.

Back in the classroom, invite the children to add to their list of what litter is. Then, add their ideas about why litter is annoying and harmful. Finally, lead a discussion about how each of them can help clean up more litter or encourage others not to litter. Follow up by letting the children decorate litterbags to use at home or make posters to encourage a cleaner, litter-free environment.

Questions. "Do you remember when you threw out some litter instead of discarding it in the trash can? What material did you throw out? Why did you do it?" (Perhaps there wasn't a convenient place for discarding the material.) "What could you do to keep from littering?"

Evaluation. Observe the children's cooperation and interest during the litter walk and follow-up activities. Note their abilities to classify items according to their material. Record your observations on a checklist.

Beautifying Our Environment

Science Processes.   Observing and communicating.

Take your class on a field trip to observe the different things people have done to improve the natural environment. You may point out trees or bushes planted along a boulevard, flowers planted to enhance a public area, and private yards that have been carefully cultivated for passersby to enjoy.

After returning to school, generate a discussion on ways the class might beautify a public area. Help your class decide on one project. For example, they might choose to work in small groups and plant tree seedlings in an area that is eroding. (In many areas you can get seedlings free or for a nominal cost from the U.S. Forest Service). Your class may decide to plant daffodils or tulips at the school. They may choose to sow wildflowers in another public spot or to fix a planter for others to enjoy. Plan your strategy for your beautifying project—ordering plants, planting, and caring for the plants. Divide the class into committees according to responsibilities. Carry out your project over a period of time.

Questions.   This activity should generate many questions during different stages of the project. Ask: "Are those bushes planted in sun or in shade? What type of care is evident in this area? Which areas did you see that you thought were unusually beautiful? Would these plants grow best in the sun or in the shade? Let's decide what we must do to carry out our project."

Evaluation.   Help each group make a list of their responsibilities and a checklist. Have them check off each item when they complete it. Encourage children to write a summary of their project with sketches and drawings. Observe children's behaviors such as interest, contribution to the project, and responsible behavior.

OUR ENVIRONMENT CHANGES

As children explore nature, they will observe many changes that take place in the environment. Teachers can guide children to examine the changes that take place in plants and animals, that are produced by weather phenomena, and that occur throughout the day or from season to season. Teachers should think about many natural changes that would be of interest to children.

Leaf Diaries   ☐ ☐ ☐

Science Processes.   Observing, using time and space relationships, communicating, inferring, and predicting.

Take your children outdoors. Have each child select a leaf on a tree or bush to observe. The students should tag their leaves at the stem or mark their initials on the chosen leaf with permanent marker. Encourage your children to go outside at least once a week to observe the changes that occur in their leaves. Help them start a diary and record their weekly observations. Many children will want to make drawings of their leaves to help them describe the changes they see. Let your children follow the changes throughout the autumn season until the leaves fall. The students will enjoy putting their leaves in their diaries after they fall from the trees.

Questions.   Ask questions that lead the children to observe their leaves in depth. For example, ask: "What can you tell us about the unusual markings on this leaf? What patterns do you see in the veins of your leaves? How do the tops and the bottoms of your leaves compare? Have your leaves changed over the past week?" They can predict when they think their leaves will fall and observe how close they come to their predictions. Ask: "What different things might have caused the changes in your leaves?"

Evaluation.   Use partner checks for weekly discussions on changes noted in the leaves. Review the children's leaf diaries for completeness, detail in observations, neatness, clarity in communication, and creativity.

Changes in Shadows   ☐ ☐ ☐

Science Processes.   Observing, measuring, using numbers, communicating, predicting, inferring, and using time and space relationships.

The changes in the position of the sun throughout the day produce changes in the lengths of shadows. Have your children work in small groups. The children in each group can work together and draw around the shadow of one member of the group. Be sure your students draw around the person's feet. Begin your drawings early in the day. Take your children outdoors again in the middle of the day. Ask them to predict if the shadows will be the same or different. Ask your "shadow casters" to step into their footprints and to try to stand in the same position to cast the same shadow formation as they did before. Let the members of each group draw around the shadow again—this time using a different colored piece of chalk. Repeat the process again at the end of the day.

Some areas in cities never receive direct sunlight because they are constantly in the shadows of tall buildings. If you have access to such areas, encourage the children to note the angles and lengths of the shadows throughout the day. Have the children locate the buildings that block the sun at different times of the day.

Questions.   "Where do you think your shadows will be an hour from now? How long do you think they will be?" After making predictions and measuring at the correct time, check them by asking: "How close did our actual predictions come? Why do you think the shadows changed?"

Evaluation.   Provide a worksheet for your students to fill out. Include questions such as the following: "The length of the first shadow at __ o'clock was __. The length of the second shadow at __ o'clock was __. I predicted that the third shadow at __ o'clock would be __ long. It was __ long. The shadows changed because ____

_____

_____."

WE CAN FIND MANY INTERESTING THINGS IN OUR ENVIRONMENT

Plants, animals, and weather are just a few of the natural phenomena in our environment. An important part of our jobs as educators is to cultivate children's sensitivity to the intricacies of nature—to the wonder and beauty to be found in it.

☐ ☐ ☐   Mud Puddle Observations

Science Processes.   Observing, communicating, measuring, using time and space relationships, inferring, and predicting.

Have you ever stopped to really observe a mud puddle? On the next rainy day, take the children out a few at a time to observe the rain falling and collecting in a puddle on the sidewalk or on the ground. Ask them to notice how the raindrops hit the water and splat and how the water mixes with dirt and becomes muddy. If water runs off from the puddle, encourage your students to suggest reasons for the runoff.

Have your children mark off the edges of the puddle with tongue depressors as shown in Figure 8.2. Stick one depressor in the center of the puddle to measure the depth of the water and mark it on the tongue depressor.

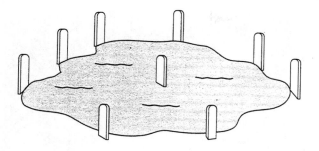

Figure 8.2
Mud puddle observation.

Take your children to observe the puddle every day until it dries up. Children will be able to notice how the water recedes from the outline made by the tongue depressors and how the water level drops on the tongue depressor placed in the center of the puddle. Let the children dictate an experience chart about the changes they observed.

Questions. Encourage the children to think of many ways to describe how the raindrops hit the puddle and how formations look as water runs off or evaporates from the puddle. After observing the puddle for two days, let them predict where the outline of the puddle will be on the next day and where the water line will be on the tongue depressor. Help them measure to see how close they came to their predictions.

Evaluation. Observe which children communicate their observations freely and in descriptive ways. Observe their skills at measuring, predicting, and inferring. Use a checklist of the science processes in this activity. Note which children use these skills well.

Bark, Bark, Bark

Science Processes. Observing and communicating.

This lesson focuses on something we see often but probably haven't taken much time to notice—tree bark. Take children outdoors and let them identify tree trunks, branches, twigs, leaves, and tree roots that are above the ground. Gather the children around a tree, preferably one with a large trunk. Ask children to describe the tree trunk's covering. They may mention the bark's color and texture. Have the children further observe the bark's odor and patterns. Explain that the bark provides a protective covering for the tree and that the tree's roots that are above the ground are covered with bark. Try to find a place where a branch has been cut off or fallen off a tree. You can probably find evidence that bark has covered this "wound." Let the children describe what they see. Look at more trees. Help the children describe the bark and compare the bark of several trees. Collect any bark specimens you may find on the ground.

Distribute plain paper and old crayons. Show children how to make bark rubbings by holding a paper onto a tree's bark and rubbing with the flat side of a crayon.

This child learns about texture as
she makes a bark rubbing.

Encourage them to make and compare several rubbings of different kinds of bark.
Display the rubbings on a bulletin board along with any pieces of bark you collected.

Questions.   "Tree bark and people's skin have some things in common. What are
they?"

Evaluation.   Observe the children's cooperation, ability to handle art materials to
make rubbings, and skill in using their senses to express what they saw. Record your
observations on a checklist.

☐ ☐ ☐   Nature Scavenger Hunt

Science Processes.   Observing, measuring and using numbers, comunicating, and
classifying.

Take your children on a nature walk and help them find a variety of interesting
things in nature. Give them a worksheet (Figure 8.3) and let them tape the items onto

```
┌─────────────────────────────────────────────────────────────────┐
│                                                                   │
│  Name _____                            │
│  Find the following things:                                       │
│                                                                   │
│  3 tiny things          something as long as this   something red │
│                         space                                     │
│                                                                   │
│                                                                   │
│  something yellow       a leaf with a hairy        a leaf with a  │
│                         surface                    slick          │
│                                                    surface         │
│                                                                   │
│                                                                   │
│  a seed that travels by  a seed that travels by    2 seeds that   │
│  flying                  sticking to the coats of  animals eat    │
│                          animals                                  │
│                                                                   │
│                                                                   │
│  something soft         something hard             something sticky│
│                                                                   │
└─────────────────────────────────────────────────────────────────┘
```

Figure 8.3
Nature Scavenger Hunt.

it with transparent tape. Get permission to collect natural items in advance. If children aren't allowed to collect objects, let them substitute crayon drawings for the real objects. Adjust the items in the following worksheet to fit your environment and your children's abilities; for instance 3- and 4-year-olds might find just four items.

Questions.   When the children return to the classroom, encourage them to compare and classify the items they found in several categories. For instance, some might find sticky objects that stick or prick their fingers, while others might find moist sticky items that adhere to their fingers.

Evaluation.   Assess children's worksheets. Note which concepts were difficult for them.

Trail Mix   ☐ ☐ ☐

Science Processes.   Measuring and communicating.

Children can make bags of trail mix to "sustain" them on a nature walk. Prior to a nature walk, set up an assembly line of ingredients using the recipe in Figure 8.4. Let each child move through the line, spooning the various ingredients into a small plastic bag. Have each child keep the bag of trail mix until the walk or have the children mark their names on the bags and collect the bags to distribute once you are outdoors.

Figure 8.4
Trail mix recipe.

```
TRAIL MIX

Spoon into a bag:

    10 ml coconut

    10 ml peanuts

    15 ml raisins

    15 ml chocolate
         chips


Shake your bag to
mix. Save it for
the nature walk.
```

Questions. "Which trail mix ingredients do you like best? What other ingredients could we add to make a good trail mix? Where does each ingredient come from?"

Evaluation. Note the children's abilities to follow directions and measure ingredients.

☐ ☐ ☐ Nature Booklets

Science Processes. Observing, communicating, using numbers, and using time and space relationships.

Enhance an experience with nature by using booklets that each child can add to and personalize. Make booklets from two folded sheets of paper, as shown in Figure 5.1, and reproduce our nature booklet, as shown in Figure 8.5. Vary it as necessary to include items in your environment. Take the children outdoors and complete several items from the booklet. Allow plenty of time. Finish the booklet on one or more trips outdoors, or let children complete it at home on their own. In a final session, let them finish the cover. They might make a drawing, rubbing, or collage for the cover. Display the booklets in your classroom library center or reading area for several days; then let the children take their booklets home.

Questions. "What part of your nature booklet did you enjoy most? Why did you enjoy it so much? What areas of nature would you like to explore more?"

Evaluation. Check the children's nature booklets for completion, care, neatness, and level of language. Note the children's cooperation and interest in the outdoor experiences.

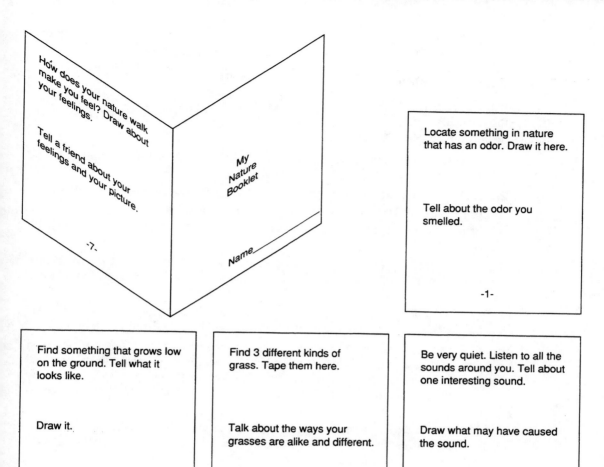

How does your nature walk make you feel? Draw about your feelings.

Tell a friend about your feelings and your picture.

-7-

My
Nature
Booklet

Name_____

Locate something in nature that has an odor. Draw it here.

Tell about the odor you smelled.

-1-

Find something that grows low on the ground. Tell what it looks like.

Draw it.

-2-

Find 3 different kinds of grass. Tape them here.

Talk about the ways your grasses are alike and different.

-3-

Be very quiet. Listen to all the sounds around you. Tell about one interesting sound.

Draw what may have caused the sound.

-4-

Find a spider's web. Look at it carefully, but don't touch it. Draw the spider's web.

Point out some things that show how skillful the spider is at building a web.

-5-

Look for a bird's nest. Don't touch or disturb it. What is the bird's nest made of?

Draw the bird's nest here.

-6-

How does your nature walk make you feel? Draw about your feelings.

Tell a friend about your feelings and your picture.

-7-

Figure 8.5
Making a nature booklet.

NOW IT'S YOUR TURN

It's your turn again! We hope your mind has been working on ways to vary and extend the concepts and activities suggested in this chapter. Try the following exercises to help formalize your thinking.

1. Design another nature activity to focus on classifying. Use resources in your local community.

2. Develop some extensions of the concept "caring for the environment." Plan some ways to keep the concept alive throughout the school year.

3. Plan some nature activities that emphasize extending children's divergent thinking ability.

4. Suppose you live in the city where opportunities for observing/studying nature are more limited than those in a rural area. Plan at least two nature activities adapted for city living.

5. You will notice that there are many aspects of nature not mentioned in this chapter. Select one of those areas that interests you, and plan a related activity.

6. Television offers many excellent nature-oriented programs. You can also find nature films appropriate for young children. Videotape a suitable program offered on television or select a film that your children might enjoy. Plan a motivating introduction and a follow-up activity. Evaluate the effectiveness of this presentation.

7. Make an informal survey among the children in your class to find out what their interests in nature are. Plan some nature activities based on their expressed interests. Incorporate these activities into your yearly plan.

SELECTED CHILDREN'S BOOKS

Anderson, L., & Svedberg, U. (1988). *Nicky the nature detective*. New York: R & S Books.

Avoy dos Santos, J. (1983). *Giants of smaller worlds*. New York: Dodd, Mead.

Barrett, N. (1989). *Picture library series*. (10 titles). New York: Franklin Watts.

Coldrey, J. & Goldie-Morrison, K. (1986). *Danger colors*. New York: Putnam.

Cristini, E., & Puricelli, L. (1983). *In the woods*. Austria: Verlag Neugebauer Press.

Florian, D. (1989). *Nature walk*. New York: Greenwillow.

Johnson, J. (1988). *Sanitation workers A to Z*. New York: Walker.

Locker, T. (1984). *Where the river begins*. New York: Dial Books.

Rius, M., & Parramon, J. M. (1986). *Let's discover the countryside*. Woodbury, NY: Barron's.

Ryder, J. (1990). *Under your feet*. New York: Macmillan.

Selberg, L. (1982). *Our changing world*. New York: Philomel Books.

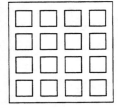

Chapter 9

The Earth and Its Weather

PEOPLE examine natural phenomena such as the weather every day. Most people are interested in the weather, especially when dramatic weather changes occur or when weather hampers their activities. Even though the Earth and its weather are familiar, children need opportunities to focus on them and to learn more about them. When the children's attention is drawn to the Earth's features and its weather, they can find many intriguing things to explore. Children learn that studying familiar phenomena can be rewarding and interesting. This chapter presents the following concepts about the Earth and its weather:

- Our home, the planet Earth, is covered by liquids, solids, and gases.
- We can observe and describe many kinds of weather.
- Weather and seasons affect people's activities.
- The Earth's surface is changed by people and by natural phenomena.

OUR HOME, THE EARTH, IS COVERED BY LIQUIDS, SOLIDS, AND GASES

When we stop to notice, we realize what a vast array of surfaces cover our Earth. The various landforms include mountains, hills, and valleys; plains and plateaus; islands and peninsulas. These landforms cover only about 30 percent of our Earth. The other 70 percent is covered by various bodies of water—brooks, streams, rivers, lakes, and oceans. A more extensive look at the Earth's terrain also reveals many kinds of soil that support an infinite variety of plant life. Not only is Earth covered with a variety of solid and liquid forms, but it is also surrounded by various gases.

A sensitive study of the surfaces of the Earth—the beauty, order, intricacy, variety, and creativity found in the masterworks—can be awe–inspiring. Our job as teachers is to help children notice and appreciate the interesting surfaces that cover our planet. Teachers can share many pictures with the children to show them surfaces not found in their immediate environment. Children also need many firsthand experiences in looking at and working with the materials that make up these different surfaces. The activities in this section focus mainly on landforms and bodies of water. Concepts related to air are presented in this chapter in the section on weather. Chapter 11 also includes several activities concerning air and its properties.

□ □ □ Looking Down

Science Processes.   Observing and communicating.

"If you were in a spaceship looking down on the Earth, what might you see?" Children today might give many enlightening answers to that question. They've witnessed televised space launches and have seen photos of the earth taken from space. Provide some interesting illustrations for the children to look at and talk about. Ask children to describe what the Earth looks like from a plane. Talk about how things look different from high in the air than they look on the ground. Let children describe what they see close-up when they walk around outdoors. Provide varied and interesting pictures of ground and aerial views to aid your discussion. Help children focus on the fact that the Earth is covered by many interesting land and water formations and by clouds.

Questions.   "What covers our Earth? What different types of water formations do we see on the Earth? What landforms? Do the clouds look the same all the time? In what ways do they change? How does the Earth look different from way out in space and up close?"

Evaluation.   Note the children's interest and the detail and sophistication of their answers.

□ □ □ Feeling Different Earth Surfaces

Science Processes.   Observing and communicating.

On a warm day take the children on a barefoot walk to allow them to experience the different surfaces that cover our earth. Let them feel and describe the various types of soil. They may walk on loam, sand, clay, mud, and rocks. They may also find areas soaked with water or covered with grass and leaves. If there are natural bodies of water nearby, let the children put their feet in the water and describe how it feels. Refrigerate or freeze a soil sample and let children feel the cold or frozen surface.

In some areas teachers may have difficulty locating a variety of earth surfaces within walking distance. If taking a barefoot walk is a problem in your area, bring "the earth" to the children. Bring small plastic tubs filled with soil samples found in your area. Let the children put their feet in each tub and describe to a partner what they feel. Note the adjectives they use to describe what they feel. You might need to supply new terms to help them enlarge their vocabularies. As the children feel the different types of surfaces, remind them that the Earth is covered with a variety of soils such as these. Encourage children to go home and survey the different land surfaces around their homes and come back and share their findings with one another.

Questions. "How does the soil feel to your feet? How is this surface like that one? How are these surfaces different? Which surface looks like the soil at your house?" As a culminating question, ask: "How many of the Earth's surfaces can you name?"

Evaluation. Notice the children's descriptive terms as they feel the different surfaces. How discriminating are they in telling about what they feel? Notice their ability to compare and contrast the different soils.

Digging Deep

Science Processes. Observing and communicating.

Take a shovel outside and dig deep into the earth. Point out the layers of dirt in the topsoil and the subsoil. Have the children compare and contrast the different layers of soil describing the feel of the soil, the different colors, and the things they find in them. When children have finished digging, have them fill the hole and leave the surface natural looking.

Questions. Ask questions that encourage detailed descriptions and comparisons, such as, "How are the layers of soil alike? Different? What colors do you find in the soil? Are the colors of each layer alike or different? How? Are the soil particles in this layer rough and jagged or smooth? Are the particles of soil in this layer larger or smaller than a marble—a pebble—a grain of sand? Do you find anything living in the soil? Do you notice any decayed plant or animal matter? What do you think it was before it decayed?"

Evaluation. Note children's interest and ability to observe closely and describe what they observe.

Nature Boxes

Science Processes. Observing, communicating, and using time and space relationships.

After children have had time to study and discuss the collection of pictures in the science center, divide them into small groups to make nature boxes depicting different land and water forms. Provide boxes, different types of soil, and aluminum foil or small bowls for making lakes. Help your children gather mosses, grasses, leaves, and twigs. Let the groups use the gathered materials to make a natural-looking scene. Some might make lakes in their nature boxes by filling small, plastic bowls or shaped heavy-

The Earth is full of wonders. There are many interesting things to discover, even in a mud puddle.

duty, aluminum foil with water. Encourage the children to construct islands or peninsulas in their lakes. Some children may wish to use big rocks to form mountains. They might represent mountain streams with crumpled, plastic wrap. They could cover the soil with moss and make trees out of twigs. Plexiglass coverings would help preserve their nature scenes. Remind the children to spray the materials in their nature boxes with water every day to keep them fresh and green. After the children have completed their nature boxes, let them share their creations with their classmates.

Questions. "What landforms and bodies of water did you make? What problems did you encounter in building your nature box? How did you solve them?"

Evaluation. Note children's interest in making nature boxes, their creativity in building the different landforms, and their problem-solving abilities. Note the children who are leaders and those who are cooperative followers. Notice how well the groups work together.

Dirty Work

Science Processes. Observing, classifying, measuring, using time and space relationships, predicting, inferring, and communicating.

Soil can be classified according to what is found in it. Sandy soil has mostly sand, a little clay, but almost no humus (decayed plant and animal matter). Sandy soil doesn't hold water well. Clay soil has mostly clay, a little sand, and humus. It holds water quite well. When it is wet, clay is very sticky; clay becomes very hard when it dries out. Loam has some gravel, sand, and clay mixed with a large amount of humus. The looseness of loam lets water and air move through it easily. Loam has a rich, dark brown or black appearance. Because it is rich in minerals and loose enough to allow water and air in it, loam is an ideal soil for growing plants.

Gather samples of soil for your children to examine. Explain the different types of soil. Provide three different types of soil for the children to test for water retention. Firmly pack each type of soil into a jar. Pour 125 milliliters (1/2 cup) of water into each of the jars of soil. Be sure that the children pour the water into the jars at the same time. Help them use a stop watch or the second hand on a clock to determine how long it takes the water to go through the soils to the bottom of the jar.

Questions. "Which soil will hold the water the longest? Why do you think this particular soil held the water longer?"

Evaluation. Note children's interest as they test their soils and the accuracy with which they carry out their experiment.

More Dirty Work

Science Processes. Observing, classifying, and communicating.

After children have examined the various soils in the classrooms, give them a homework assignment to collect a small bag of soil from an area around their homes. Put tagboard labels on the science table describing each of the three types of soil previously studied. Display the labels along with plastic cups filled with soil samples (Figure 9.1). Let the children compare the soil samples from their homes to those at the science table. Then have them place their soil samples with the type of soil that is most like theirs.

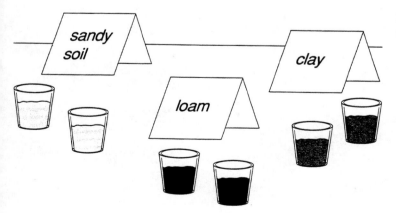

Figure 9.1
Classifying soil samples.

Have magnifying lenses at the table for the children to use. Encourage them to feel their soil samples. Provide an index card for the children to fill out to describe their sample.

Questions. "What is the same about your soil from home and the sample it is most like? What is different? Did you find other kinds of soil near your home? What were they like?"

Evaluations. Check the children's answers on their cards to assess their understanding of the three types of soil.

Art Forms from the Soil

Science Processes. Observing and communicating.

Follow up your soil study with an art activity using at least one type of soil. You might provide clay for the children to make sculptures. Perhaps your children would enjoy using mud as finger paint. If so, try to find mud of different colors for the children to combine. The children might enjoy working with sandy soil to make sand and dirt designs in empty baby food jars (Figure 9.2). In this activity children fill the jars with several layers of dry sand and dirt. They poke holes in the layers along the insides of the jars with a toothpick or another thin instrument to allow one layer of sand or dirt to seep down into the next to make interesting designs. In setting up this activity, be sure that the dirt and sand are dry and are of contrasting colors.

You may wish to use one of these activities, to have all three activities available for the children to choose from, or to assign children to create their own art project using soil in some way.

Questions. Your questions will vary depending on the art projects in your class. You might ask such questions as, "How does the clay feel as you knead it and mold it? How did your sculpture change after it dried? What happened to the water in the clay? How does the mud feel? Are the textures alike or different? How? How did you

Figure 9.2
Sand and dirt design.

get your design to work in your sand sculpture? What would you do differently to improve it?"

Evaluation.   Observe children's interests as they work with the different art forms. Notice how creative their art projects were. Note descriptive words as children tell about the soils.

Rock Histories

Science Processes.   Observing, inferring, and communicating.

If rocks could talk, they could divulge some interesting history. The three basic types of rocks—sedimentary, igneous, and metamorphic—were formed in different ways. *Sedimentary rocks* are formed from materials such as clay, silt, sand, gravel, or the remains of plants and animals. Some of the materials may have been caught up in streams or rivers and settled to the bottom of the water. These sediments have accumulated over several thousand years with one layer pressing down on the layers beneath it. The chemicals in the materials have cemented them together. People can recognize sedimentary rock by the layers within the rock, by tiny particles of sand found in the rock, or by fossils imbedded in the rock.

Igneous rock is formed by heat or fire. Hot, molten materials form magma below the earth's crust and push their way up to the surface, sometimes breaking up or melting the rocks in their path. As the magma breaks through the cracks and cools, it often forms crystals. People can identify igneous rocks by their glassy appearance or the crystals found in them.

Metamorphic rocks are sedimentary and igneous rocks that have been changed by heat and pressure. Metamorphic means "changed in form." Either the materials in the rock have been rearranged or chemical changes have occurred in the rock. Slate, marble, quartzite, and hard coal are types of metamorphic rock. To identify metamorphic rock, look for grains in the rock or for fossils that appear to have changed. Young children do not need to know the names of the three types of rocks, but adults will need some knowledge of rocks to foster the children's intelligent observation and deep appreciation of rocks.

Gather pictures of various environments from which rocks come. You might have pictures of different bodies of water such as rivers, streams, and oceans. Your picture collection should include photos of volcanoes, mountains, and cliffs that show stratified rock. Collect some examples of each type of rock. Using your pictures and your rocks, tell the children stories about how each of the three types formed long ago. Put the pictures and rocks in the science center for children to examine. Have them collect other interesting rocks to add to the collection. As the children study the rocks, point out interesting features in them, such as fossils, layers, grains, or crystals. Tell them how these features might have gotten into the rocks. Encourage the children to compare similar rocks.

After the children have studied rocks and their origins for many days, have them pick their favorite rock and look for "clues" in that rock that might suggest its origin.

Encourage the children to dictate or write stories telling where their rocks might have come from, making their stories realistic by using the clues they find in their rocks.

Questions. "What interesting features can you find in your rock? How do you think they got there? Who else in the class has a rock similar to yours?"

Evaluation. Notice how logically they relate the facts in the stories of their rocks. Note their interest level and the details included in their stories.

Rock Observations

Science Processes. Observing, communicating, using time and space relationships, and measuring.

Let each child choose a rock to examine and predict what the rock looks like on the inside. Supervise the children carefully as they break their rocks apart by placing each rock in a paper bag and hitting it with a hammer. Ask them to compare the colors on the inside and the outside of the rocks. Encourage them to test the hardness of their rock by scratching it. Remind them that the softer the rock is, the easier it is to scratch. Ask: "Can it be scratched with your fingernail or a penny?" Supervise as the children try to scratch the rock with a steel table knife or adult-size scissors. Have the children test to see if the rock leaves a mark when it is scratched on a surface. Let them look for interesting features in their rock. Let older children describe their rocks by filling out a form like the one in Figure 9.3.

```
Color on the outside _____ Picture of rock

inside _____

Hardness of rock: soft _____ scratch with fingernail

              medium _____ scratch with penny

                hard _____ scratch with knife

           very hard _____ won't scratch

Does your rock leave a mark? _____

Describe the rock. _____

_____

Describe interesting features found in your rock. _____
```

Figure 9.3
My rock.

Besides answering the questions in Figure 9.3 children may wish to weigh the rock before cracking it apart, measure its circumference, and describe its shape. They may also compare their rock with a classmate's rock.

Questions.   "What are five words you could use to tell about your rock? What new things have your learned about rocks today?"

Evaluation.   Check the accuracy of children's data sheets.

WE CAN OBSERVE AND DESCRIBE MANY KINDS OF WEATHER

Even young children are aware of weather. They known that on some days their parents or caregivers gladly let them play outdoors, but on other days they must play inside or don rain gear or heavy clothing to go to school and home. Educators can help children deepen their understanding of weather phenomena by having them focus on its many aspects and record weather data regularly. They can help them make and use some simple tools and charts to measure different aspects of weather. In this section you will find suggestions for helping children observe, describe, measure, and predict the weather.

Weather Walks

Science Processes.   Observing and communicating.

Take the children on a series of walks in different weather conditions. At least four walks could be planned to give children a good sample of your local conditions. For example, you might take the children out in warm, sunny weather; cool or cold, sunny weather; warm, rainy weather; and cold, rainy or snowy weather.

Take a writing tablet with you on each walk. Pause in a comfortable place (in rainy weather, you might gather on a porch) and have the children help you list words to describe the weather. Draw their attention to aspects such as temperature, position of the sun and shadows, clouds, condition of the ground and surroundings, and wind. Be sure to date your list.

After returning to the classroom, reread your list. Have each child draw or write at least one page for each class, weather-walk booklet. You will make a separate weather booklet for each of your walks, so you might want to use a different format for each booklet. For example, you might use bright yellow for your warm, sunny-walk pages. For a rainy-walk booklet, you might let children do watercolor paintings and add words or sentences to them describing the walk. After a walk on ice or snow, children might do crayon drawings and then paint over them with a strong solution of table salt or Epsom salts and water. After they dry, a crystalline "snowy" effect will be left on the pages. Help the children review their contributions to each booklet.

Have a small committee of children bind the pages together. Display the booklets in your class library area.

After two or more weather-walk booklets are completed, guide the children in looking through the booklets to review the details in the pictures and writing and to discuss the similarities and differences in the types of weather on the walks.

Questions.   "What do you like about sunny, warm weather? What do you like about cooler, rainy weather? Do you like changes in weather? Why?"

Evaluations.   Observe the children's abilities to describe and record aspects of the weather. Note the details shown in children's artwork and written language. Mark your observations on a checklist or make notes of unusual examples for children's anecdotal records. You might also wish to compare each child's contributions to your weather-walk booklets and find evidence of progress in the child's communication over time.

As these children take a walk on a rainy day, they list words to describe the weather.

Weather Forecasters

Science Processes.   Observing, communicating, measuring, and using time and space relationships.

Groups of children can take turns acting as weather forecasters and reporting the weather. Organize a rotation of groups of children to gather and report weather. Each day help the group take the temperature, generate several words to describe the weather, and predict the next day's weather.

Have your weather forecasters present their weather report. You might help children cut the front out of a large box to make it look like a television set (Figure 9.4). Your weather forecasters can stand behind the box and give their weather reports. Children might use paper microphones, maps, or charts as props. Children could also go to another classroom to share their weather reports. You might arrange for the weather forecasters to read their weather reports as part of morning announcements on the intercom for a period of two weeks. As children become adept at weather reporting, you might videotape their reports and play them back for other children to enjoy. You might have each group of weather forecasters record their predictions on a chart, the chalkboard, or a calendar. The next day, take a minute or two to compare the predictions to the actual weather.

You might follow up the children's weather reports by having the children view videotapes of local television meteorologists. Children could discuss the meteorologist's

Figure 9.4
"Television set."

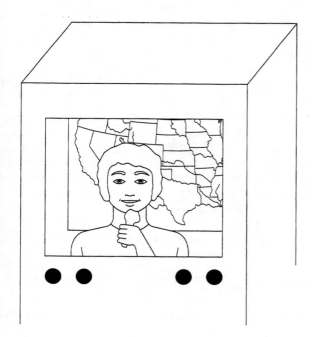

styles and props. They might write letters or send pictures of "weather news" to the television meteorologists. As a special event you could arrange to visit a local television studio to meet the meteorologist and crew. Sometimes meteorologists visit classrooms.

Questions. "What are the many factors that we might include as we describe the weather? (wind, temperature, humidity, clouds, precipitation) What are some things that helped you decide on your weather prediction?"

Evaluation. Help the class evaluate each weather group's report by discussing some things they thought were well done and some things that could be improved. Note the children's communication skills as they describe the weather. Which children comment in detail on the weather? Which children use a wide vocabulary? Which children are particularly poised? Which children need help and support in oral language?

Clouds, Clouds, Clouds

Science Processes. Observing, communicating, classifying, and using time and space relationships.

Clouds play an important part in the weather. Dark, heavy clouds indicate impending storms or accompany rain or snow. On some days the sky is cloudless. Big, fluffy clouds or high, wispy clouds often accompany fair weather. On still other occasions the children cannot observe distinct clouds because the sky is partially or completely overcast.

To help the children focus on different kinds of clouds, take them outdoors to observe various cloud formations. Let the children describe what they see and talk about the weather conditions that are present. Explain that, although snow and rain come from clouds, not all clouds bring rain or show. Help the children make a list of words that describe the clouds they see. Have the children add pictures to your list. As you observe different clouds on another day, refer to your previous list and pictures; help the children make comparisons.

Provide different art materials after each observation for the children to make pictures of clouds. After one, they might draw on blue paper with chalk. Another time, they could glue cotton balls to blue paper to represent clouds pulling the cotton into the shapes they want. Encourage the children to show higher and lower clouds in their pictures. After another observation, the children could use sponges of various shapes to print white or gray clouds on blue paper. For a sensory experience, they might use shaving cream to form clouds on dark-colored trays or covered tabletops.

After several observations of clouds, prepare a large display area. Have children choose their favorite cloud pictures and display them under the captions "Fair Weather Clouds," "Overcast Weather," and "Bad Weather Clouds."

Questions. "What are some similarities and differences in clouds? How do you think the clouds will affect today's weather? Tomorrow's weather?"

Evaluation. Note the children's interest, abilities to describe and compare clouds, and abilities to show details in their artwork.

Taking the Temperature   □ □ □

Science Processes.   Observing, communicating, measuring, and using time and space relationships.

"It's 80° today. You can wear shorts." "Bundle up! The temperature's below freezing." Children often hear comments like this at home and at school. They are aware of temperature and thermometers. Although most young children should not be expected to read a thermometer independently, individual or small-group experiences can help children realize that thermometers are tools that people can read and use.

Use a large, simple thermometer. Each day for several weeks, have individuals or small groups of students help you read the thermometer. Explain that the numbers and the level of the mercury or alcohol in the thermometer help us determine the temperature. Explain that the higher the level is, the warmer the temperature.

You might have the children look at the thermometer each day at about the same time. You might help them take pairs of temperatures such as these: temperatures indoors and outdoors, temperatures in the sun and in the shade, temperatures in the morning and in the afternoon, or temperatures on thermometers laid under a white cloth and under a black cloth. In cold weather, the children might also hold a thermometer out in the air and one inside their jackets and compare the results.

The children should record temperature data. They can make temperature readings part of their weather reports or write temperatures on a calendar or on a chart. Second or third graders can "set" a thermometer model by moving a ribbon or strip of paper up and down to indicate the temperature (Figure 9.5).

Questions.   Where children make pairs of temperature readings, ask: "How can you explain the differences in these temperatures?" Use temperature data for several days and ask: "What trends or patterns do we see here?"

Evaluation.   Evaluate children's interest and abilities in reading thermometers. Note their abilities to communicate about temperature data.

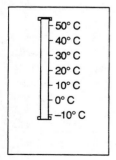

Figure 9.5
Paper thermometer model.

☐ ☐ ☐   Rain Gauge

Science Processes.   Observing, communicating, measuring, ordering, and using time and space relationships.

You will want to plan this activity for a time when rain occurs most frequently in your area. Organize the children into groups to make simple rain gauges. They can use sturdy scissors to cut the tops off straight-sided containers such as plastic bottles or paper milk cartons. Second and third graders can attach a vertical strip of masking tape to the inside of their containers and use ballpoint pens to mark centimeter units on the tape.

The groups should decide on several outdoor locations in which to place their rain gauges—in open spaces, near buildings, under trees, or on stairs. When rain is expected have the children place their gauges outdoors, securing them so they do not blow away. After a rain, the children should collect their gauges and compare the levels of rainwater in them. Older children can read the water level in centimeters; younger children can observe the water level and cut paper strips to match its depth. Have the children arrange the gauges in order from greatest to least amount of water. If any gauges have the same water level, place them side by side. Guide the children in recording and comparing their rain data for several rainy days.

If it snows in your area, the children can also measure amounts of snowfall in different locations by inserting a stick or ruler into the snow and marking its depth. Have the children arrange the measurements for snowfall in order from deepest to shallowest. You might also have children loosely fill their rain gauges with snow, bring them indoors, and record and compare the water levels when the snow melts.

Questions.   "How can you explain any differences in amounts of rain in the gauges (or depths of snow in different locations)? What are your predictions for the amounts of rain we will collect on the next rainfall?"

Evaluation.   Note on a checklist the children's cooperation and neatness in making the rain gauges. Observe their abilities to discuss the data and to put it in order.

☐ ☐ ☐   Collecting Wind Data

Science Processes.   Observing, communicating, measuring, using time and space relationships, and using numbers.

Wind affects weather conditions in a number of ways. The children can feel the wind and see evidence of the wind as it moves objects such as leaves and flags. In this activity the children will focus on the wind by making a wind vane and learning how to measure and describe the wind's direction and force. Divide the class into small groups. Help each group of children make a simple wind vane (Figure 9.6). They will need to cut out an arrow from poster board and make slits in it to insert a straw. They should tape the arrow and the straw together. Help each group place its wind vane in a location where it can be anchored. Use a long thin nail and place the straw over it. You can drive the nail into the ground or an appropriate wooden surface. You can also

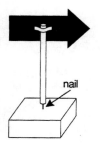

Figure 9.6
Wind vane.

use a large nail with a broad head, set the nail head-down, tape the head in place, and slip the straw over the pointed end of the nail.

Give the children some orientation terms to help them describe the direction of the wind. Young children can use directions such as "toward the school," "away from the school," "toward the front of the school," and "toward the back of the school" to describe the directions in which their wind vanes point. Older children can use north, south, east, and west. As the wind blows, have the children observe their vanes and discuss the wind's direction. They should record their data on a chart or on the calendar.

Meteorologists use the Beaufort scale to determine wind speed. Beaufort (pronounced BO-fort) was a British admiral who devised the scale in the early 1800s. It worked so well that people still use it today. Young children can use the version of the Beaufort scale in Table 9.1 to determine wind speed.

Prepare a chart with all or some of the data shown in the table. Help the children observe the effects of the wind and agree on a word to describe its speed. Second and third graders can also use the numerical data to describe wind speed.

Table 9.1
A version of the Beaufort scale of wind speed.

What to Look for	Wind Words	Wind Speed (kilometers/hour)	Wind Speed (miles/hour)
No leaves move. Smoke rises straight up.	Calm	less than 2	less than 1
Smoke drifts slowly. Leaves move. Wind felt on face. Small flags wave.	Breeze	2–19	1–12
Dust and papers blow. Branches move and sway. Waves are seen.	Stronger winds	20–50	13–31
Big trees sway. Branches break. Damage is done.	Gale, wind storm, hurricane	51–120+	32–74+

Have children observe and record wind data for several days and then compare their findings. They might also compare winds in the early morning and in the afternoon. Your class weather forecasters could make wind data part of their weather reports.

Questions. "Besides the ones in our chart, what other effects did the wind have? (You might want to add some of the children's responses to your chart.) Besides using our wind vanes, what other ways might we use to determine the wind's direction?"

Evaluation. Observe the children's cooperation and motor skills as they construct their wind vanes. Note the children's abilities to relate their observations of the wind to the data on the chart.

WEATHER AND SEASONS AFFECT PEOPLE'S ACTIVITIES

Weather affects the way people dress and the activities in which they participate. Weather also affects people's moods sometimes. The weather at any time is determined by factors such as wind, water and humidity, and temperature. Seasons also play a role in weather conditions.

This section features a variety of activities to make children more aware of changes in the weather and the way weather affects their lives. In the activities, children use several communication forms and science processes.

□ □ □ Month-by-Month Weather Book

Science Processes. Observing, communicating, using numbers, and using time and space relationships.

Each month help the children prepare a poster of highlights of the weather and classroom events. Use a poster board and write the month and year at the top. As dramatic changes and weather phenomena occur, help children dictate or record descriptive words on the poster. At the end of each month, have them choose some temperatures to represent the monthly highs and lows. Let the children gather a few natural specimens and tape these to the poster. For example, in September, leaves will probably be green, while in late October, some leaves will have turned color. In February, deciduous trees will have no leaves in most areas, but the children can find bare twigs to attach to the poster. Take a photograph of your class and attach it. Make note of special classroom events, especially those that are influenced by the weather. For example, if your class studies local harvests in October, make note of some of your activities and the weather conditions. If you take a walk in the rain or to observe spring flowers in April, include these things, too.

Each month the children can add a poster to make a giant, accordion-style book. The "pages" can be put together with tape or metal rings (Figure 9.7). After you have completed pages for a few months, have the children review what the weather has been like and predict how it is likely to change in the next few months. Have the

Figure 9.7
Accordion book.

children examine their photos and discuss the clothing they wore. Have the children make and attach labels of the seasons. For example, in your area September may be considered summer, whereas October and November are fall and December is winter. Be sure to review your weather book toward the end of the school year.

Questions. "If you choose two months in our weather book and compare the weather during them, can you tell how it affected our activities? How did the weather help us take part in some activities? Did weather ever prevent us from doing things? What? When?"

Evaluation. Children could make their own month-by-month weather books; you could check them for completeness and depth of detail. Note children's interest in the project and their abilities to compare weather phenomena and to discuss its affects on people.

Weather Collages

Science Processes. Observing, communicating, and using time and space relationships.

Cut out large cardboard letters for the words of the seasons: F-A-L-L, W-I-N-T-E-R, and so on. Divide the class into small groups. During each season, have each group of children take a letter and make a collage of seasonal materials on it. For fall, one group could glue and tape on autumn leaves on one of the letters. Other groups could collect nuts, seeds, and dried grasses to attach to their letters. Each group could also write appropriate weather words on their letter or add little sketches of things people do in the season.

Display and discuss the finished letters. Discuss how the season's weather affects people's activities. As the next season arrives, make collage letters again and compare them to the letters for the previous season.

Questions.   "What are some differences in the weather we had in fall and winter? What are some similarities? What things remain the same in all the seasons? What things change?"

Evaluation.   Note on a checklist the children's cooperation and neatness as they work with their collages. Observe the children's abilities to describe and compare the materials they used in their weather word collages.

□ □ □ Dressing for the Weather

Science Processes.   Communicating and using time and space relationships.

Cut several sheets of paper for each child about 12 by 20 centimeters (5½ by 8½ inches.) Help each child make a drawing of himself or herself dressed in the clothes they have on. The figure should be fairly large. Next, help each child figure out where

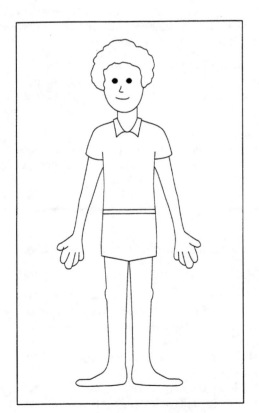

Figure 9.8
Dressing for the weather.

to cut a hole in a second sheet of paper so that when that sheet is placed on top of the figure, the face will show through (see Figure 9.8). On the second sheet the child should draw clothing to dress the figure for a weather condition. For example, a child might draw rainy weather gear, a snowsuit, or a bathing suit for warm weather. Help each child complete several "outfits" and label each one with words to name or describe the weather. Next, help the children arrange their pages on top of the figures they drew. Each child should make a cover for the booklet; the cover may or may not include a hole for the face to show through. Help the children punch holes through all their pages and the cover and put the pages together with brads or yarn ties. Let the children exchange and browse through each other's books. Encourage discussion of how the clothing that they have drawn fits the weather. You might show the drawings to a small group, covering up the weather words. Then let the children tell what kinds of weather they think the clothes are appropriate for. Use the books in your class library area before the children take them home.

Questions. "What makes this outfit suitable for the weather? What weather word (descriptive words) could go with this picture?"

Evaluation. You might ask each child to draw at least three pages for her book. Then check the pages for neatness, detail, and completeness. Encourage the children to add details such as shoes, boots, and hats to their pictures. Note each child's ability to tell about her book pages.

Seasonal Animal Stories

Science Processes.   Observing and communicating.

Weather affects animals as well as people. Create a simple story using pellon felt board pieces to suit the animals and weather conditions in your area. The story might be like one of the following.

Geese Migration
The geese in the lake sensed that winter was coming. The days grew short. It didn't get light early in the morning, and sunset came in late afternoon. The air grew chilly on most nights.

The geese gathered together. They ate and ate. They started to leave their lake and fly south for the winter. They flew high in the sky in a big "V" pattern. Different geese took turns leading the "V." After many days of flying the geese settled in another lake. The weather was warmer. The geese found food to eat for the winter.

What did they do when spring came? The geese gathered together again and flew back to their lake in the north. Their wonderful sense of direction let them find their home lake. In the spring, the days were longer and warmer again. The geese found lots to eat.

The mother geese laid eggs. When their babies hatched they ate and grew large and strong all summer long. The next fall, the parents and babies made a long trip to the south again.

A Dog for All Seasons

Bo was a lucky dog because he lived in a large yard with a fence. Bo could run and play. Bo had a dog house where he lay when it was cold or rainy. Bo had a girl, Vicki, who played with him and took care of him.

In warm weather, Bo rested during the hot parts of the day. He lay in the shade. Vicki watched Bo pant to cool his body. Bo liked to run and play in the cooler parts of the day. Bo drank lots of water in the summer.

When fall came, the air and ground were cooler. Bo's coat grew thicker. Vicki gave him a little more food to eat to keep his body warm. In the afternoons, Bo lay in the sun. At night he slept in his dog house.

In the very cold weather, Bo stayed in his dog house more and more. Sometimes the water in his dish froze, and Vicki brought him fresh water. Vicki put a rug in Bo's dog house to help him stay warm. When it was very, very cold, Vicki brought Bo into the basement to sleep.

Vicki and her mother helped to keep Bo safe and comfortable in different seasons. Do you have animals that you care for, too? What special things do your animals need in different seasons?

Tell the story. Ask the children to add details to the story. Allow the children to use the pellon pieces to tell their own versions of the story. The children might also draw pictures on pellon and use them on the felt board.

Questions. "What are some ways cold (hot) weather affect animals and people?"

Evaluation. Make notes of children's attention and interest as you and they tell stories.

☐ ☐ ☐ Good Weather, Bad Weather

Science Processes. Observing, communicating, and classifying.

Prepare a large display area and add the captions "Nice Weather" and "Weather Hardships." Discuss weather conditions that are "nice" for people; for example, rain waters crops and lawns; it "refreshes" the earth. Talk about rain that causes problems—floods, washing away crops, and making people cancel outdoor events. Explain that sometimes people welcome snow—it is pretty and fun to play in, but sometimes snow causes hardships—accidents, power failures, and school and work closings. Discuss the idea that winds supply gentle breezes to cool the earth but winds can be harsh and destructive when tornadoes and hurricanes occur.

Provide magazines and newspapers and have children select pictures to fit your categories—nice weather and weather hardships. Have the children pin or tape up their pictures, describe the pictures, and tell why they chose the category they did. Continue the display and picture search over a period of several weeks.

Questions. "Tell about some times when the weather caused problems for you and your family. Some people like snow (rain, high wind), but others think it causes problems. What do you think?"

Evaluation. Note the children's abilities to communicate and justify the classifications they made. As part of your evaluation, have the children choose a weather condition such as rain. Have them fold a piece of paper in half and draw something to illustrate "rain helps us" and "rain causes problems." Check the children's pictures for detail and logical thinking.

Relating to the Weather

Science Processes. Observing and communicating.

Gather many pictures that show different weather conditions. The children might help you select pictures from newspapers and magazines. Have each child choose a picture and write a story about it. To personalize the pictures, each child might draw a picture of himself, cut out the figure, and glue it onto the weather picture. You could also photocopy the children's class pictures and let them use these as parts of their figures.

Let the children tell about their pictures and write their names on them. Bind them together in a class book and place the book in your library center.

Questions. "When you put yourself in the picture, what did you see and hear? What did you feel? Do you like the weather condition you chose? Why or why not?"

Evaluation. Judge each child's story and oral description of the story for progress in use of expressive vocabulary and use of appropriate weather words.

THE EARTH'S SURFACE IS CHANGED BY PEOPLE AND NATURAL PHENOMENA

The earth's surface is constantly changing. Wind, water, ice, and other elements of nature cause some of these changes. Wind, rain, and many weathering conditions wear down the surface of the earth; in other places the earth is being built up by natural phenomena such as volcanic eruptions, earthquakes, and the accumulation of soil in new areas. Mountains rise out of the sea in some places and sink into the sea in other places.

People also cause changes in the earth's surface. They build dams and levees to control water. They construct houses, office buildings, roads, bridges, and shopping centers. As people build, they make radical changes in the natural surface of the earth. The soil is bulldozed away in one area and deposited in big mounds in other areas. To prevent erosion, people sensitive to protecting the earth will replant where they have torn away the natural coverings of the earth. However, people often show a lack of responsibility and fail to protect our natural surroundings. Some people oppose or mourn the irresponsible actions that others make in the name of "progress." They take political action or use advertising to bring attention to changes they consider undesirable.

Teachers can help children become aware of the different ways the earth's surface is changed. This section offers adults an opportunity to foster children's appreciation for our Earth and sense of responsibility for caring for it.

☐ ☐ ☐ ## People Change the Surface of the Earth

Science Processes.   Observing, communicating, using time and space relationships, and inferring.

Take the children for a walk to help them notice the changes in the Earth's surfaces brought about by people. Help children locate dramatic changes in the contour of the land caused by construction. Children may notice areas around roads and bridges that are built up or other constructions that cut right into the earth. Point out places where erosion has occurred. Discuss the causes and the possible solutions to the problem of erosion. Help the children notice the things people have done to prevent erosion. When you return to the classroom, make a class list of ways people change the Earth's surface. Let each child select one item from the list and illustrate the change using collage materials and crayons. Be sure each child dictates or writes about that change on his illustrated page. Compile a class book entitled "People Make Changes in the Earth's Surface." Place the book on the science table for children to look at.

Questions.   As you map out your walk ahead of time, plan the changes you might point out and the related questions you might ask the children. For example, be sure to include some application questions where children solve problems and some evaluation questions such as "Is this change good? Why or why not? Do you think this change took a long time or a short time? Why?" You could also ask: "What did they do to the earth when they built this road (or house, shopping center, or playground)?"

Evaluation.   Note children's interest in and sensitivity to surface changes. Observe their book illustrations for detail and comprehension.

☐ ☐ ☐ ## Make Changes at the Sand Table

Science Processes.   Observing, communicating, using time and space relationships, and inferring.

Bring pictures from magazines, calendars, and newspapers that illustrate natural and people-made changes to the Earth's surfaces. Be sure to include pictures of tornadoes, hurricanes, and earthquakes. Discuss these illustrations with the children and talk about how each of these phenomena affects the Earth's surfaces.

Place a bulletin board for pictures illustrating changes near the sand table. Encourage the children to make changes in the contour of the sand by simulating different phenomena. They may turn on a fan, under supervision, to notice the changes wind can cause. They may wish to use a sprinkling can to make "rain." They can build roads, tunnels, bridges, dikes, and levees. The pictures on the bulletin board should offer children suggestions. This activity is not for one class period but should be made available for several weeks to encourage the children to vary and build upon their ideas. Add different materials to the sand tray to motivate them and give them new ideas.

Questions. As children work at the sand table, ask: "What will happen if we pour the water on this mound of sand? How could we keep our tunnel from caving in? How could we move the sand without moving it with our hands? What are some ways nature changes the earth? How do people cope with frightening events such as tornadoes, hurricanes, or earthquakes? How can people keep safe during a bad storm or an earthquake?" (You may have an earthquake or tornado drill to help children refine their answers to these questions.)

Evaluation. Notice children's interest in this project. Listen to their comments at the sand table to determine what types of changes they are aware of.

Testing the Air and Water for Purity

Science Processes. Observing, ordering, using time and space relationships, communicating, and inferring.

The Earth is changed by the people. People cause changes in the land, the water, and the air. Help children test the water and the air to see if they notice signs of pollution. Children may wish to test the water in two different ways. They may collect rain in a jar and pour the rain water through a coffee filter into another container. Have the children examine the coffee filter and look for signs of impurities. The children could also melt snow and test it using the same process. Children may wish to collect water or snow from different areas and compare their results.

To test the air for impurities, have groups of children hang out white cloths in different places for several days and then examine the cloths carefully to see whether they have collected impurities. For variety, children may wish to hang out various types and textures of materials. They may put out strips of tape with the sticky side exposed, loosely woven or tightly woven material, sandpaper, or plain paper. The children may wish to cut the material they are testing in half and leave one half inside to use for comparison with the half that has been outdoors. The children may also wish to arrange the materials from the dirtiest to the cleanest.

Questions. "How has the coffee filter (cloth, tape) changed? What do you see on the material? How do you think it got there? What are some things that people do to make our air (water, snow), dirty? What are some things you have done before that have caused the water or air to be dirty? What could you do to keep our air and water clean?"

Evaluation. Notice children's abilities to test and collect data, make comparisons, and relate air and water pollution to people.

☐ ☐ ☐ Protecting Our Earth

Science Processes.   Observing, communicating, inferring, and predicting.

"A ship off the coast of California has spilled thousands of gallons of oil in the ocean. The ship's anchor knocked a hole in the side of the boat and caused the oil leak. Sea birds are coming to land all coated with oil." "The redfish have been pulled off the market because of the high content of lead in the fish." Almost daily, news articles cover information about distressed animals or other forms of nature that have been devastated because of human error.

Have the children collect pictures and articles about wildlife and environmental problems from newspapers and magazines. Plan discussions focusing on these dilemmas—the problem, how it happened, the effect on the land and/or animals, how people might remedy the problem, what might happen to our environment if the problem is not remedied.

After several environmental discussions, have each child focus on one distressed animal and write a story about that animal telling what happened to it. Children may choose to give their story a happy or sad ending. Younger children may select a newspaper or magazine picture and dictate a story to a tape recorder about the animal in the illustration.

Questions.   Tell about an experience you know of where people have not taken care of animals or the natural environment. Ask children: "What would you do about this situation?"

Evaluation.   Note children's sensitivity in their discussions and their stories. Are they realistic in their solutions? What degree of understanding do they demonstrate regarding the problems?

☐ ☐ ☐ Conservation Projects

Science Processes.   Observing, using time and space relationships, communicating, and inferring.

Even young children can work on conservation projects when they become aware of and sensitive to wasteful habits we have developed. Bring to children's attention a few of the wasteful habits people have. Mention habits such as leaving on lights and televisions when they are not being used; using too many paper towels, an excess of toilet paper, or construction paper; letting the water run more than necessary; or neglecting to recycle and reuse materials. Let them add their own ideas about wasteful habits. Write these ideas on an experience chart and add to them on subsequent occasions.

Let the children discuss which of these habits they, as a class, are most guilty of. Let them vote on one conservation project to work on as a group. They may choose to use only one paper towel, to recycle many different types of paper, to stop wasting water, or to keep the door shut to conserve heat. Children will need to exhort each

A family does its part in the recycling effort.

other to remember to conserve. Perhaps they can find a way to collect data showing the savings that resulted from their conservation project.

As a follow-up to this project, plan a school project or a homework assignment. If the children choose a school project, help them plan and carry out their strategy to involve the whole school. If they choose a home assignment, show them how to survey to determine where the waste really occurs in their families. Help them base their conservation project on that area of waste. Encourage your children to think of ways to motivate the entire family to work on the conservation project. After families have worked on the project for a week or two, have children report on the results of their family conservation endeavor.

Questions. "What did we (our school, the family) do to keep from being wasteful? How did our project work? Was it successful? Were some members more helpful than others? Do we notice a change since we began conserving? What is the difference?"

Evaluation. Note children's abilities to work together as a unit. Which ones readily cooperate? Which ones have to be reminded? Observe reporting of data on family projects. Do children show an interest in the project? Do they give clear reports? Do they demonstrate an understanding of and appreciation for the conservation process?

NOW IT'S YOUR TURN

You live on the Earth and observe its weather conditions daily. We have described some ways to attune children to observing the Earth and weather carefully and focusing on various aspects. Now it's your turn to "tune in" and do some investigations yourself. The activities in this section will help you plan for children's further study of the Earth and its weather.

1. Collect nature pictures to help you teach the concept "Our home, the earth, is covered by liquids, solids, and gases." Gather pictures of different land and water formations. See the introductions to the concept at the beginning of this chapter to give you ideas for the pictures you will need. You may find interesting pictures on calendars, posters, and in nature magazines.

2. What do you know about rocks? If you feel that your basic knowledge is weak, do a little research on rocks. Study the three basic types of rock formations. Purchase a paperback rock book. Try to collect some of the rocks illustrated in the book. Start a picture file of the different settings in which rocks are formed. Share your newfound information with children.

3. Is there a "rock hound" in your community? Invite him or her to come to your classroom and share a rock collection with the children.

4. To help you "tune in" on different types of weather, keep your own weather diary for at least two weeks. As a minimum, note the temperature and the relative humidity, use the children's modified Beaufort scale or a complete Beaufort scale to determine the wind speed, and use at least four words to describe the weather each day. After keeping your own weather diary, think about some aspect of your findings that the children could understand. Share some of your weather data with the children.

5. Read about relative humidity and ways that meteorologists measure it. Plan a way to draw the children's attention to relative humidity.

6. Air temperature affects the way people feel and how they dress in cold weather; wind speed or windchill affects us, too. Use the windchill chart in Table 9.2 along with a Beaufort scale to determine the windchill on at least three cold, windy days. Once you know the wind speed in kilometers per hour and the temperature, see where the appropriate row and column intersect to find the windchill. Compare your windchill results to windchill data reported on television or in the newspaper. Share your techniques and findings with adult colleagues or with 2nd- and 3rd-graders.

7. Our activities have focused on temperature, observation of general weather conditions, amounts of precipitation, clouds, and wind speed. What other aspects of weather could you bring to young children's attention? What variations could you add to our activities? Plan and implement at least two more ideas.

8. Collect several pictures of people around the world whose clothing suits the climate in which they live. Be sure to include pictures that show older and younger children, people of different ethnic groups, and people of different socioeconomic status. Show the pictures to a group of children. Encourage them to describe and compare the pictures, to compare the clothing shown to their own clothing, and to make inferences about the climate based on the clothing in the pictures.

9. How do you rate when it comes to conservation? In teaching the activity on conservation, did you become aware of some of your own wasteful habits? Now is the time to change. Talk with a friend about your wasteful habit. Plan a strategy for change. Carry out your plan with diligence. Report the results to your friend.

Table 9.2
Windchill chart.

Actual temperature (°C)	Wind Speed (km/h)							
	6	10	20	30	40	50	60	70
20	20	18	16	14	13	13	12	12
16	16	14	11	9	7	7	6	6
12	12	9	5	3	1	0	−0	−1
8	8	5	0	−3	−5	−6	−7	−7
4	4	0	−5	−8	−11	−12	−13	−14
0	0	−4	−10	−14	−17	−18	−19	−20
−4	−4	−8	−15	−20	−23	−25	−26	−27
−8	−8	−13	−21	−25	−29	−31	−32	−33
−12	−12	−17	−26	−31	−35	−37	−39	−40
−16	−16	−22	−31	−37	−41	−43	−45	−46
−20	−20	−26	−36	−43	−47	−49	−51	−52
−24	−24	−31	−42	−48	−53	−56	−58	−59
−28	−28	−35	−47	−54	−59	−62	−64	−65
−32	−32	−40	−52	−60	−65	−68	−70	−72
−36	−36	−44	−57	−65	−71	−74	−77	−78
−40	−40	−49	−63	−71	−77	−80	−83	−85

(Left axis label: Windchill temperature (°C))

10. Select one of the concepts presented in this chapter. Plan a way to blend it with another area of the curriculum. For instance, you may develop an art appreciation lesson based on a topic related to one of the concepts. You would select many prints or other art forms that depict that topic. You might develop a music appreciation lesson on Grofe's *Grand Canyon Suite* linking your lesson into the study of rock formations. You may have other ideas for blending one of these concepts with history, math, or geography. Share your ideas with your colleagues.

SELECTED CHILDREN'S BOOKS

Allington, R. L. & Krull, K. (1981). *Beginning to learn about autumn (spring, summer, winter)*. Milwaukee, WI: Raintree.

Ball, J. A., & Hardy, A. D. (1989). *What can it be?: Riddles about the seasons*. Morristown, NJ: Silver Burdett.

Bannan, J. G., & Jacobs, L. (1989). *Earth watch books: Letting off steam: The story of geothermal energy*. Minneapolis: Carolrhoda.

Bannan, J. G., & Jacobs, L. (1989). *Earth watch books: Sand dunes*. Minneapolis: Carolrhoda.

Bender, L. (1989). *The story of the Earth series: Cave*. New York: Franklin Watts.

Branley, F. (1990). *Tornado alert*. New York: Harper & Row.

Burstein, F. (1990). *Anna's rain*. New York: Franklin Watts.

Catchpole, C. (1983). *Deserts*. New York: Dial Books.

Catchpole, C. (1983). *Jungles*. New York: Dial Books.

Catchpole, C. (1984). *Grasslands*. New York: Dial Books.

Chisholm, J. (1982). *Finding out about our Earth*. Tulsa, OK: EDC Publishing.

de Paola, T. (1975). *The cloud book*. New York: Holiday House.

Greene, C. (1983). *Hi, clouds*. Chicago: Children's Press.

Kaufman, J. (1987). *Earth and space*. New York: Western.

Martin, B., Jr., & Archambault, J. (1988). *Listen to the rain*. New York: Henry Holt.

Otto, C. (1990). *That sky, that rain*. New York: Harper & Row.

Parramon, J. M., & Wensel, U. (1981). *Autumn*. New York: Delair.

Peters, L. W. (1988). *The sun, the wind, and the rain*. New York: Henry Holt.

Simon, S. (1989). *Storms*. New York: Morrow.

Tresselt, A. (1951). *Autumn harvest*. New York: Morrow.

Updegraff, I., & Updegraff, R. (1981). *Rivers and lakes*. Mankato, MN: The Children's Book Co.

Vendrell, C. S., & Parramon, J. M. (1985). *The four elements: Earth*. Woodbury, NY: Barron's.

Zolotow, C. S. (1989). *The storm book*. New York: Harper & Row.

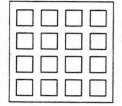

Chapter 10

Space

Y OUNG children encounter news about space almost daily. As they watch television, they hear about the rocket that is ready to be launched on a space probe. Children see many amazing photos of planets taken in space via high-tech photography. Many of today's youngsters are familiar with astronauts, often by name, and they are acquainted with some of astronauts' adaptive habits in space. Other aspects of space—the sun, the moon, the stars, and night and day—children can see with their own eyes. Through these daily experiences, young children observe how the sun, moon, and stars directly influence their lives.

Although children today have much more exposure to information about space than children have in the past twenty years, we must remember that concepts related to space are very abstract for young children. Therefore, teachers need to be selective in choosing activities. They need to present each concept related to space with a sensitivity to the developmental level of their children.

This chapter includes four concepts about space with related activities for each concept. The concepts we present are:

- We can see many things in the sky.
- The sun gives us light and heat.
- Nine planets have been identified in our solar system.
- People have explored space and want to know more about it.

WE CAN SEE MANY THINGS IN THE SKY

Some animals fly in the sky and so do some objects made by human beings. What else can we see in the sky? During our activities we can help the children take special notice of the clouds and our all-important sun. We can help them plan time at night to observe our moon, many stars, and the planets. Skywatching can be fun and informative. For young children, learning about the bodies in the sky is an important part of exploring our physical world. The activities in this section are intended to deepen and extend children's powers of observation and communication as well as their understanding of our universe.

☐ ☐ ☐ Look Up! What Do You See?

Science Processes.   Observing, communicating, predicting, and using time and space relationships.

Start this activity indoors. Ask children what they might see in the sky outdoors. Make a list of their answers. Next, take the group outdoors and observe for several minutes. Caution the children not to look directly at the sun. Make a list of what you have observed and compare it with your pre-observation list. Invite the children to talk about things they have seen in the sky at times other than today. Have them identify natural things on your list—the sun, clouds, or insects—and things made by people—planes, kites, balloons. Underline the natural ones. Ask the children to draw a picture that shows at least two natural things (perhaps the sun and birds or the moon and stars) and at least two things made by people.

Second and third graders can observe the sun's position at various times of the day—perhaps at 8 A.M., 10 A.M., noon, and 2 P.M. Remind the students to make their observations quickly and not to look directly at the sun. After making one observation, they can predict approximately where the sun will be at their next observation.

Questions.   "How would a nighttime picture be different from what you have drawn?" Ask the children to observe the sky for the next several days and suggest things to add to your list of things we can see in the sky. Then ask: "What can we add to our list of things seen in the sky? Are our additions natural or made by humans?"

Evaluation.   Ask the children to point to the natural things and things made by people in their pictures. Use the pictures to check their levels of understanding. Assess the children's facility in adding to the list and discussing items on the list.

☐ ☐ ☐ Moonlighting

Science Processes.   Observing, communicating, and inferring.

This activity works best in the winter, because it is dark early and winter nights are often crisp and clear. At the beginning of the month, help each child make a calendar on large paper. Ask the children to go outdoors with a family member and observe the moon as many nights as possible. Each child should draw on his calendar what he noticed about the moon—its size, shape, and position in the sky. If it is too stormy or overcast to see the moon, direct him to draw raindrops or clouds on the appropriate space on the calendar.

About once a week, take time to let the children talk about their moon-watching experiences and to encourage them to continue gathering moon data for the rest of the month. Perhaps you could note some of their special moon observations on your classroom calendar, too. Help the children describe gradual changes they see in the moon's shape. At the end of the month help them make some generalizations about the changes they observed in the moon's shape.

Questions. "By next week, what do you think the moon might look like? How many nights this week were clear enough to see the moon?"

Evaluation. Check each child's calendar to see that he or she gathered data regularly. Note each child's interest in the project. Have each child write and illustrate a story about the moon watch project. Evaluate the stories noting the details and skillful use of language.

Our Moon's Phases

Science Processes. Observing and communicating.

After the children have observed the moon for a week or two, discuss the apparent changes in its shape over the period of several nights. Let the children sketch and describe moon shapes they have seen during the period of observation or at other times.

Help 2nd and 3rd graders see why the moon seems to change shape. Supply a large light-colored ball to represent the moon. You might have the children draw "moon craters" on the ball. Let a child hold the ball and darken the room. Use a bare light bulb to represent the sun. Have the child stand or kneel to be on the same level as the "sun." Then the child should move the ball slowly in a counter-clockwise direction around her head which represents the earth. Help the class to notice that the ball (moon) glows with reflected light and that its lighted part changes from fully lighted (full moon) as the "moon" orbits the "earth." Let several children take turns holding the ball in this demonstration while the class compares the way the ball looks to what they have actually observed in their moon watch.

Questions. "How can we describe the shape of the moon (at various phases)? How does what you have seen in this demonstration compare to the sketches you made when you observed the moon?"

Evaluation. Check the children's moon calendars for completeness. Note the children's abilities to follow directions and their willingness to describe what they see.

Starlight Stories

Science Processes. Observing, communicating, and using time and space relationships.

Talk to the children about things they can see in the night sky besides the moon. As the children mention stars, introduce the word *constellation*—a pattern of stars that may appear to resemble an object or person. Tell a few stories about the constellations and point out the positions of the stars as you tell each story. Start with a simplified story about the Big and Little Dippers. You might present a version similar to this one: "Some ancient Greeks made up stories about the stars. They imagined that the Big Dipper was a huge bear and that the Little Dipper was her son. They said that the king of the gods, Zeus, put the bears in the sky to keep them from harm. Some storytellers still say that the bears have long tails because Zeus stretched them when he threw the bears into the sky."

Using a constellation book as a reference, punch holes in heavy paper to represent the stars in the constellations. Make bigger holes to represent the brighter stars. Place the paper on an overhead projector focusing the light on the chalkboard. The "stars" should shine through the paper onto the board. Now take the chalk and draw the outline for both the Big and the Little Dippers. You might sketch in the bears' shapes, too.

Tell your children about the constellation Orion, the hunter. Using the dark paper on the projector, point out Orion's shoulder, hips, belt, and sword hanging by his side. Explain that people imagined that Orion had a big dog named Canis Major and that Procyon, the brightest star in the constellation, represents the big dog's eye.

Tell your starlight stories at the time of the year when these constellations can be seen in the sky. In the winter, the Big and Little Dippers can be seen in the northern sky and Orion can be seen in the southeastern or southern sky. Both constellations are low on the horizon early in the evening.

After telling your stories, give each of your children a diagram of the constellations to take home. Encourage them to look for the constellations with their families at night.

Questions. When telling the stories ask questions such as, "Why might Zeus have thrown the bears into the sky? If you could think of another name for the constellation Orion what would you name it? What would you call his dog? What story would you tell about him?"

Evaluation. Have the children tell about the observations they made with their families. Make a checklist of those who followed through with the family assignment. Mark the degree of interest each child shows in the family assignment.

☐ ☐ ☐ Creating Star Stories

Science Processes. Communicating and using time and space relationships.

After the "Starlight Stories" activities, have children work in small groups and create their own starlight stories for imaginary constellations. Provide a few simple books about constellations for children to use for inspiration. Give each group a piece of heavy construction paper and let them punch holes in the paper to represent the stars of their constellation. Let each group place their picture on the overhead projector and share their constellation stories with one another. Encourage the children to ask each other about their creative constellation stories.

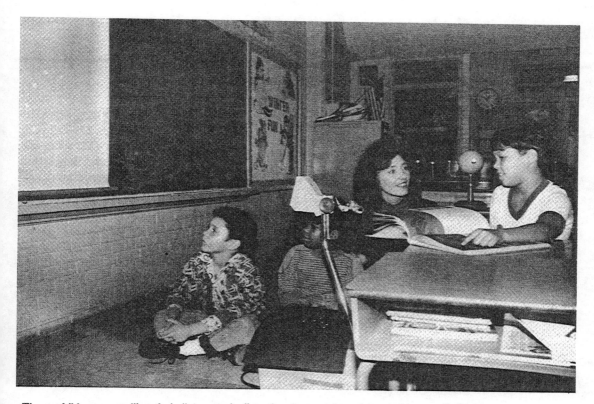

These children are telling their "star stories" to the class as they show their constellations on the overhead projector.

Questions. "What other stories might we tell for the constellations? What makes a good star story? Was yours a good one based on these qualities?"

Evaluation. Notice how well the children work together in their small groups—who are the leaders and who are the cooperative followers? Which children initiate the creative story task? Which children are good at embellishing the stories? During group presentations notice the children's communication abilities, problem-solving skills, and logic in their stories.

THE SUN GIVES US LIGHT AND HEAT

We are so accustomed to seeing the sun shining that we often take it for granted, but let the sun dip behind the clouds for a few dreary days, and we all begin to complain. We could not exist without the sun. Perhaps young children cannot understand the far-reaching effects of life without the sun, but even a 3-year-old can see the light from the sun and feel its heat. Young children can understand in an elementary way the concept of night and day.

Life Without the Sun

Science Processes. Communicating and inferring.

On a sunny day while the children are out on the playground, bring their attention to the sunshine—how bright it is, how it helps us see, and how it warms us. Take the children into a classroom that has been darkened as much as possible. Talk about the difference between the bright sunlight and the dark room. Discuss some things that might be hard to do in the dark. Then lead the discussion into a pretend situation. Ask: "What would we do if we didn't have the sunshine for one week?"

After the discussion tell a feltboard story similar to the following.

Helja of the Arctic Circle

Helja lives near the Arctic Circle where the sun never shines in the wintertime. (Place dark felt background on board.) When Helja gets up on the morning, the sun is not shining; it is still very dark outside. Helja dresses in very warm clothes. Because the sun is not shining, it is very cold outside. (Dress felt doll in many layers of clothing.) When the school bus arrives to pick Helja up, it is very dark. (Show felt bus with lights on.) All day Helja works at school while it is still dark outside. Helja and her parents play games indoors, read, and watch TV because it is too dark and cold to play outside. (Show appropriate felt pieces to demonstrate.) The winter seems long, dark, and dreary. Helja's family is glad to see the spring finally come with its warmth and light. (Show bright felt background with sun and green grass.)

Questions. To answer the question, "What would we do if we didn't have the sun for a week?", many children will respond "It would be very dark." Follow up with questions such as "What could we do to help us see in the dark?" Elicit many answers from the children. Build new questions on the children's responses, always reinforcing the concept that the sun gives us light and heat. Encourage the children to use the felt pieces and make up their own stories describing the contrast between life with and life without the sun. They may want to make a few extra props for their feltboard stories.

"How is Helja's life different from yours? How would you feel if you lived near the Arctic Circle and didn't see the sun for several weeks?"

Evaluation. Observe the children's contributions as they tell their feltboard stories. Note the detail that they use in telling their stories, the originality they employ, and the depth of understanding they demonstrate.

Testing the Heat from the Sun

Science Processes. Observing, predicting, and inferring.

Choose a sunny day for this experiment. Select two aluminum cans. Let your children feel both cans and describe whether the cans are hot or cold and alike or different in temperature. Take the children outside to place one can in the sunshine and the other in the shade. In about 30 minutes take your children outside again. Ask them "Which can do you think will be warmer?" Let the children feel the cans. Encourage them to explain why the can in the sun is warmer. In your discussion reinforce the concept that the sun gives us heat.

Let your children test objects to determine how they respond to the sun's heat. For example, have two pieces of aluminum foil, light fabric, dark fabric, wood, clay, and two jars of water for your children to test. Let the children work with partners placing one object in the sun and its duplicate in the shade. Encourage the children to predict what will happen and to test their predictions by feeling the cans and comparing their temperatures. Have the children share their findings with the class.

Questions. "Which object will be hotter? Why? Which objects absorbed a lot of heat? Which objects absorbed less heat? If we are playing outside on a cold day, where can we stand so we will be warmer?"

Evaluation. Notice whether or not the children are able to replicate the experiment and the clarity with which they report their findings to the group.

Light and Shadows

Science Processes. Observing, communicating, using time and space relationships, and inferring.

While the children are playing outside, have them point to the sun. Warn them not to look directly at the sun. Bring the children's attention to the brightness of the sun pointing out the many objects that seem to gleam and glisten in the sunlight. Draw the children's attention to leaves that seem to have brighter colors when the sun shines on them and to leaves that seem translucent when the sun shines through them. Have them describe how their friends' hair looks when the sun shines on it and how the sunlight affects the appearance of other parts of their bodies.

After the children have noticed how the sunlight affects objects around them, tell them that things can block the light of the sun. Point to a child's shadow. Ask the group what is making that shadow. As the children come to the understanding that the child's body is making the shadow, explain that opaque objects, like our bodies, block the rays of the sun. Encourage all of the children to block the light of the sun with their bodies to make shadows. Direct them to make short shadows, tall shadows, fat shadows, thin shadows, scary shadows, funny shadows, still shadows, and galloping shadows. After their body shadow play, have them search around the playground for at least one object that is blocking the light of the sun to make a shadow. Encourage them to report to the class telling or showing what they found.

Questions. "How does the sunlight change the way objects look? What causes shadows? Name some things that make shadows."

Evaluation. Note the children's responses to the questions. Assess the depth of understanding revealed by them.

Blocking the light of the sun to create funny shadows is lots of fun.

☐ ☐ ☐ Night and Day

Science Process. Communicating.

Ask the children if they have ever been outside at night and watched the moon and stars. Let them describe what they saw, heard, and felt. Encourage them to tell how the nighttime is different from the day. Be sure to point out that the sun's light gives us day; but when the sun is not shining on our part of the earth, we have night. Have the children discuss the differences between the things we do at night and the things we do in the day-time. Explain that some people may do different things than we do at night. For instance, many of us watch TV, do homework, and sleep at night, but some people work at night. Lead into a discussion about people who work while we sleep.

Follow up your night and day discussion with a home assignment. Ask the children to go home and talk with each family member about what he does at night and what he does during the day. Have the children record their answers. Some children will be able to take their own notes. Other children may have their parents record the notes for them. Some children may tape record answers. When the children share their family responses in class, make two big lists, "Things we do at night" and "Things we do in the day."

Questions.   As children contribute answers to the day and night discussions, help them compare night and daytime activities. Encourage them to notice likenesses and differences in their family activities. Ask: "Are there activities on our chart that everyone in this class does at night? (During the day?) Could we do those things during the day? (At night?) Why or why not? What makes it nighttime? Daytime?"

Evaluation.   Observe children's abilities to compare daytime and nighttime activities and family differences. Observe their abilities to summarize how day and night affect our activities.

Day and Night Book

□ □ □

Science Process.   Communicating.

Have children make a classroom day and night book. Provide yellow construction paper with crayons and markers for each child. Write the caption "In the day I . . . ." on each child's yellow paper. Let the children draw pictures of things they do in the daytime. On another day provide dark blue paper, chalk, and paper scraps for the children to use to illustrate nighttime activities. On each child's blue sheet put the caption "At night I . . . ." Children can choose to draw on the dark paper with chalk, cut and paste to make a collage, or combine chalk with paper collage. Have the children write or dictate a sentence describing what they have shown on each page. Bind the pages into a class book with each child's yellow page on the left and blue page on the right. Read the book to the entire group. Then display the book in the library center for children to read often.

Questions.   As the children do their artwork encourage them to add details to their pictures. Ask: "What else do you do before you go to bed? (Before you come to school?)"

Evaluation.   Note the originality of the children's artwork and the details they add to their pictures.

NINE PLANETS HAVE BEEN IDENTIFIED IN OUR SOLAR SYSTEM

Ancient people noticed that certain bodies in the sky seemed to "wander"; they changed their relative positions in the night sky more rapidly than the stars did. Therefore they named the bodies "planets" which means "wanderers." Nine planets revolve around our sun. Ancient people identified and named the individual planets Mercury, Venus, Earth, Mars, and Jupiter. Other planets were not discovered until more recently; for example Pluto was not discovered until 1930. Scientists are constantly learning more about the planets and their moons, so the knowledge base is changing rapidly. Sophisticated telescopes, computers, and space probes all help scientists learn more about our solar system and the space beyond.

Table 10.1
Basic facts about our solar system.

Body's Name	Size	Characteristics	Moons	How It Got Its Name
Sun (a star, not a planet)	Huge compared to Earth; more than 100 times as large.	The center of our solar system; the source of heat and light for the earth; *very* hot—a ball of gases that gives off energy through nuclear reactions (rather than by burning); has sunspots.	Has no moons; 9 planets travel around it.	Named for the Latin word *Sol,* which means sun.
Mercury	Much smaller than Earth.	Has very long days and nights; the side that faces the sun is *very* hot; no known air or water.	None	Named after the swift messenger of the Greek gods.
Venus	About the size of Earth.	Shrouded in heavy clouds; the Earth's "twin" in size; can be seen often as a beautiful, bright "star."	None	Named for Venus, the goddess of beauty.
Earth	————	The only planet with known life; covered by oceans and land masses; has atmosphere and temperature appropriate for living things.	1	Named for the nurturing "mother," Terra Mater who was the earth mother in Roman mythology.
Mars	About half the size of Earth.	Has a reddish surface; can be seen as a bright body in the sky; has two small moons; has polar ice caps, volcanoes, mountains, and other features similar to Earth.	2	Named for Mars, the Roman god of war, perhaps because of its "angry" reddish color.
Jupiter	The largest planet; *much* larger than Earth.	Has a gaseous surface and mysterious large red spot on its surface; has cloudy belts or bands around its equator.	At least 16; four discovered by Galileo and others more recently.	Named for the supreme Roman god.
Saturn	Very large; almost as large as Jupiter.	Is famous for its beautiful rings—they are composed of ice and rocks; like Jupiter, rotates quickly on its axis, but takes many years to complete its long journey around the sun.	At least 20 moons; some large, some quite small.	Named for the Roman god of reaping.
Uranus	Very large; the fourth largest planet.	Rotates in a different position from other planets—like a top spinning on its side; has faint rings.	At least 15 moons.	Named for the god of the sky.
Neptune	Very large; the third largest planet.	Like Jupiter, Saturn, and Uranus, explored by Voyager space probe in late 1980s; surrounded by frozen clouds of methane gas; has a blue hue; has rings.	6 moons; one has icy volcanoes on its surface.	Named for the god of the sea.
Pluto	Small; probably the second smallest planet.	Most recently discovered planet; in late 1900s, actually closer to the sun (and earth) than Neptune is; very cold; probably has an icy rough surface.	1 moon, about half of Pluto's size.	Named for the god of the underworld—a dark, mysterious place.

Though educators cannot help children make many direct observations of other planets and their moons, classroom activities based on books, pictures, and other visuals can take on real meaning for first through third graders. Children can show their understanding through creating various expressive forms such as pictures, models, and spoken and written words. The list at the end of this chapter suggests several children's books on planets. Some basic information about our sun and its nine planets appears in Table 10.1.

Learning About Planets

Science Processes.   Observing, communicating, using numbers, and using time and space relationships.

To help children learn more about the planets in our solar system, divide the children into 10 groups; assign each group a planet or the sun. Help the children use books to find pictures of their planet or the sun and to learn about some of its characteristics. As the children work, circulate and help each group pull out key information that they can understand.

After children have completed some research, help each group write a story or make a poster telling, in their own words, some basic facts about their planet or sun (Table 10.1). Help the children translate phrases and terms such as 93,000,000 miles (the distance from the Earth to the sun) or 140,000 kilometers (Jupiter's diameter) to terms they can understand more readily. Phrases like *very, very far, even farther,* or *much, much larger* than Earth will be more intelligible to children than will the use of large numbers.

Each group should also make a picture or model of their planet or the sun based on what they have learned. If children draw pictures, guide them to show size differences between the largest and smallest planets. Help them make the sun *very* large in comparison to the planets. It could be painted on several sheets of newspaper. The children might paint pictures to show "actual" planet colors and features or decorate balls or round balloons to represent their planets and the planet's moons.

After the written work and pictures are completed, help the groups share their information with others. Because the bodies in our solar system are far apart, perhaps you can have the children display their models in a long hallway. The class can walk along and pause by each body for its group's "show and tell." Encourage the children to question each other and to comment on the models and reports.

Questions.   Choose two planets or a planet and the sun and ask: "In what ways are they alike and different?" After the children have reported on all planets, have them summarize by asking the general question, "What have we learned today?"

Evaluation.   Note each child's cooperation and interest in completing the group project. Note the details shown on the planet models and summaries. Assess the children's speaking and listening abilities during the planet reports. Make a simple test to suit the level of understanding of 1st through 3rd graders. Be sure to include information brought out in the children's research and projects.

□ □ □ Planet Facts Game

Science Processes.   Communicating and using time and space relationships.

After the children have done group research on planets and heard each others' reports, let groups of interested children make planets games. One game might be done in a domino format so the children can match domino parts with names of planets to parts with facts about the planets. Another game could be a simple version of Rummy where children collect facts about the same planet. The children might also design a game with a pathway to move markers on as they answer questions about the planets and sun. As children make their games, help them include appropriate content. Ask the children who designed a game to introduce it to the class. Make the games available at a learning center.

Questions.   As the children play their games, ask specific questions about the content children are working with. "What color is Mars' surface? What planets have rings? What do you like about this game?"

Evaluation.   Write notes for the children's anecdotal records as they create the games. Notice who is able to include pertinent data in their game.

□ □ □ Planet Graph

Science Processes.   Observing, communicating, classifying, and using numbers and measurements.

If your children have made planet models and displayed them in the hall, why not culminate your study of our solar system with a planet graph? Have the children make small pendants by taping a tiny triangular-shaped piece of paper to a toothpick. Each child should write her name on the pendant. Encourage children to select their favorite planet and designate their choices by affixing their pendant with a tiny piece of clay in front of the model of their choice. After each child has voted on his favorite model, take the group for a walk down the hall and discuss the graphing results.

Questions.   "Which planet was the favorite planet? How many more chose Earth than Venus? Susan, why did you choose Jupiter?"

Evaluation.   Notice children's comments as they give reasons for their choices.

PEOPLE HAVE EXPLORED SPACE AND WANT TO KNOW MORE ABOUT IT

Today's young children have grown up in an age of space exploration. Unlike many adults, they cannot remember a time when space probes and people in space were not in the news. Most children are interested in spaceships, space suits, and space

As the children look at this moon rock, they are able to have a first-hand experience with objects found in space.

adventures. They like to imagine that they are exploring space. Educators can help children learn more about people's exploration of space through experiences with pictures, models, and role-playing.

Getting Started

Science Processes. Observing and communicating.

Show the children pictures of spaceships, astronauts, and equipment used on space journeys. You might use a short videotape, a taped television newscast, or magazine and newspaper pictures about space travel. You might write to NASA (see address at the end of Chapter 4) to ask for free or inexpensive pictures; NASA makes many beautiful, up-to-date, informative posters available. Let children discuss what they have seen.

Questions. "What do the pictures tell us about what astronauts see as they travel out in space? Where do they sleep? Where do astronauts store things? How are astronauts' chairs like our classroom chairs? How are they different?"

Evaluation. Notice the children's interest and abilities to answer questions. Ask the children who can draw representationally to draw a picture to show the details of a spaceship.

"Spacey" Problem Solving

Science Processes. Observing, communicating, inferring, and using time and space relationships.

Pose a problem to the children such as ones that follow.

- How can an astronaut exercise in a small spaceship?
- In a spaceship with little or no gravity, soup would spill out of a bowl. Milk would "float" out of a cup. How can astronauts eat and drink these things?
- When an astronaut goes to sleep, she might roll out of bed or even "float" around the spaceship. How could we prevent this from happening?

Let groups of children work on the problems; plan how to present the answers. They might demonstrate their answers, draw pictures, make models, or use some other techniques. Have the small groups present their answers to the class.

Questions. "What problems do astronauts have in space that they don't have on Earth? Would you like to be an astronaut in spite of the problems you might encounter?"

Evaluation. Find ways to appreciate each answer the children offer. Note which children or groups devise especially creative or insightful answers.

Space Suits

Science Processes. Observing, communicating, and using time and space relationships.

Help the children examine pictures of astronauts' clothing. Direct their attention to various features such as the head coverings and foot coverings. Point out the heavy gloves that astronauts sometimes wear, the devices that help them communicate, and the things that help them breathe when they are outside the spaceship. Ask the children to talk about what they see using many descriptive words.

Tell children they are going to make their own space suits. Help them make a list of things they might need and figure out which things you or the children can provide. You might use basic materials such as foil, plastic garbage bags, clear plastic wrap, ice cream cartons or other boxes, and large sheets of paper in many creative ways. You can use plastic tubing for "air hoses" and other connecting parts.

Help each child make a "space suit." Let the children model their suits and show each other the special features they have included. Have the children save their suits for the "Space Journey" or conduct the journey just after the suits are completed.

Questions. "How is this space suit like our regular clothing? How is it different? What features do you especially like about this space suit? Which part was hardest to make? What problems did you solve as you made your suit?"

Evaluation. Note the children's enthusiasm and creativity in making their space suits. Note the details they included and the problems they solved. You might take pictures of the completed space suits as examples of the children's creativity and problem-solving abilities.

A Space Journey

Science Processes. Observing and communicating.

Gather pictures of the earth, the moon, and a planet or two. You might also obtain some slides of several of the bodies in our universe. Use a tape or record of "space music"; orchestrations like Horst's "The Planets" or "2001—A Space Odyssey" will add wonderful background music to your simulated space journey.

Seat the children, dressed in their space suits, in a small area. They should be comfortable, but not too far apart. (Spaceships aren't very spacious!) Darken the room. Narrate the following story and ask the children to imagine along with you.

Blasting Off!

"We're astronauts! This morning we got up very early. We got into our suits. We drove in a special van to our spacecraft. We're on the spaceship. Is everyone in place? Are your seat belts fastened? It's time for the countdown. Count along with me . . . 10, 9, 8, 7 . . . oh wait, mission control has signaled a delay. Everyone check your computer. Check your seatbelts everyone. OK, countdown can proceed. 6, 5, 4, 3, 2, 1 . . . BLAST OFF."

"We're pressed back in our seats. We feel really heavy. It's very noisy. Now we can see back on the ground." (Show a picture.) "What do you see?" (Let several children respond.) "Now we're high above the earth. When we look back at earth, we see some swirling clouds. We can see land and oceans." (Show pictures.) "It's not so noisy now. What can you see?" (Let several children respond.) "How are you feeling now?" (Invite other children to respond.)

"Now that we're *very* high above the earth we relax and unbuckle our seat belts. We're ready to move about our spaceship. But wait! There's not much gravity. We'll have to move slowly and carefully. Our spacecraft is not very large either. We'll have to move in our small area without bumping each other. Let's all get up and do a space chore." (Have children pretend to do various chores.)

"It's time to be seated again." (Now let several children describe the "space chores" they did or tell how it felt to be "weightless.") "Let's settle back now. Our spacecraft is moving very fast and for a long time. Let's look out the window. Here we are. We're close to the moon. What do we see?" (Use the moon picture and ask children to describe some of its details.)

"If you could keep going on our space journey, where would you like to go?" (Let several children talk. Comment that even in a fast-moving spaceship, journeys take a long time.)

(Continue the story—perhaps describing eating or sleeping in a spaceship.) "Now it's time to come back to the planet Earth. As we come nearer to our home planet, the Earth looks larger and larger. Our ship has special "brakes" and special ways to slow down. Fasten your seat belts. Hang on tight. We're about to land . . . closer . . . closer . . . bump, bump, bump. . . . We've landed! We've made it back to Earth! Let's give a cheer! People from NASA drive out on the runway to pick us up. Let's disembark from our spacecraft and step back on the ground. We get into a van to go back to the air base. We're glad to be safely home."

After your story invite children to talk about the parts of the journey they liked and what they would change. As an extension of your space journey you can also encourage children to role-play being astronauts in the dramatic play center or block center. Children might also enjoy creative movement exercises to space music.

Questions. "How was our journey different from a trip you've taken in a car or on a bus? Would you like to take a real space trip? Where would you like to go?"

Evaluation. Have the children draw a picture or write a story about their simulated space journey. Check for richness of detail shown in the pictures or stories. Note the children's cooperation, enthusiasm, and willingness to describe parts of the space trip.

☐ ☐ ☐ Rocket Models

Science Processes. Observing, communicating, and using time and space relationships.

Display pictures of rockets. Talk about details in the pictures. Help the children point out the launching pad, the rocket stages, and the parts and shape of the rocket.

Have the children use cylinders from paper towel rolls or tissue rolls, juice cans, paper, foil, tape, and other materials to create their own rocket models. Encourage them to add details such as rocket "fins," decorative emblems, and pointed nose cones. Ask the children to explain their rockets to each other. Either display the rockets on a "launchpad" created from a box or table or hang them from the ceiling with thread.

Questions. "What details have you used to make your rocket look realistic? How are these two rockets alike? What things are different about them? What problems did you solve as you made your rocket?"

Evaluation. Note the details shown in children's work, the care taken in rocket construction, and the children's abilities to describe and compare their rockets.

☐ ☐ ☐ A Space Mural

Science Processes. Observing, communicating, and using time and space relationships.

Toward the end of your unit on space, involve the children in making a space mural. You could use black or dark blue paper as a background or children could paint or fingerpaint the background in a suitable color. Start out by assigning groups to make various parts of the mural. Groups could construct planets, moons, constellations, spaceships, satellites, and stars. One group can add glitter to or small bits of foil to various places on the background. Children who have ideas for other details should be encouraged to add them.

Invite another class of children to view your mural. You could serve Milky Way punch (milk with blue food coloring and ice) and star-shaped crackers to your guests. For a smaller version of a space mural, groups of children could make box diorama of space scenes.

Questions.   As the children work on the mural, encourage them to describe what they are doing and what objects they are representing. Help the children evaluate their mural: "Did you do a good job? What could you improve? What are the mural's most outstanding features? Why did you choose those features?"

Evaluation.   Note the children's cooperation, care, and interest as they complete the mural. Mark on a checklist the children's abilities to communicate and evaluate their work.

NOW IT'S YOUR TURN

As you have read our chapter on space, we hope that many related ideas have occurred to you. Now it's your turn to put your ideas with ours and think about ways of applying and extending them. You might also choose exercises from our list to expand or to update your knowledge of space and space travel.

1. Conduct a moon or star watch yourself—perhaps a month before you plan to conduct such an activity with children. Note any ideas to help children learn from their stargazing (or moongazing) experience.

2. Find a star map for the current month or season. Star maps are available in *Science and Children, Odyssey, Natural History,* and other publications. Find some constellations on the map that are familiar to you. Choose an unfamiliar constellation. Locate it in the night sky; read the story of that constellation. Plan a way to share what you have learned with the children or with other adults.

3. On a star map or newspaper feature on meteorology, find information about planets that are currently visible in the night or early morning sky. Locate a planet and view it several times. Devise an informational take-home sheet for the children and their parents to use as they observe and learn more about the planet.

4. Start a file on space news or expand your existing file. Clip magazine and newspaper articles and pictures to use with your children this year and in the future. As "space news" is shown on television, consider videotaping programs or segments to use in your classroom.

5. Plan an activity for children in which they can explore people's roles during the night and day. In your activity focus on the relationship between the sun and the Earth that causes night and day: When parts of the Earth's surface are toward the sun, those parts have light and "day"; when the Earth rotates on its axis and parts of the Earth turn away from the sun, it is night.

6. In the activities we have suggested in this chapter, children can use a variety of creative forms of expression to show what they are learning. We have described books, pictures, role-playing, discussions, models, and murals as suitable expressive forms. Plan a different form that the children could use during this unit or devise a unique variation of one of our ideas. Write a detailed description of how you would guide them in implementing your ideas. How would you evaluate the

children's work? Write a description of things you would look for as you examine the children's products.

7. Plan a series of activities for a child who is especially interested in space or one who needs an extra challenge. Suggest some ways for the child to do some individual research and share information gained with others.

SELECTED CHILDREN'S BOOKS

Bennett, D. (1988). *Day and night.* New York: Bantam Books.

Branley, F. M. (1981). *The planets in our solar system.* New York: Thomas Y. Crowell.

Branley, F. M. (1981). *The sky is full of stars.* New York: Thomas Y. Crowell.

Branley, F. M. (1988). *The sun: Our nearest star.* New York: Harper & Row.

Carle, E., Briggs, R., Popov, N. Y., Hayashi, A., Calvi, G., Dillon, L. & D., Chengliang, Z., Brooks, R., & Anno, M. (1986). *All in a day.* New York: Philomel Books.

Gibbons, G. (1983). *Sun up, sun down.* New York: Harcourt Brace Jovanovich.

Moche, D. L. (1985). *If you were an astronaut.* New York: Western.

Muirden, J. (1987). *Going to the moon.* New York: Random House.

Simon, S. (1985). *Jupiter.* New York: Morrow.

Simon, S. (1985). *Saturn.* New York: Morrow.

Snowden, S. (1983). *The young astronomer.* Tulsa, OK: EDC Publishing.

Thompson, C. E. (1989). *Glow-in-the-dark constellations.* New York: Grosset and Dunlap.

Williams, J. A. (1985). *The inter-planetary toy book.* New York: Macmillan.

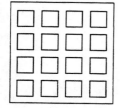

Chapter 11

Water, Air, and Light

WATER, air, and light are all around us. Because they are so readily available, they are easy to study and to use in activities. They are so common that children often take them for granted. However, when children become involved in exploring the properties of water, air, and light, they can learn valuable concepts.

In this chapter we present eight concepts and activities to help the children understand each concept. The concepts are presented in this order:

- Water has many unique properties.
- Water has different forms.
- Water is a solvent.
- Air is real.
- Air exerts pressure.
- Light helps us see.
- Light travels through some materials, but not others.
- Light can be reflected.
- Sunlight is composed of many colors.

WATER HAS MANY UNIQUE PROPERTIES

Water has a wide range of interesting attributes: it flows; it exerts pressure; it has weight; and it has no shape of its own, but takes the shape of its container. Because water is so versatile and intriguing, children are attracted to water play. They need many opportunities to explore and experiment in order to discover some of water's unique properties.

□ □ □ Water Play Fun

Science Processes.   Observing, communicating, measuring, using time and space relationships, and inferring.

Water play can be an ongoing activity for several days. The many variations you provide will help the children explore and discover some of the unique features of water.

Fill a water table or a large tub with water. Collect a variety of plastic and metal containers, including sieves and funnels, for the children to use in pouring water. Some days, supply interesting objects such as corks, seashells, rocks, and sponges for children to use. Other days, give the children dishes or doll clothes from the dramatic play center to wash. You might provide fishing poles with magnets on the lines and

This child is discovering some of the unique properties of water.

put magnetic and nonmagnetic objects in the water. On some occasions give the children a variety of boats. Never overstimulate the children with too many items cluttering the water; present only one type of object at a time. Allow the children to explore with few interruptions, interjecting questions and problem situations sparingly, especially at first. After the children have had opportunities to explore and make discoveries that interest them, begin to ask questions to lead them to new discoveries.

Questions. "How does the water feel when you pour it over your hand? How did you make that cork bounce up and down without touching it? Which container holds the most water?" Base your questions on the children's actions as they play in the water.

Evaluation. Observe the children as they use various materials in the water. Make note of the concepts they appear to understand as they experiment. Ask questions to verify their grasp of different concepts.

Waterfalls

Science Processes. Observing, communicating, using time and space relationships, predicting, and inferring.

Children can observe water and other liquids flowing in many daily activities. Water flows from drinking fountains and faucets. Children observe liquids being poured from cartons and pitchers. As the children watch water, adults can confirm the concept that water flows by verbalizing what children are observing. Say: "Notice how the milk looks when it *flows* out of the pitcher" or "The water is running from the hose and *flowing* down the hill in little 'rivers.'"

Show the children pictures of waterfalls and encourage them to discuss how the water flows down the slopes. Ask: "Do you think you could make a waterfall on the playground? How would you do it?" Help the children gather the needed materials such as pitchers, shovels, rocks, and bricks. Connect a water hose out on the playground. Encourage the children to experiment building a waterfall.

Questions. "What makes the water flow over your waterfall? How could you make it flow in another direction? Which waterfall flows farther? Why does it flow farther?"

Evaluation. Note the children's abilities to solve problems. Observe evidence of their understandings of gravity, directionality, force, and speed.

Waterwheels

Science Processes. Observing, communicating, using time and space relationships, predicting, and inferring.

Construct a waterwheel by stapling cups cut from egg cartons between two aluminum pie pans (Figure 11.1). Poke holes through the centers of the pans and insert a pencil for your waterwheel to turn on. (Older children will enjoy making their

Figure 11.1
Waterwheel.

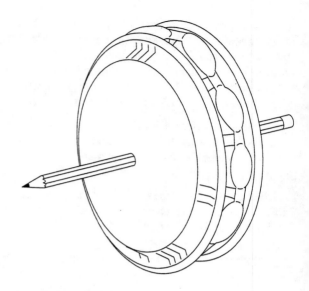

own waterwheels.) Place the waterwheel and some pitchers at the water table. Demonstrate how to pour the water to make the wheel move. Help the children experiment with the waterwheel guiding them by your questioning to change the speed and direction of the wheel.

Questions. "How can you change the direction in which the wheel is moving? What can you do to make it go faster? Why did it slow down?"

Evaluation. Observe the children's experimentation with the waterwheel. Make note of those who demonstrate an understanding of changing direction and speed by controlling the flow of the water.

□ □ □ Siphons

Science Processes. Observing and using time and space relationships.

For snack time provide each child with two cups and a straw. Put juice in one cup. Ask the children if they can think of a way to move the juice from one cup to the other by using the straw. Make it clear that they are not allowed to carry the juice in their mouths to spit it into the other cup, but they can carry it with the straw. If any child figures out how to siphon the juice have him demonstrate for the others. If your children don't solve the problem on their own, demonstrate how to suck the juice up into the straw, how to cut off the air flow at the top of the straw with your tongue or finger, and how to release the juice into the other cup by removing your finger or tongue from the top of the straw.

On another day, give the children a clear plastic tube and show them how to siphon water into a container placed at a lower level. Allow plenty of time for children to experiment. Ask them to siphon water from the water table so it can be cleaned and fresh water provided. To ensure sanitary conditions for these activities show the children how to use an air pump to create a vacuum in the tube.

Questions. "How could we stop the flow of the water? What are some other ways we could use siphons?"

Evaluations. Observe the children's actions in coping with the siphoning problems to see which children demonstrate an understanding of the siphoning technique and which ones don't.

Water Flow Charts

Science Processes. Observing, communicating, using time and space relationships, and predicting.

Scout the hardware store and your kitchen to find items that change the direction of water flow (Figure 11.2). For instance, collect plastic tubing, pipes, and joints that can be put together in different configurations. In the kitchen gather funnels and sieves. You might also punch holes in different configurations in plastic jugs. Place these items at the water table. Allow plenty of time for the children to experiment freely with the materials and to enjoy pouring water through the different items.

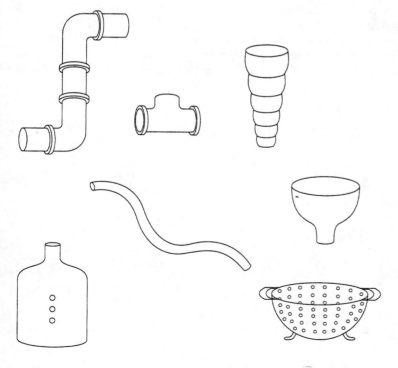

Figure 11.2
Items to change the direction of water flow.

After the children have explored without interruptions, ask them questions about the direction in which the water flowed through each container. Cut and laminate sheets of poster board 25 by 35 centimeters (10 by 14 inches). Use a grease pencil to mark one of the posters with arrows, designating the water flow (Figure 11.3). Ask: "Which container directed the flow in the same direction as the arrows marked on the poster?" Have the children test their predictions by pouring water through the containers they chose. After testing their understanding by using arrows you have drawn, have the children select a container and draw their own arrows predicting the direction of the water flow. Encourage them to work in pairs and make "arrow riddles" for each other to solve. Be sure to suggest combining plastic pipes in different ways.

Questions.   Encourage predictions and verifications. Ask questions such as "How can I make the water flow this way?"

Evaluation.   Note children's experimentation with the water and the containers. Notice the accuracy of their diagrams showing the water flow.

Changing the Shape of Water

Science Processes.   Observing, communicating, using time and space relationships, and inferring.

Provide clear containers of as many different shapes as possible at the water table. Include plastic bags and water balloons of various sizes. (Young children need to be carefully supervised in using plastic bags and balloons.) Hold up a clear, plastic glass full of water and ask the children to describe the shape of the water in the container. Then ask: "Can you think of a way to change the shape of the water?" Let each child fill a container and change the "shape" of the water by pouring it from that container

Figure 11.3
Posters showing direction of
water flow.

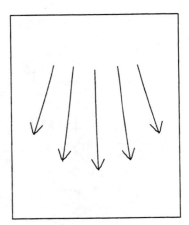 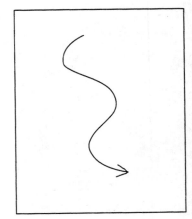

to another. Provide laminated poster boards for children to draw a picture of the shape the water assumes in various containers.

Questions.   At the completion of each step of this activity, ask: "What is the shape of water?"

Evaluation.   Note children's answers to your final question. Were they able to make appropriate inferences from their experimentation?

Float-Sink Test

Science Processes.   Observing, classifying, using numbers, predicting, and inferring.

Some things float in water because they are lighter in weight than the water that they displace; thus they stay on top of the water. When objects are heavier than the water that they displace, they sink. To understand this concept, children need many opportunities to test objects in water to determine whether they will float or sink. You can give the children a variety of experiences with the float-sink test by providing a different classification of objects to test every day.

One day provide small water-safe toys. Another time let children test objects from the kitchen. The next day, provide foods such as fruits, vegetables, and nuts for children to test in the water. Make a float-sink chart on a bright colored manilla folder (Figure 11.4). Laminate your chart to protect it from water. Encourage the children to test items and place them in the appropriate place on the chart.

Questions.   "Do you think this object will float or sink? Why do you think it sank? How many more objects do we have on the 'float' side of the chart than on the 'sink' side?"

Evaluation.   Note the accuracy with which children record their results. Observe their predictions to determine which children seem to understand the basic concept.

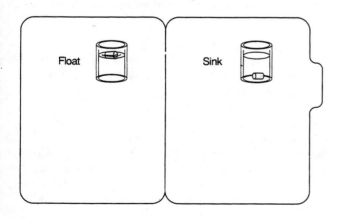

Figure 11.4
Float-sink chart.

☐ ☐ ☐   Sink the Boat

Science Processes.   Observing, measuring, using numbers, and inferring.

Provide the children with small pieces of aluminum foil. Direct them to design boats that will float and carry cargo. Ask them how many dried beans they think their boats will carry before they sink. Have the children test their predictions by counting the number of beans their boats actually hold before sinking. Encourage them to improve the designs of their boats so they will hold more beans. Have them test their boats again to see if they actually hold more beans. If the children remain interested in this activity, let them construct boats out of oil-base clay or other materials on another day. Encourage them to predict and test the capacity of their boats using buttons, small pebbles, or paper clips for cargo.

Questions.   "Whose boat held the most beans? Why did her boat hold more than yours? How could you make your boat hold more? What makes a good boat? Is yours a good boat? Why or why not?"

Evaluation.   Notice the children's problem-solving abilities as they construct their boats. Note whether they can refine their predictions with each experiment. (Do their predictions get closer to the actual number each time they test their boats?)

WATER HAS DIFFERENT FORMS

Water can exist in three different states: as water freezes, it becomes a solid; as it condenses, water becomes a liquid; and as water evaporates it forms a gas. These interesting transformations of water seem very abstract to children. However, as they are given opportunities to experiment with water and other liquids in different states and to observe how they change, children can develop specific knowledge about the three states of water.

☐ ☐ ☐   Cooking Noodles

Science Processes.   Observing, measuring, predicting, and inferring.

Sometimes water changes into steam—a type of gas. To observe the change that water can make from a liquid to a gas, help a group of children cook noodles. As children pour the water in the pan, let them feel and describe the water using many descriptive terms. Ask them to predict changes the water might undergo as it gets hot. Before the children put the noodles in the water, ask them what they think will happen to the noodles when they are added to the cold water and what the noodles will look like after they are cooked. Direct the children to observe carefully as the water begins to boil and cook the noodles. Help each child, standing at a safe distance, hold a large spoon with a long, insulated handle above the water. Ask: "What is happening to the bottom of the spoon you are holding?" (Steam will be condensing into water.) Ask: "Where do you think this water came from?" You could even have each child remove the spoon from over the steam, wait a minute to be sure it's cool, and feel the bottom of the spoon. As the water boils down ask: "Where does the water go?" Point out that the steam rises and seems to disappear into the air. After the noodles have been cooked and drained, let the children put butter, salt, and pepper on them and eat them. Have them describe the changes they observed and tell why they think those changes occurred. Have children dictate a list describing the changes that occurred in their cooking experience.

Questions. "What changes occurred in the water? How do the noodles change as they cook? How does the butter change on the hot noodles?" Elicit many descriptive words from the children.

Evaluation. Notice the details they include in their contributions to the discussion and the list.

Where Did the Water Go? Observing Evaporation

Science Processes. Observing, predicting, and inferring.

The children will need many opportunities to observe the phenomena of evaporation. On different occasions set up the following activities for children to experiment with.

Outdoors on a warm, sunny day, provide wide paintbrushes and buckets of water for the children to use to "paint" the sidewalk, the steps, or the building. Ask: "How do the steps look when you paint them? What is happening to the water? Where is it going? Why do you think it is doing that?"

Indoors, provide brushes and water to paint the chalkboard. Let them blow on it or use child-made fans to speed up the water evaporation process. Introduce the term *evaporation* as the children describe the process they are observing. Explain that the water doesn't actually disappear; instead, tiny particles of water move into the air. The water changes into a gas.

Tell the children that you can often *feel* a difference when water evaporates. Have children roll up their sleeves to paint one arm with water and leave the other arm dry. Let the children describe the way each arm feels as the water evaporates. Point out that water cools as it evaporates.

Set up materials and equipment for the children to wash doll clothes outdoors. Provide a clothesline and clothespins. Bring children's attention to the water dripping from the clothes as they hang them on the line. Ask them what they think will happen to the clothes during the day—what will happen to the water in the clothes. Again, bring out the term *evaporation* and help children understand what is actually happening to the water.

Questions. As you question the children during these activities, focus on evaporation: what individual children are observing, what they perceive to be happening, and where the water is actually going. In asking questions, adults will want to elicit many descriptive words from the children. Ask: "What's the word to use when water dries up or disappears into the air? How did we make water evaporate? How do you think water evaporates?"

Evaluation. Observe children's reactions and discussions as they explain the changes in the water as it evaporates. Give feedback on children's responses where appropriate.

☐ ☐ ☐ Orange Ice

Science Processes.   Observing, predicting, and inferring.

Water, like many other liquids, can change from its liquid form to a solid. Allow the children to produce and observe this change as they make orange ice. Provide ingredients for the children to make their own orange juice—mixing water with orange juice crystals or orange juice, sugar, and water. This step is important because it will help the children understand that orange juice has no "magic powers" that cause it to respond differently from water. Let them pour their orange juice into ice trays or small paper cups. They may wish to add to their orange juice mixture one of the following: cherries, raisins, pineapple chunks, grapes, banana slices, or apple slices. Place the orange juice mixture in the freezer. Ask the children to predict what will happen to their juice—how it will change—how the fruit will change. Urge children to be specific in their predictions and their inferences as they talk about the changes the orange juice makes from liquid to solid. When the juice has frozen, allow children to eat their "orange ice."

Questions.   "What happened to the orange juice? Is it the same juice we put in the freezer? How did it change? Describe your orange juice in its liquid state. Describe it in its frozen state."

Evaluation. Note children's responses to determine the depth of their understanding of this concept.

☐ ☐ ☐ Melting Chart

Science Processes.   Observing, using time and space relationships, measuring, communicating, predicting, and inferring.

Help the children collect data and make a graph as they observe water as it changes from its solid state to a liquid state (Figure 11.5). Give children ice cubes and have them put them in aluminum pans in different places to see which ice cubes will melt the fastest. Let them choose where to place ice cubes: for example, outside in the sun, in a sunny window in the room, under a table, in a closet, on top of a heater, or under a tree. Have the children predict which ice cubes will melt the fastest. As the ice cubes melt, have the children record their data on strips of paper and place them on the graph.

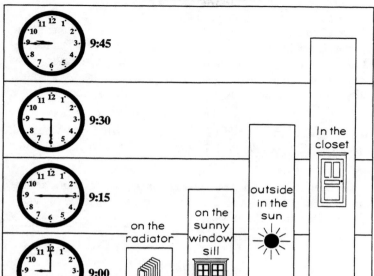

How long did it take
for the ice cubes to melt?

Figure 11.5
Graph of melting ice.

Questions. "Which will take the longest time to melt? Which cube will melt most quickly? Why do you think so? Why did the ice cubes in the shade take longer to melt than the ice cubes in the sun?"

Evaluations. Observe children's responses as they collect their data and discuss their findings. Note their degree of understanding and their skill in recording the data on the graph.

We Use Water in Many Ways

Science Process. Communicating.

Try to imagine life on earth without water. Of course, we couldn't survive. We use water for drinking, cooking, bathing, recreation, and for almost every situation in which we are involved. To help children develop a better understanding of our dependence on water, ask: "What are some of the ways you used water before you came to school today?" Encourage them to name as many uses of water as possible. Record their answers on an experience chart. Remind them that even their toothpaste has water in it. For example, help them extend their experience chart suggesting many categories of uses of water. Tell them the dye in their clothes was mixed in a solution of water.

You may wish to work on this experience chart over a period of days, adding to the list as children have new ideas. After the children have discussed their ideas in detail, let them make a water book showing the many uses of water. Each child can contribute at least one page to the class book by coloring a picture showing one of the ways he uses water. Show the child how to give the water in his picture a glimmering effect by cutting a piece of transparent, plastic wrap and gluing it over the water. Have each child dictate or write a sentence on the page describing how he uses water. Combine the pages and make a class book. Keep the book at the science table for children to read.

Questions. "What other details can you add to your picture? What else would be near the water in your picture? What do you think life might be like if we had no water for a week?"

Evaluation. Notice the variety of ideas the children have to contribute to the experience chart and the different categories of ideas they suggest. Observe the detail and elaboration that children show in their drawings.

WATER IS A SOLVENT

Because many substances dissolve when they are mixed with water, water is called a solvent. For example, when salt is stirred into water, the tiny particles become smaller and smaller until they seem to disappear. Actually, the salt does not disappear; it adds a salty taste to the water as the small bits of salt break down and spread out evenly into the water. In the following activities, the children will experiment by mixing different substances in water to determine how they react.

☐ ☐ ☐ The Chocolate Milk Solution

Science Processes. Observing, measuring, communicating, and inferring.

Combine snack time with a science experiment. Let each child make her own chocolate milk from "scratch"—mixing cocoa and sugar with a little water in a cup, then adding dry milk and more water to the solution. As the children measure and mix, encourage them to describe in detail what they observe happening to the ingredients as they dissolve in water. (A large amount of the sugar and milk will dissolve making a concentrated solution, but only a small amount of the cocoa will dissolve.)

Questions. "What is happening to the sugar (cocoa, dry milk) as we mix it with water? When it seems to disappear in the water, we say it dissolves. Which is dissolving faster—the sugar or the cocoa? How can you tell the sugar is dissolving? Does it feel any different? How? Does it sound different? Listen as you stir. How does the water change as we mix the ingredients? Why does it change colors? Does it taste different? Why? Name some of the other things we might mix with water. What would happen?"

Evaluation.   Notice the children's ability to follow directions and to measure. Observe their interest as they mix the solutions and their responses to your questions.

Visual Solutions

□ □ □

Science Processes.   Observing, predicting, and communicating.

In this activity the entire group of children can observe different substances dissolving in water. Direct the children to bring any substances from home that they wish to test. They might bring a variety of substances such as salt, sugar, flour, lemonade crystals, gelatin dessert mix, soap powder, mud, sand, syrup, or oil. Encourage your children to think creatively about what they will bring to test.

Cover an overhead projector with clear plastic wrap to protect it from the water. Place a clear, flat-bottomed, glass container of water on the overhead projector. Let each child bring his ingredient and stir it into the water as the other children observe the results on the screen. Change the water in between the children's turns. As some substances are mixed with water, children will be able to see the little particles projected on the screen and to watch as the particles grow smaller, become less distinct, and finally dissolve.

After this group experience with the overhead projector, give children time to test ingredients on their own at the science table. Place different ingredients and labels for them in each cup of an egg carton. Provide clear plastic cups, water, and small spoons for mixing each substance with water. Encourage children to make predictions before they test the substances. Have them compare the ways different substances react when mixed with water.

Questions.   "What do you think will happen when you mix this with water? Which one dissolved faster? How can you tell it has dissolved?"

Evaluation.   Have children work with a partner at the science table and establish an effective way to record their data as they experiment.

AIR IS REAL

Even though people cannot see air and ordinarily do not smell it, air is a real substance. We feel air in a variety of circumstances; we sense breezes and gales or can sometimes hear or feel the breathing of another person close to us.

Air is all around us. Layers of air surround our Earth. People live in the trophosphere, a layer of air that supports life and includes most weather conditions. About 32 kilometers (20 miles) above the Earth other layers of air begin—the stratosphere, mesosphere, ionosphere, and exosphere. Air is about 78% nitrogen and about 21% oxygen. Small amounts of other gases such as helium, neon, argon, krypton, xenon, and carbon dioxide are also found in the air.

Educators can use the activities in this section to help children internalize the idea that air is real and is almost everywhere.

☐☐☐ Capturing Air

Science Processes.   Observing, communicating, and using time and space relationships.

Ask: "How could you capture some air?" If materials they suggest using are available, let the children demonstrate some of their ideas. Provide some plastic or paper bags and have the children catch some air in the bags. Some may blow into the bags; others may scoop the bags through the air to get air inside; some may try other methods.

Have the children share their ideas about how to keep the air in the bags and how they can tell there is something inside. Most of them will suggest closing the bags in some way. They may push on their bags to show that they have something inside or point out that their bags look "full." If the children do not suggest it, prompt them to release the bag's openings and feel the air as it rushes out.

Have children see if they can catch air inside a straw, bag, or other container *everywhere* in the classroom. Some children should try to capture air near the floor, others near windows, others under their chairs, and so on. After the children succeed in capturing air in several locations, discuss the fact that air is found almost everywhere on our Earth. For 2nd or 3rd graders you might introduce the word *vacuum*—absence of air. Show a plastic straw and ask what is inside the straw. Show children how to hold a finger over one end of a straw, hold the straw in a vertical position, and put it under water. The finger presses against the air at one end. Water holds air inside the straw at the other end. Ask children how they might "see" the air that is inside the straw. If you tilt the straw and release your finger, some air will come out as bubbles. Let several children try to replicate the activity. You might want to have straws at your water play area so that children can experiment further with this idea. Ask: "Where did the bubbles go? Did any sink?" Have the children observe that most bubbles travel straight up in water. Point out that they seem to disappear, but as they reach the top, they move back into the air and cannot be seen.

Questions.   "What are some other substances that are hard to see? How do we know that they are real? Although air is available for us to breathe almost everywhere on the surface of Earth, what are some places or situations where people need special equipment in order to breathe?"

Evaluation.   Note on a checklist the children's interest and the originality and logic in their responses. Provide materials to work with air at the water table and note which children do so voluntarily.

☐☐☐ Air Bag Creatures

Science Processes.   Observing, communicating, using time and space relationships, and measuring.

Organize the children into small groups. Give each group a clear or light-colored plastic bag. Have the children use crayons or permanent markers to create a creature on the bag. The children could then fill the bag with air and close it with a twist tie.

Have each group "introduce" their creature to the class and describe the details on it. Have the children compare the size of their creature to their size and to the size of different objects in the room. Let them compare the weight of the bag to the weight of other objects. Have some children fill (or partially fill) another bag with objects such as books, crumpled newspaper, or pieces of plastic foam. Ask: "What fills your 'creature bags?' Compare the weight of an air-filled bag to one filled with another substance." The children will find that their air bag creatures are very light in comparison to the bags filled with other objects.

When using plastic bags, remember to discuss safety; children should not place the bags over their heads. After using the plastic bags, children might want to place them in a container for recycling plastics.

Questions. "Will your air bag creatures float above the ground or not? How can you find out? If you made a smaller air bag creature and put it in water, what would happen?"

Evaluation. Make notes of the children's cooperation and creativity as they work together to make their creatures. Note their abilities to compare their creatures with other objects.

Air in Solids

Science Processes. Observing, communicating, classifying, predicting, and inferring.

Air occupies the space all around the earth. Air is also found in water, soil, and in porous materials. Remind the children that they were able to capture air in many places in the classroom and that they saw air bubbles come from their straws under water.

Help the children gather a variety of materials—some soil and sand; samples of porous materials such as bricks, sponges, foam rubber, bread, wood; and rocks with holes and crevices in them. Have them predict whether or not they will see air bubbles rise as they submerge each object in water. Record their predictions. Then let the children take turns placing the objects in water, waiting several seconds, and seeing if bubbles appear. They can also note the size of the bubbles and whether the bubbles rise, cling to the objects, or move to the sides of the container. On your chart record which objects contained "lots of air," "some air," and "no air."

Some air is also dissolved in water. To show this have the children fill a plastic glass with warm water and one with cold water. Label the glasses, set them aside for an hour or two; then compare the glasses. Help the children infer that air is found in many "solid" objects and also in water.

Questions. "What are some other porous materials we could test to see if they contain any air? A sponge has many air spaces in it. Will it float or sink in water?"

Evaluation. Note on a checklist the children's abilities to predict, record results, and classify objects.

AIR EXERTS PRESSURE

Air exerts pressure in all directions. When people blow up a balloon or work with soap bubbles, they force air into a "container"—the balloon or the soap film. The air presses against the container and inflates the balloon or bubble. Air mattresses, tires, and rubber rafts are filled with air. The air exerts enough pressure to inflate them and also to support people—or even cars, in the case of tires—on top of them.

Moving air is called wind. When air moves, it exerts pressure or pushes against objects. The harder the wind blows, the more pressure it exerts. The activities in this section help children experience and understand more about air pressure and its effects on people.

☐ ☐ ☐ Wind Moves Things

Science Processes. Observing, communicating, and using time and space relationships.

Take the children outdoors. Ask the children to sit very still to observe and to describe some things that are moving. As they name things moved by the wind, ask them questions like "What moves that piece of paper across the playground?" or "Why is that bush swaying?" Help them to understand that wind is moving air. Explain that we do not see wind directly, but we see its effects on many objects because when air moves, it presses on objects and moves them.

Help the children make a long list of things that could be moved by the wind. Ask: "Could the wind move you? Could it move a house?" Perhaps the children will respond

What happens when we run with streamers? Air helps to hold them up.

that wind moves light or pliable things. Perhaps some have experienced a terrific wind storm, tornado, or hurricane and know that at times the wind *can* move people and heavy objects such as cars and houses.

Pass out streamers and let the children stand holding the streamers to see if the wind moves them. Ask the children to "make wind" to move their streamers. Some might blow on the streamers; some might run with them or use other approaches. Help children discuss the air or moving air they felt as they moved the streamers.

Back in the classroom, let children make fans and feel the moving air as they fan themselves (Figure 11.6). Display the fans on a bulletin board entitled "Our Fans Make Breezes."

Questions. "When are some times when moving air or wind feels good? When does it feel unpleasant?"

Evaluation. Mark the contributions of children in the discussions on a checklist. Note the children's abilities to follow directions and do neat work as they make their fans.

Air Boats

Science Processes. Observing, communicating, predicting, inferring, and using time and space relationships.

Show the children pictures of various kinds of sailboats. Ask: How do the boats move? Be sure the children realize that wind presses against the boats' sails and moves the sails and the boats along with them.

Provide time and materials for the children to make little sailboats. One simple design uses plastic foam for the body of the boat and a paper sail attached with a toothpick. Encourage the children to use different shapes for the boats and the sails and to discuss their designs with their classmates.

Let the children experiment with their boats and ways to move the boats. They could sail the boats outdoors in tubs of water using the wind for power. They could also use their fans to move the boats. Some might blow on the sails to move the boats along.

Figure 11.6
Fans.

Pose some problems such as these: "Your boat is in the corner of the tub. How can you move it to the opposite corner? Can you ever move your boat *into* the wind? How? If you blow in this direction (demonstrate), which way will your boat go? Will your boat go faster in a breeze or a strong wind?" Allow some time between your questions for the children to work with their boats to try to solve each problem.

Help the children come to some conclusions about what they have learned. Working with sailboats is an appealing activity, so you might want to repeat it or offer free time for those children who want to continue to play with their boats.

Questions.   "What moved our boats? What other vehicles does air move? What are some other ways the air or the wind helps people?"

Evaluation.   Note children's abilities to solve the problems you pose and to discuss their results. Note children's care and neatness in constructing the sailboats.

☐ ☐ ☐   Sitting on Air!

Science Processes.   Observing, communicating, and using time and space relationships.

Show the children a picture of a person sitting in midair or flying on a "magic carpet." Discuss whether the picture is "real or pretend." Ask: "Have you ever sat on air?"

Set a doll on the tabletop and point out that she is sitting on the table that rests on legs. Ask: "How could you help the doll to sit on air?" If the children do not suggest it, place a plastic or paper bag under the doll and inflate the bag. Now the doll is raised above the tabletop and is sitting on the air-filled bag.

Place something large and flat but relatively light on a tabletop. You might use an empty plastic swimming pool, a large tray, or a cardboard box. Put a few dolls in the container and challenge the children to raise the dolls and container so they are all supported by air. The children might suggest working together and inflating several bags to raise the container and the dolls above the table's surface. Ask: "What are the dolls and containers resting on?" Point out that the air inside the bags presses hard enough to inflate the bags and to raise the other objects.

Arrange for a trip to a service station. Have the attendant show the children several ways that air is used. He might describe air brakes, fans, or vacuum cleaners that he uses. Ask the attendant to demonstrate inflating an inner tube or tire. Supervise children as they take turns sitting on the tire and feeling the support of the air inside. Perhaps children could carefully feel the end of the air hose and the great pressure and force of air as it leaves the hose.

Back in the classroom, help children write a group composition about their experiences. Be sure to write thank-you letters to the service station attendant.

Questions.   "Are there other times when you have sat on air or laid down on air? Describe them (or draw pictures)."

Evaluation.   Note the children's interest, cooperation, and abilities to communicate about their experiences.

LIGHT HELPS US SEE

Natural and artificial light sources illuminate our world. Without light, people could not see. Light travels from a source to objects and then to our eyes in straight lines. Thus, we are able to see the objects. The following activities will make the children more aware of this phenomenon, which they probably take for granted.

Candlelight in the Classroom

Science Processes.   Observing and communicating.

Ask: "What do you need in order to see? The children will probably reply, "Our eyes." Without commenting, darken the classroom as much as possible. Ask: "Why does the classroom look different than usual?" Lead them to discuss the fact that we need healthy eyes to see, but that we also need light.

Have the children stay seated. Light a candle and carefully carry it around. Help them to realize that the candlelight travels in all directions. Carefully hold the candle so that it illuminates one child's face, another child's shoes, and other objects around the room. Encourage the children to describe what they see and how things look different depending on where the candle is placed. Next, use a flashlight and shine it on various objects. Help the children realize that light from the flashlight does not travel in all directions, but only straight ahead. Discuss what can be seen. Show the children how light travels from its source, to an object, then back to our eyes. Have a child or two trace the path of the light to his eyes.

Turn on the lights and let the children describe what they see now. Help a child or two trace the path of light from the source (window or overhead light) to various objects and back to a child's eyes. For example in Figure 11.7 light travels from the candle to the pencils and is reflected to the child's eyes. Thus the child sees the pencils. Help the children list many sources of light; encourage them to include some "unusual" ones such as campfire light, penlights, stoplights, or Christmas tree lights.

Talk to the children about safety with light sources. Tell them they must enjoy candlelight only under adult supervision and never leave candles unattended. Explain

Figure 11.7
Tracing a path of light.

that they must not taste or touch the substances inside flashlight batteries. Remind the children to handle light bulbs with care, if at all, because light bulbs can shatter if dropped. Tell them they should handle only the switches of lamps, not the "insides."

Questions. "Does the candle or flashlight light the whole room? What do you notice about colors in candlelight, flashlight, and normal, classroom light? When light comes from our overhead fixtures, how does it help us to see our chairs? To see each other?"

Evaluation. To assess their understanding of this concept have the children fold a paper in half and draw two pictures: a well-lighted scene and a dimly lighted scene. Have them include at least one light source in each half of their picture.

☐☐☐ Peeker Boxes

Science Processes. Observing, communicating, and using time and space relationships.

Help each child make a peeker box from a shoe box or cracker box. The children can cut paper figures and tape them inside the box. They should cut a peeker hole in the front of the box. They can peek inside but won't be able to see much. Next, direct the children to cut a small hole or two in the tops of their boxes. They can cover these holes with tissue paper, waxed paper, or leave them open. The children can display their boxes on a table and take turns viewing each other's scenes. Through your discussion questions, help the children understand that they can see their scenes because light enters their boxes through the holes, hits the objects, and then travels to their eyes.

Questions. "What do you like about this box? How does the light help us see the scenes inside our boxes? What was it like when there were no holes at the top? Why was it so dark?"

Evaluation. Note each child's skill and creativity in completing the box. Note the children's cooperation and interest in examining each other's boxes. Do their answers to your questions demonstrate an understanding of the concept?

☐☐☐ Light Travels in Straight Lines

Science Processes. Observing, communicating, classifying, and using time and space relationships.

Ask: "What are some sources of light?" Write each of the children's responses on cards or pieces of paper and have them group the cards according to these sources: natural (sun, moon, fire, stars, and fireflies) or artificial (made by people—lamps, candles, electric lights, neon lights). Ask: "How does light travel from the sun?" They could demonstrate with a ball and straight rays traveling off in all directions.

Have a child hold a flashlight pointing downward. Turn off the overhead lights. See if the children can see any beams of light coming from the flashlight. Hold chalk dust-filled erasers over the flashlight. Gently tap the erasers together and let the particles of chalk dust fall down. Have the children describe what they see.

Divide the children into small groups. Give each group a paper toweling tube and ask them to take turns looking at a light source through the tube. When they "line up" the tube with the source, they will see it. If they "aim" away from the source, they will not see it. Let the groups experiment with a 1- to 2-meter length of old garden hose. If the hose is held straight, the children can see light through it. If it is bent, they will not be able to see through the hose.

Finally, let the groups of children take several note cards and cut small holes in them in the same position. They can stand the cards up using spring clothespins. Have them take turns arranging the cards so they can see light through the series of holes (the holes will have to be lined up).

Questions. "What else could we use to show that light travels in straight lines?" (Perhaps you can gather equipment beforehand to let children explore some of their suggestions.)

Evaluation. Ask children to draw or describe the travel of light from a given source to their eyes. Note the children's ability to suggest and classify light sources as well as their cooperation in group work.

LIGHT TRAVELS THROUGH SOME MATERIALS BUT NOT OTHERS

Light passes through transparent materials such as window glass, cellophane, or acetate. When we look through these materials, we see a clear image. Other materials, such as sheer fabric, waxed paper, or "cloudy" glass let some light pass through. When we look through these materials we see a shadowy or less distinct image. Such materials are known as translucent. Many objects block light—are opaque—so light cannot pass through them and we cannot see through them. Examples of opaque objects are cardboard, metals, and people's bodies. Shadows are cast when opaque objects block a beam of light.

Transparent, Translucent, Opaque ☐ ☐ ☐

Science Processes. Observing, predicting, classifying, and communicating.

Gather a group of children near a window. Show them various materials and let them experiment with them by trying to see through the materials. Introduce the words *tranparent, translucent,* and *opaque* and let the children predict which objects fit in each category. Hold various materials (bits of fabric, various weights of paper, colored cellophane or Easter grass, and small solid objects) up to the light and let the children decide if light passes through the objects or if they are opaque.

Let the children work in groups and tape bits of material to the windows to form pleasing designs. They might make designs of all opaque materials or all transparent materials, or they might mix materials. Have them describe their results verbally or in writing.

Questions. "What are some other transparent materials? Translucent or opaque materials? What types of materials do we use for windows? For sunglasses? For porch roofs? Why do we choose these materials?"

Evaluation. Note the accuracy with which the children classify the materials. Observe the children as they look at materials and try to sort them into "transparent," "translucent," and "opaque" categories.

Overhead Images

Science Processes. Observing, communicating, predicting, inferring, and using time and space relationships.

Show the children a leaf (or other small object); then place the leaf on an overhead projector to let the children see its shadow on the screen. Invite them to come closer to see how the light travels from its source, through lenses and mirrors, and onto the screen. Let a few take turns tracing the path of the light with their hands.

Show the children other small objects such as scissors, a pinecone, a rock, or a twig. Let them make predictions about what kinds of shadows the objects will cast on the screen. Let the children take turns placing the objects on the stage of the projector and describing what they see on the screen. Encourage them to move the objects to different positions to see how the shadows change. Finally, place or tape two file folders—standing up—around the front and sides of the projector (the sides not next to the screen). Place some "mystery" objects (blocks, a dead insect, or a ball) on the stage and let the children guess what the objects are.

Questions. "How are the shadows of the two objects alike and different? Will this object look different when it is placed in one position or another?"

Evaluation. Note evidence of the children's understanding of the path of light from the bulb to the screen. Project a "mystery object" and, based on its shadow's appearance, ask second and third graders to draw what it might look like.

Outdoor Shadow Play

Science Processes. Observing, communicating, and using time and space relationships.

Take the children outdoors on a sunny day. Have them look at the shadows their bodies cast. Lead them to discuss how light travels from the sun and to observe how people's opaque bodies block the sun and cast shadows. Have the children make and describe various shadows—tall ones, skinny ones, round ones, short ones, or shadows with "holes" in them.

Divide the children into groups of two or three. Pass out pieces of chalk. In each group, have one child stand still while the others trace around his shadow. When the tracings are complete, let the other children try to stand so their shadows fall within the tracings.

Return to the shadow tracings later in the day and see how the lengths, widths, and directions of the shadows have changed.

As follow-up, read the poem "I Have a Little Shadow" (Robert Lewis Stevenson) aloud. Have the children draw pictures of themselves and their shadows. Encourage the children to play shadow tag at outdoor time.

Questions. "What might our shadows look like at supper time? When might our shadows be the shortest—early or late in the day or at noon?"

Evaluation. Have children draw pictures of their experience and write about it. Judge the pictures for detail and ability to show the light source (sun), persons, and shadows. Outdoors ask the children to explain why their shadows are cast on the ground.

Shadow Puppets

Science Processes. Observing, communicating, and using time and space relationships.

Have the children make a stage for shadow puppets in a large box (Figure 11.8). Help them cut out one end of the box and tape interfacing (a stiff, lightweight, sewing fabric) in the opening. Provide scraps of opaque and translucent materials for the children to use to make shadow puppets to fit inside the stage. The children should tape their puppets to straws or dowels so they can be held inside the box.

Figure 11.8
Shadow puppet stage.

Let groups of children develop stories for their puppets and take turns giving shadow puppet shows. They need a strong light held or placed behind the puppets so their shadows are cast on the screen. The children should show their shadow puppet shows to small groups in the beginning to practice their scripts.

Questions. "Suppose you wanted a light spot in your puppet. How could you make one? Trace the path of the light and tell what blocks the light and causes the shadow."

Evaluation. Note the children's creativity and problem-solving abilities as they make their shadow puppets.

LIGHT CAN BE REFLECTED

We see things because light travels from a source and then reflects from objects and back to our eyes. Different materials reflect light differently. In general, light colors reflect more light back to our eyes than dark colors do; dark colors absorb more light than lighter colors do. Texture also affects light reflection. Usually smooth surfaces reflect more light than bumpy or textured surfaces do. Children can explore these ideas in concrete ways using activities like the ones described here.

☐ ☐ ☐   Exploring Reflections

Science Processes.   Observing, communicating, predicting, and using time and space relationships.

Ask: "Do you know a good reflecting surface you probably use every day? It helps you get dressed, fix your hair, and see how you look. What is it?" (A mirror.) Explain that a mirror is an excellent reflector of light because it is smooth and shiny. Point out that people can see clear images of themselves in good reflectors like mirrors.

Divide the children into small groups and give each group a mirror (Plastic mirrors are safe and durable. You might tape the edges of glass mirrors and caution the children to handle them with care). Darken the classroom. Show the children how light travels from a flashlight to a mirror and produces a reflection. If the mirror is in a horizontal position and the flashlight is held at an angle as shown in Figure 11.9, a reflection will

Figure 11.9
Reflecting light.

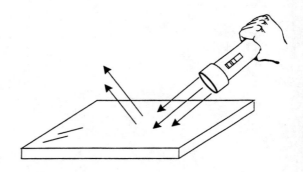

appear high on a wall or on the ceiling. Have a few children trace the path of light from the flashlight to the mirror to the reflection.

Encourage the groups to predict where reflections will appear when they hold their flashlights and mirrors in various positions. Have the children check their predictions. Let each group show the others various things they tried with their flashlights.

Discuss reflective surfaces they see in everyday life. Be sure the children consider clothing signs, advertisements and billboards, and jewelry items that reflect light. Make a list of the children's responses. Have each child prepare a page for a class book on reflections. You might provide foil and other "shiny" papers as well as crayons and markers.

Questions.   "When are some times when people need reflective surfaces? When do we want to block or dim the reflection of light? When I aim the flashlight at this mirror (held horizontally), you see a reflection on the ceiling. How does it get there?"

Evaluation.   Judge the children's appropriate pictures and descriptions of items or situations in which light is reflected.

More Work with Reflectors

Science Processes.   Observing, communicating, predicting, inferring, and ordering.

Gather 15-centimeter (6 inch) squares of colored paper and solid color fabrics, aluminum foil, and several flashlights. The children's families could contribute some of these. Divide the class into small groups. Supply each group with a flashlight and help one member from each group select at least four colored squares in a wide range of colors and a foil square.

Instruct each group to arrange their squares from the lightest to the darkest. Use one group's supplies to demonstrate how light travels from a source (the flashlight) to a reflective surface (the square) and to their eyes (Figure 11.10). Have a child or two

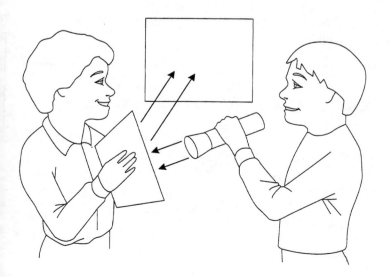

Figure 11.10
Tracing a path of reflected light.

trace the path of light. Ask each group to work in an area where they can tape a plain white paper to the wall. Demonstrate how they should hold a square in front of them and aim the light at the square to see a reflection on the paper "screen." Explain that we see the reflection or "glow of color" on the screen because light travels from the source to the square and then is reflected onto the screen.

Have each group predict which squares they think will be good reflectors and then test their squares to determine which are and which are not. Help the children discuss their findings and make a list of the colors that reflect light well and those that do not. Guide the children to come to some conclusions about how color affects reflection.

Questions.   "Where do we see reflections in the daytime? At night? What reflective surfaces (if any) do you have on your shoes and clothing?"

Evaluation.   On a checklist mark your observations concerning the children's abilities to work cooperatively, handle equipment responsibly, make accurate judgments, and communicate their findings.

SUNLIGHT IS COMPOSED OF MANY COLORS

Most children have seen or heard of a rainbow. With a natural rainbow or a rainbow produced by using a prism in the sunlight, we see a spectrum of colors (Figure 11.11). The prism breaks sunlight into different colors because the colors in light have different wavelengths. As light (a combination of colors) enters the prism, the prism bends (refracts) the colors with shorter wavelengths more than those with longer wavelengths. Red light has the longest wavelengths; as red light enters the prism, these rays are bent (refracted) the least by the prism. Rays of orange light have the next longest waves. The prism bends these rays a little more than it does for red light, but not as much as it does for yellow, green, blue, indigo, and violet light. Violet light has the shortest wavelengths. The prism bends these rays the most.

In the following activities children can observe the colors found in sunlight as they work with soap bubbles and with prisms.

☐ ☐ ☐   Colors in Bubbles

Science Processes.   Observing, communicating, and using time and space relationships.

Figure 11.11
Color refraction through a prism.

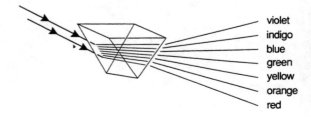

violet
indigo
blue
green
yellow
orange
red

Invite a small group of children to help you prepare a bubble solution. Mix 2 liters (2 quarts) water, 250 milliliters (1 cup) clear liquid detergent, and 30 milliliters (1 tablespoon) glycerine in a large bowl. Gather several small plastic bowls. Have the children prepare bubble wands. To do so they might bend pipe cleaners and insert them into drinking straws, twist wires into various shapes, or cut holes in thin plastic lids.

Take the children outdoors on a sunny day. Divide the class into small groups and give each group some bubble solution in a small container. Circulate as the children make bubbles. Encourage the children to describe their bubbles—their sizes, shapes, numbers, positions, colors, and how long the bubbles last. Gather the children together. Ask some to blow more bubbles while the other children look closely (and quickly) at the bubbles and note the colors on their surfaces. Explain that the curved surface of each bubble bends the "white" light from the sun breaking it up to let us see several colors. Use the word *sphere* to describe the bubbles' shapes.

The curved surfaces of the bubbles bend and break white light. The child sees several colors.

Questions. "How did the size and shape of your bubble makers affect the sizes and shapes of the bubbles? What are some other materials we could use as bubble makers?" (You might try to follow up on some of the children's suggestions.)

Evaluation. Mark on a checklist your observations about the children's interest and cooperation as they worked with bubbles. Note the children's abilities to describe qualities of their bubbles.

□ □ □ Real Rainbow Colors

Science Processes. Observing, communicating, and ordering.

Have children take white paper and crayons outdoors. Gather the children in a sunny location and have them sit down. Hold a prism to cast a spectrum of colors on the ground. Show children how light from the sun enters the prism and is bent to reflect on the ground. Let children take turns using the prism to see if they can hold the prism so light is broken into a spectrum of colors. Place white paper on the ground so the children can see the vivid colors that the prism casts. Let the children describe the colors and note their order. Tell the children that scientists and artists call the deep, blue-violet color *indigo*. Trace the path of light from the sun to the spectrum of colors on the ground. Ask children to locate colors as you name them or to tell which bands of colors are adjacent to a given color. Allow time for the children to carefully draw the spectrum's colors in their correct order. Second and third graders can also write the name of each color.

Display the children's "rainbow" pictures on a bulletin board. Help children review the bubble-blowing and prism activities and draw pictures that show something they learned about the colors in light.

Questions. "Which color in the spectrum is your favorite? What color(s) is it next to?"

Evaluation. Note children's cooperation and the accuracy of their pictures. Ask each child to compose and illustrate a "rainbow poem." Check to see that poems are completed. Make notes for children's anecdotal records of particularly expressive examples.

NOW IT'S YOUR TURN

1. Water play is messy but it is an ideal environment for children to experiment, observe reactions, and describe their observations—to develop physical knowledge about water. Write at least three lesson plans using water play. State objectives, materials, procedures, questions you will ask, and ways to evaluate.

2. Choose one other concept about water, air, or light that has not been mentioned in this chapter. Plan ways to develop that concept in your classroom.

3. Children learn best in a curriculum that blends different subject matters. In your study of light, air, and water, plan at least two or three art, music, or drama activities based on the theme of light, air, or water. Be innovative in your planning. You may build on old ideas, but create something new that captivates children's attention.

4. Plan a field trip into the community to learn something new about light, air, or water. Bring in career-oriented aspects with this field trip.

5. What is something you have wanted to know about related to air, light, or water— something that you have never really understood? Now is the time to find out. Do a little research in science books. Experiment. Clarify a concept that has been hazy in your mind. Write this experience up and share it with others.

6. Choose a concept about water, air, or light that you think might be difficult for a child with limited language ability. Plan some activities to enhance the child's knowledge as well as strengthening the child's vocabulary.

7. Water play has a soothing effect on hyperactive children. Plan a water play activity for a hyperactive child. Be sure to include your introduction, the limitations you will set, and the concepts you intended to present in this activity in your plans.

SELECTED CHILDREN'S BOOKS

Gibbons, G. (1983). *Boat book*. New York: Holiday House.

Gibbons, G. (1983). *Sun up, sun down*. New York: Harcourt, Brace, Jovanovich.

Lloyd, P. (1982). *Air*. New York: Dial Books.

Rius, M., & Parramon, J. M. (1985). *The four elements: Air*. Woodbury, NY: Barron's.

Rius, M., & Parramon, J. M. (1987). *Life in the air*. Woodbury, NY: Barron's.

Smith, N. F. (1981). *Wind power*. New York: Coward, McCann & Geoghegan.

Watson, P. (1982). *Light fantastic*. New York: Lothrop, Lee & Shepard.

Watson, P. (1982). *Liquid magic*. New York: Lothrop, Lee & Shepard.

Wilkes, A., & Mostyn, D. (1983). *Simple science*. London: Usborne Publishing.

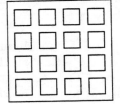

Chapter 12

Heat, Sound, and Machines

THIS chapter focuses on two energy forms—heat and sound—and provides activities that help children explore transfer of energy and force with machines. It provides many hands-on experiences and some discussion lessons to help the children understand these important and intriguing aspects of our physical world.

The information in the chapter is built around nine concepts:

- Heat comes from many sources.
- Heat helps and harms us.
- Heat changes some things.
- Friction causes heat.
- Sound comes from many sources.
- Sound is caused by vibrations.
- Sound travels through many materials.
- Machines help people.
- People use many kinds of machines.

HEAT COMES FROM MANY SOURCES

Heat comes from natural sources such as the sun, fire, and lightning. People use fires and electrical appliances and burn gas and other fuels to produce heat. Heat can also be produced in mechanical ways; the friction created by surfaces rubbing together causes heat. Scientists also have produced tremendous amounts of heat by nuclear fission and fusion.

Heat is a form of energy related to molecular motion. All substances are composed of tiny particles called molecules that are always moving. The faster they move, the more heat they produce.

Heat travels in three ways—conduction, convection, and radiation. When heat travels in a substance such as a metal spoon, scientists picture the molecules as moving, bumping into each other, and making other molecules move. Thus, they say that heat energy is passed from one area to another through this process called conduction. Many metals are good conductors of heat. Plastics, air, water, and other materials do not conduct heat as well; often they are called insulators. Convection is the way heat travels in gases and liquids; molecules of heated gas or liquid move from one place to another. Heated molecules rise, cooler molecules fall, and a convection current occurs. Heat energy from the sun travels by radiation in the form of invisible rays. When these rays strike solid, opaque objects, some energy is absorbed and the materials become warmer.

Finding Sources of Heat

Science Processes.   Observing, communicating, and ordering.

Have the children sit in a sunny location. Say: "Describe what you see and feel." After several answers, focus the discussion on the warmth of the sun. Ask: "What are some other sources of heat or warmth?" Record their answers.

Take the children to actually feel sources of heat in the building or outdoors. In warm weather, the sidewalk, fence, and building's surfaces may be warmed by the sun. Indoors, with your close supervision, the children may be able to hold their hands near water pipes, stoves, the coils in the back of a refrigerator, surfaces of other appliances, or electric light bulbs to feel their warmth. You might have them touch the cooler ones after you have tested them yourself.

Ask the children to investigate more sources of heat at home. Be sure they understand that they should do this with the guidance of an adult. Discuss what the children find and add it to your list.

Guide the children to make pages for two class books. One could be entitled "Warm as a _____" and the other, "Hot as a _____." Have each child explain what she drew for her page in each book.

Questions.   "Where is the hottest place in our room? Where is the coldest place? Where are the warmest and coldest places in your homes?"

Evaluation.   Note on a checklist the accuracy and detail of the children's drawings. Observe their interest and abilities to name and describe sources of heat.

Feeling and Observing Heat

Science Processes.   Observing, communicating, ordering, predicting, and inferring.

Set up three learning stations in which children can feel and observe heat. Rotate groups of children through the stations so that each child has a chance to participate in each activity.

In one area, furnish five closed, opaque containers of water of various temperatures—ice water, cold water, room temperature water, warm water, and hot water. Have the children feel the outsides of the containers and then put them in order from coolest to warmest. Help the children discuss how they use water of various temperatures.

In another area, help the children put one drop of food coloring in each of two small transparent containers—one of hot tap water and the other of cold water. Direct them to watch carefully and describe what they see. Ask: "Where does the food coloring go? How does it move? Does it move in the same ways and at the same rate in the hot and cold water? If not, what are some differences?" The children can also draw what they see.

In a third area, use two or more containers of hot tap water and spoons (plastic, wooden, steel, silver) to put into the water (Figure 12.1). Caution the children about putting their hands in hot water, even from the tap. Have them predict how the spoons' handles will feel after the spoons are placed in the water. Ask: "Will all the spoons feel the same? Will they get warm at the same rate?" Have the children take turns putting the spoons in the water and feeling the handles. Supervise to be sure the children do not spill the hot water or put their hands into it. Help the children explain that heat travels from the water through some of the spoons (steel and silver), but not through others, to the spoon handles.

After the children have participated in the experiences, help them discuss their findings and come to some conclusions like these: "Our hands can feel differences in temperature. Food coloring moves faster in hot water than in cold. Heat travels through some materials better than others." Have the children move around pretending to be the food coloring in the hot water and in the cold water.

Questions.   "When we want to stop the travel of heat, what materials do we use—in pot holders or pot handles, for example? When are some times you can safely use your sense of touch to feel heat? When should you be careful when feeling hot objects?"

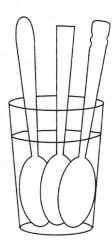

Figure 12.1
Spoons in hot water.

Evaluation.   Check the children's attention and their abilities to describe and draw conclusions about what they observe.

HEAT HELPS AND HARMS US

Like many things, heat can help or harm us. A suitable range of temperatures is necessary for all life forms. Warm-blooded animals—mammals and birds—maintain a relatively constant body temperature. Their bodies metabolize or "burn" food to keep their bodies warm. The body coverings of warm-blooded animals—feathers, fur, or hair—help insulate their bodies to keep in heat. When the weather is cold, birds fluff out their feathers to make air spaces that help to keep their body heat inside. Most fur-bearing animals grow heavier coats in winter if they live where the weather is cold. The body temperatures of cold-blooded creatures change within a wide range; although their body temperatures fluctuate to match the temperature of their surroundings, they need some heat to survive. Plants also need heat to grow and reproduce.

People wear clothes not only because of social customs but also because clothing helps maintain comfortable body temperatures. In cold weather several layers of clothing help to keep body heat in. In warm weather most people wear fewer and lighter clothes so that air circulates around their skin to cool them. Houses and shelters help animals and people escape some of the extremes of outside weather, thus making maintenance of body temperature easier.

Besides needing heat to survive, people use heat for a wide variety of purposes. Home heating keeps people comfortable. Various heating devices help us cook our food, dry our hair and clothes, and iron our clothes.

Despite its many benefits, heat can be harmful. Fires can kill animals, plants, and people and can destroy property. Appliances are also dangerous if not handled with care. Too much heat in homes, classrooms, and outdoors can make people uncomfortable or sick. The sun's rays can cause painful and dangerous sunburn.

The activities in this section will help children become more aware of the ways that heat helps and harms people and other animals. As children explore the topic, they will become more aware of the sources of heat in their surroundings and of ways to use heat safely.

☐ ☐ ☐   Keeping Heat In, Letting Heat Out

Science Processes.   Observing, communicating, measuring, predicting, inferring, and using time and space relationships.

You might use this activity in cold weather and again in warm weather. Use a felt or paper doll and clothes. Dress the doll in several layers—underwear, shirt and pants, sweater, jacket, hat, socks, shoes, boots, and mittens. Ask: "What might the weather be like when you would dress this way?" Explain that clothing keeps us warm because it keeps body heat in. Point out that, similarly, blankets are not warm in themselves, but they keep body heat in when they are piled on top of a person.

Now dress the doll in underwear, shorts, and a short-sleeve shirt. Lead the children to discuss weather conditions for this type of clothing. Help them realize that with less clothing, body heat can escape and people will feel cooler. Have the children examine their own clothing and point out features that keep body heat in or let body heat out. Help them understand that where the body is covered, clothes keep in body heat. Features like cuffs, drawstrings, and elastic help clothes to fit the body and retain heat. Point out that loose clothes let body heat escape.

Have a child volunteer to tell how today's temperature makes her feel—comfortable, cool, or warm. Have the children predict how she will feel if she wears a heavy jacket and then wraps herself in a blanket. Have the child don the insulating layers and describe how she feels. A 2nd or 3rd grader could also hold a thermometer close to her body and read the thermometer with and without the insulating layers. Let other children wear the jacket and blanket and describe how they feel. Children could also try laying the jacket and blanket across one arm or leg and describe the effects in comparison with their other arm or leg.

Provide a container of warm, tap water. Let the children feel the water's temperature. Older children could use a thermometer to measure its temperature. Ask: "What will happen to the water's temperature if we leave it on the table for several minutes?" Let the children propose some ways to keep the water from cooling. Have them gather materials to try out some of their suggestions using several samples of warm water. The children should feel (and perhaps take the temperature of) their water samples after 15 minutes and after 30 minutes. Help the children draw some conclusions about keeping heat in and helping heat escape.

Questions. "What are some features of your warmest clothes that help to keep you warm? What features do your hot weather clothes have? How do they help to keep you cool? If you ran a restaurant and needed to keep foods hot, how would you do it?"

Evaluation. Note on a checklist the children's interest and abilities to express themselves. Have children draw or select catalog pictures to show clothes that keep them warm and clothes to keep them cool. Have children point out features of the clothing that insulate or that let body heat escape.

Animals Keep Warm in Cold Weather   ☐ ☐ ☐

Science Processes. Observing, communicating, inferring, and using time and space relationships.

Read to the children about how animals adapt to winter. You might show some pictures of animals in winter and have the children describe what they see. Try to include some pictures of animals migrating, animals in shelters, or animals seeking food. Explain that they metabolize their food to keep their bodies warm. Let children tell about the ways their household pets stay warm in winter.

Provide materials for the children to make models of the ways animals keep warm in winter. For example, children could use sticks and grass to make a snug bird's nest.

Children might use playdough or modeling clay to depict a gopher or bear in its den. Sand, water, sticks, and a plastic container could be used to build a beaver's dam. Some children could use a hanger, paper, and strings to make a mobile to show geese in flight to a warm place for the winter.

Have the children write some information about their models to share with their classmates. Leave the models on display for a few days. If the children have made models of animals that live in similar geographic areas, they might group their models together against a large background showing that habitat.

Questions. "What did you show about your animals' habits in your models? What problems did you solve as you made your models?"

Evaluation. Mark on a checklist the degree of detail in the children's models and their abilities to convey facts accurately through their models and words.

▢ ▢ ▢   Safety with Heat

Science Processes. Observing, communicating, and inferring.

Use puppets to present some safety guidelines for using heat. The puppets might present some ideas like these.

- Mr. Cool uses hot pads as he handles pans on the stove. He uses a long spoon with a cool plastic handle to do his stirring. He keeps the pan handles in positions where he will not bump them and where his young son Mike can not grab them.

- Ms. Cool plugs in the iron carefully. She grasps the iron by its plastic handle and puts it away after using it. She makes sure Mike does not play with the iron.

- Ms. Cool adds sticks to the campfire very carefully. She stirs the fire with a long stick. Ms. Cool and Mike stay at a safe distance from the campfire. They do not play with or near the fire. The family makes sure the fire is out before they leave it.

- When Mr. Cool wants to light a candle, he gets matches from a special container. He strikes the match away from his body; he makes sure the match is out before he throws it away. Mr. Cool tells Mike he can light matches when he is older and when he learns to do it safely.

Have the children suggest and role-play other situations in which safety with heat is necessary. Help each child make a small, heat-safety poster to take home and discuss with his family.

Questions. "What could you say or do if you saw a baby going close to the fireplace? What could you say or do if an older child gave you some matches to play with?"

Evaluation. Observe the children's attention and their suggestions for aspects of safety with heat. Check the children's posters for accuracy of ideas. Help each child discuss his poster as another gauge of understanding of ideas.

HEAT CHANGES SOME THINGS

Heat changes the ways many things feel. For instance, water left in the sun for an hour feels different than water that has been in the refrigerator. Eating hot soup feels different than eating cold soup.

Heat also changes states of matter. Extremely hot temperatures can turn rocks into molten lava. Water freezes, exists as a liquid, or is turned to water vapor or steam, according to its temperature.

Children can easily see the changes heat causes in some foods. As bread is toasted, it changes texture, color, and taste. Heat causes some molecules of water in the bread to move off into the air, making the toast crispier and drier than the bread was before it was toasted. Heat causes chemical changes in some of the bread's ingredients as the bread is toasted. As sugar and flour cook, they turn brown and become slightly sweeter in taste. Heat causes popcorn to undergo even more dramatic changes. As popcorn kernels are heated, the small amount of water in each kernel expands enough to break the kernels' outer layers and force the corn to pop. The children can also observe the changes of states of matter that heat causes in some foods. For example, butter melts as it is heated; eggs solidify.

As these children cooked playdough they experienced heat in the steam rising from the pan and the hot finished playdough. They have also learned that heat changed the texture of the playdough.

In the activities in this section, the children will examine some of the ways heat changes things. The activities feature cooking experiences, which are fascinating to most youngsters.

☐ ☐ ☐ Changing Bread with Heat

Science Processes.   Observing, communicating, predicting, and inferring.

Divide the class into small groups. Then give each child one fourth of a piece of bread. Have the children examine the bread using several senses by asking: "What does it feel and smell like? Does it make a noise when you rub it with your finger? Does it bend? What color is it? What does it feel like in your mouth? What does it taste like?"

Have the children predict how the bread will change when it is toasted. Write down some predictions. Now prepare some toast in an oven or toaster and serve each child one fourth of a piece. Lead the children to examine the toasted bread and compare it to the untoasted bread by asking the same questions again.

Help the children prepare "painted toast." Mix small amounts of milk and food coloring, and let the children paint designs on white bread using clean paint brushes. They should use a minimal amount of milk and then toast the bread. Their designs will show on the toast! After the children show each other their designs, they can eat their painted toast.

Questions.   "What made the bread change color and texture? What are some other foods that change colors or textures when they are cooked? What are some things other than food that heat changes?"

Evaluation.   Note on a checklist the variety and detail of children's descriptions of the bread and toast.

☐ ☐ ☐ Heat Changes Eggs

Science Processes.   Observing, communicating, predicting, and using time and space relationships.

Eggs undergo changes as they are heated. Help the children understand the nature of these changes during this cooking activity. Use a hot plate to boil some water in a place where children will not disturb or spill it. Have the children look at and describe a fresh egg in its shell. Crack the egg into a dish and have a small group of children examine and describe it. Help the children talk about the egg's color, texture, and general appearance. Let them touch it gently with a spoon to establish that it is liquid, but cohesive and somewhat slimy.

Have the children predict what an egg will look like when it is cooked in the boiling water. Ask: "Will its color, texture, or general appearance change? How?" Help the children note the time. Slip an egg or two into the boiling water. Help the children determine what time it will be in 15 minutes when you remove the egg from the water.

In the meantime, use an electric skillet to fry an egg or two. The children can help put some margarine in the skillet, watch it melt, crack the eggs, and place them in the skillet. Have the children watch carefully from a safe distance and describe the effects of the heat on the eggs. Encourage them to describe subtle changes such as the eggs bubbling, parts of the eggs moving up and down, the edges of the eggs turning opaque white first, and the yolk hardening and turning a lighter yellow. Cool the fried eggs slightly and let children touch and compare their appearance to that of the raw egg.

When the boiled eggs are ready, take them out of the water and have a child or two run cool water over them. Choose another child or two to peel the eggs. Discuss the children's predictions about the boiled eggs' appearances; compare the predictions to the actual appearances of the eggs.

Let the children sample a bit of each cooked egg and describe its taste. Discuss other ways that eggs are prepared. Offer several choices and let the children graph their favorite kind of cooked egg. Have the children explain their graph results.

Questions.   Say: "Heat made the eggs harder or more solid. What are some other foods that heat makes harder? What are some foods that heat melts or makes softer?" You could make lists of the children's responses.

Evaluation.   Have children draw pictures of raw eggs, fried eggs, and hard-boiled eggs. Judge the accuracy and detail of the pictures. Note the children's abilities and willingness to describe features of the eggs and the effects heat has on them.

Popping Corn

Science Processes.   Observing, communicating, measuring, ordering, using time and space relationships, and predicting.

Make popping corn a memorable experience by using a popper in the middle of a clean sheet and seating the children on the floor around the perimeter. Caution them that they should never be closer than this to an open popper while it is popping. Have a child measure 200 milliliters of unpopped corn (about 3/4 cup) and place it in the popper. Add about 60 milliliters (about 1/4 cup) oil. (Do not plug it in yet.) Have the children predict where the corn will go as it pops. Have them point out the place farthest from the popper where they think corn will land as it pops. Place some small paper markers on the sheet at the spots the children choose. Use yarn to compare the distances of each spot from the popper.

Plug in the popper, but leave its lid off. Have the children close their eyes, pay attention to what they hear and smell, and discuss some of the things they observe. As the corn pops, discuss and compare some of the distances the corn travels. Explain that each kernel of corn contains some moisture or water. As it heats, the moisture expands enough to burst the kernel's outer shell to make the corn expand and "pop."

After it stops popping, have the children gather the popcorn and put it in a bowl. Compare the volume of popped corn to the original 200 milliliters of unpopped corn. Help each child measure out a small amount of popcorn (100–150 milliliters) and eat it. Have the children describe how the corn feels in their hands and on their tongues and how it tastes.

Ask a group of children to draw pictures representing the various steps in your popcorn-making experience. They can shuffle their finished pictures and let others try to put them in order. Let children move to music and pretend to be popcorn moving and expanding.

Questions. "What did heat do to the popcorn? What could we observe with our senses that let us know that heat was working? What other foods expand as they are cooked?"

Evaluation. Have children write and draw about the experience, perhaps recording their data on popcorn-shaped pages. Let each child tell about his page. Then make a popcorn book of the pages. Note the children's interest and contributions to the entire experience and the detail shown in their book pages.

FRICTION CAUSES HEAT

Friction is produced when surfaces of objects rub together. Smooth objects slide freely against each other, producing very little friction. Rough surfaces, with many irregularities, have more bumpy and hollow places than smooth objects do and produce more friction as they are rubbed together. This friction generates heat.

We experience the heat from friction as we rub our hands together. Indeed, rubbing our hands on the cold parts of our bodies is an effective way to warm them. As a woman uses a screwdriver to put a screw into the wall, the screw becomes warm from friction. If a workman feels a board or his saw as he cuts the board, both objects will be warm from the friction of the saw blade moving against the wood. As parts of engines move, they rub together. To decrease the resulting heat and friction, manufacturers make engine parts as smooth as possible and often use oil and other lubricants.

Children can explore friction and the heat it causes through the activities described in this section.

☐ ☐ ☐ Observing Friction's Heat

Science Processes. Observing, communicating, predicting, inferring, ordering, and using time and space relationships.

Let children predict what will happen when they rub a piece of cotton against various surfaces. Have them rub the cotton on surfaces such as a smooth tabletop, a mirror, or a person's cheek, and on the rougher surfaces of the bottom of the table, a twig, or a cement block. Some bits of cotton may adhere to the rougher surfaces. Let the children examine the surfaces, feeling them with their fingers and looking at them through a hand lens. Lead them to discuss similarities and differences in the surfaces.

Provide smooth wood blocks and rougher ones. Have the children rub the blocks together for several seconds and then feel their surfaces. Some heat will be generated by rubbing both, but the rough blocks will probably be warmer. Let the children use small pieces of sandpaper to smooth some of the rough surfaces. As they rub the wood and the sandpaper together, the children will be able to feel some heat. Help them conclude that when surfaces rub together, friction and heat are produced.

Have the children rub their hands together and feel the heat that is produced. They can also rub their arms or legs and compare the effects of hard rubbing and gentle rubbing or rubbing for a few seconds versus rubbing for a prolonged period.

Encourage the children to work in pairs to suggest and try out other materials that will produce friction and heat. They could pull a string back and forth across the edge of a table and feel the heat that is generated. They could briskly polish part of a surface and feel the heat as they rub with the rag. The children might also insert eye screws into soft wood, remove them, and feel the heat on the screw as it is twisted into the wood.

Questions. Say: "When Sally slid on the sidewalk, her skin was badly scraped. Why? Maria picked up a piece of wood her brother had sawed. The end was quite warm. Why?"

Evaluation. As part of your evaluation, present the children with three samples of wood and paper of different degrees of roughness. Ask them to put the materials in order from smoothest to roughest after looking at and feeling them. Ask: "What will happen as the wood surfaces are rubbed with sandpaper or the paper surfaces are rubbed with your hands?" From their actions and verbalizations, judge the children's understanding of the concepts you have presented.

Using Friction, Decreasing Friction

Science Processes. Observing, communicating, ordering, classifying, and inferring.

Set up several situations in which the children can work with the effects of friction. You might have them write with pencils on waxed paper, aluminum foil, writing paper, and rough-textured paper. They might make crayon rubbings on paper over glass windows, brick walls, cement sidewalks, and wood or tile floors. The children could play with toy cars on smooth floors, brick surfaces, and gravel surfaces. They might rub their dry hands together and then use a small amount of liquid soap and continue to rub them. They could try drying their hands with smooth, cotton cloth, with terry cloth, and with burlap.

After some experiences, lead the children to discuss the similarities and differences in each situation. For example, they might have found it difficult to write with the pencil on very smooth surfaces; they might have found that pencil lines look different on writing paper and rough-textured paper. Children might comment on the way towels of various fabrics felt on their skin. In drying their hands, they might have noticed that a towel of medium texture (and high absorbency) might do a better job than a very smooth or rough fabric. They might have observed that toy cars travel farther on smooth surfaces than on rough ones but "brake" better on rougher surfaces that provide more friction.

Ask the children to describe some cases in which friction is useful or helpful and other situations in which people try to decrease friction. Have children draw pictures that represent these situations. Give each child an opportunity to discuss his picture; then display the pictures on a bulletin board with categories "Friction Helps Us" and "Friction Harms Us."

Questions.   Have the children examine the soles of their shoes. Ask: "Whose shoes are good for sliding? Whose shoes provide a lot of traction? Whose shoes are designed with both smooth and rough areas?"

Evaluation.   Mark on a checklist the children's interest, cooperation, and abilities to make comparisons as they participate in the activities. Note their abilities to discuss their results, and to draw and classify their friction pictures.

SOUND COMES FROM MANY SOURCES

Even on a "quiet" day in a "quiet" setting people can hear many sounds if they "tune in" by listening carefully. People's wonderful sense of hearing lets them perceive and discriminate among sounds as small as the rustling of leaves, the hum of a refrigerator, faraway sirens, and the sound of their own breathing. Sounds enable us to communicate. People use words and intonations to convey meanings. We also respond to sound signals such as fire alarms, doorbells, telephones, and schoolbells. Music entertains us and evokes our emotions.

Sounds surround us. Helping children focus on the variety of sounds in our world can be challenging and interesting. The activities in this section will help children to focus on the many sources of sound.

Sounds come from many sources, with each sound having its distinct characteristic. These children are trying to match the sounds they hear with the pictures in the book.

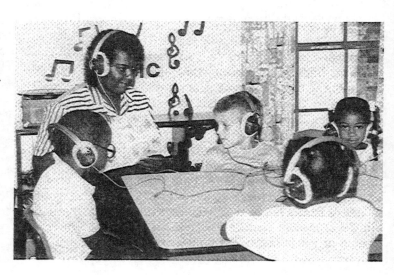

Sounds All Around   □ □ □

Science Processes. Observing, communicating, and classifying.

Gather the children into a group and explain in a low voice that soon you will be quiet and that the children should listen carefully to notice as many sounds as possible. When everyone is quiet and ready, participate in the listening exercise for about 2 minutes. Ask the children to name and discuss all the sounds they heard. Take dictation, making a long list. Then have the children listen again for sounds on the list and for other sounds. Add any further descriptions the children offer.

Help the children categorize the items on the list. You might color-code items as to whether they were sounds made by people, machines, animals, or other sources. You might classify the sounds as "loud" or "soft." Ask the children to describe or make other sounds that would fit into each category.

Remind the children that people have distinctive voices that others can often identify. Ask the children to close their eyes while you touch a child and ask that child to say a few words. Ask classmates to raise their hands and try to identify the speaker.

Questions. "What are many different words we can use to describe sounds? What are some things that make very little noise or no sounds at all?" (You might make another list entitled "Quiet as a _____.")

Evaluation. As part of your evaluation have each child draw a picture of something or someone that makes a sound. Have the children explain their pictures and pin them to the appropriate area of a bulletin board labeled "Loud Sounds," "Soft Sounds," and "No Sounds." Judge the children's understanding as shown in their pictures and descriptions and their accuracy in classifying.

Mystery Sounds   □ □ □

Science Processes. Observing, communicating, and using time and space relationships.

Have a group of children help you gather many small objects that will make sounds. You might use bells, marbles, coins, plastic or metal spoons, wood blocks, and paper clips. Prepare a mystery sound area. Cut one side out of a box; then turn the box upside down. Place a few objects inside the box. One child can use the objects to make sounds inside the box. Other children who cannot see inside can try to identify the objects by the sounds.

Help the children start with just four to six kinds of objects. Guide the child who is making the sound to produce the sound several times, giving the listeners ample opportunities to hear the sound before guessing.

As the children gain practice identifying sounds, ask them to make loud sounds and soft sounds and to let their listeners describe the sounds. Have them make several sounds "close together" and several sounds with pauses in between; again, have the listeners describe the qualities and timing of the sounds that are produced. Have the leader select two objects that make sounds of different pitches; then let the listeners tell whether the sounds were high first, then low or low first, then high.

Questions.   "What gives you clues about the sounds? What are some other things we could do with our mystery sound box?"

Evaluation.   Note the children's abilities to identify sounds and discuss qualities of sounds. If you find children who, after practice, are not able to identify many sounds, you might want to investigate their hearing abilities further through more observations or through a hearing screening.

SOUND IS PRODUCED BY VIBRATIONS

How can our voices be heard by others? How does a drum make noises? How does the sound of a car's horn alert another driver? Sound is a form of energy that is caused when objects vibrate or move back and forth rapidly. Vibrations are produced when objects are plucked, stroked, blown, or hit. Air moves across our vocal chords and makes them vibrate. When drum sticks hit a drum head, its surface vibrates and makes sounds. A car's horn has vibrating parts that make noises that can be heard at considerable distances.

When objects vibrate, sound waves travel out from them in all directions. Molecules of air vibrate and strike other molecules which also vibrate. Sound waves reach our ears and are carried by our auditory nerves to our brains. Thus, we sense sounds. The activities in this section will help children begin to associate sounds and vibrations with their sources.

☐ ☐ ☐ Lots of Vibes!

Science Processes.   Observing, communicating, predicting, inferring, and using time and space relationships,

Hang a musical triangle by a string. As the children to watch carefully as you tap the triangle with a metal spoon or a mallet. Have the children describe what they heard and saw. Ask: "What will happen if you hold the triangle very tightly as another child strikes it?" Let the children carry out the action. The children will probably notice that the sound is more quiet or dull if the instrument cannot vibrate. Ask: "What will happen if you strike the triangle and another child quickly grabs it and holds it still? Try it out." They will probably notice that the sound will be muffled or stop as the instrument's vibrations are stopped.

Have each child gently put a hand on her voice box as she hums, talks, and sings. Have the children try high, low, loud, and soft sounds. Have the children describe what they felt as their voice boxes vibrated to produce sounds.

Questions.   "What other things could we watch to observe vibrations as sounds are made? What will we see if we gently stretch and pluck a rubber band? What will we hear?"

Evaluation.   Note the children's interest and abilities to associate vibrations with sounds.

Musical Mobiles

Science Processes. Observing, communicating, ordering, and using time and space relationships.

When objects can move freely, their vibrations may be enhanced. Help the children make mobiles of various materials, strike the objects, see what sounds are produced, and compare the sounds they hear.

Mobiles can be made several ways. You might help children suspend things from a long metal or bamboo pole. They might hang seashells or nuts and bolts from strings, placing the objects in order from smallest to largest. When the children strike the objects, help them describe the sounds, focusing on pitch, loudness, and quality. They might try to find the objects that make the loudest sound and the softest sound. Guide the children to look closely at their mobiles and see their objects vibrating as the sounds are produced.

Children might use coat hangers as a basis for their mobiles and hang objects that will make noises as the mobiles move (Figure 12.2). Bells, nails, pieces of plastic, and chopsticks will make distinctive noises. Pieces of heavy-duty aluminum foil will make more subtle sounds. Metal or plastic spoons and forks may be attached in horizontal or vertical positions and will add familiar sounds to the mobiles.

Questions. "Do the smallest objects always make the smallest sounds? How did you get your mobile to balance? Which mobile do you think makes the most interesting sounds? Why?"

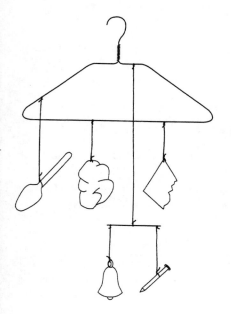

Figure 12.2
A coat hanger mobile.

Evaluation.   Record on a checklist the children's abilities to construct mobiles, to describe the characteristics of the sounds they hear, and to discuss the making of their mobiles.

☐ ☐ ☐   Musical Visitors

Science Processes.   Observing and communicating.

Arrange for some visitors to come to your classroom with musical instruments. Junior high or high school band members may be able to come as may parents or retired persons who play instruments. String instruments (guitars, violins, ukeleles, cellos) or percussion instruments (steel drums, cymbals) may be especially interesting to the children because they will be able to see the vibrations the instruments make as they are played. The children may also be able to put their hands on instruments such as a tuba, bagpipe, or saxophone and feel the vibrations as the instrument is being played.

Have the musician play a short passage for the children and then tell a bit about the instrument and how it is played. With the musician's approval, let the children take turns gently feeling the vibrating parts of the instrument as it is played. The musician might also tell the children about how she got started playing the instrument and how to take care of it. The musician might lead a short sing-along.

Have the children write a thank-you letter to the musician after the visit. Encourage interested children to make a book shaped like the instrument and to tell the story of the visit in the book.

Questions.   "What words describe the sounds you heard? What parts of the instrument vibrated as the instrument was played?"

Evaluation.   Note the children's cooperation during the visitor's presentation. Note their abilities to describe the sounds they heard and their interest in follow-up activities.

SOUND TRAVELS THROUGH MANY MATERIALS

We hear sounds travel through the air every day. Many signals and communications that we receive in everyday life are sounds that reach our ears through the air—sounds of car engines and horns, birds' songs, and sounds of conversation. Sound also travels through liquids and solids. We can hear while we are swimming under water; noises may sound distorted, but nevertheless, we hear them. When we put our ear to a watch, we hear it ticking. Sound travels through the solid materials of the watch and through some solid parts of our ears as well.

Children can listen carefully to a variety of sounds as they explore the ways that sounds travel. The activities in this section will help them "tune in" to and examine another aspect of the world of sound around them.

Making Sound Travel

Science Processes. Observing, classifying, using time and space relationships, and ordering.

Provide some experiences in which children hear sounds conducted through several kinds of materials. Explain that, ordinarily, people hear sounds that travel through the air. Ask: "How can you hear me? How does my voice get from me to you?" Listen to the children's explanations. If the children do not mention it, point out that sound waves or vibrations can travel through the air from one place to another—from your vocal chords and mouth to the children's ears. Seat the children all around the room. Make various sounds—whisper, ring a small bell, rub your hands together, or smack your lips. Have the children raise their hands when they hear you. Point out that some sounds can be heard by children nearby but not by children who are farther away.

Ask the children whether sound can be heard through water. They will probably respond "yes" and describe hearing sounds while in the shower or swimming under water. Use a water-filled balloon and rub or tap against it. It will make a small sound which some of the children can hear as the sound travels through the air. Now let the children take turns holding the balloon next to their ears and listening to the same sounds through the water. Because the sound travels faster through water than through air, most children will hear louder, more distinct sounds than before. Let children describe and compare the sounds they heard.

Sound also travels through solids. Ask the children to listen as you rub your fingernail across a tabletop. They will probably not be able to hear much. Now ask the children to put their ears against the tabletop and listen as you rub your fingernail across it again. This time they will probably hear quite a distinct sound. Explain that sound travels faster through the solid material of the tabletop than through the air. Let the children make and listen to other sounds "through" the tabletop and other solids.

Now provide an experience where sound travels through solid and air at the same time. Use a 1 to 2-meter (1 to 2-yard) length of old garden hose and whisper into one end while a child holds the other end near his ear to listen. Whisper some directions to the child such as "Wave to your classmates, and give the hose to someone else." Provide a longer piece of old hose to let the children stretch it across the room or out in the hall for talking and listening.

Provide different kinds of cups (smooth plastic, paper, plastic foam, and metal cans) and strings (yarn, nylon twine, metal wire, and cotton string) and let children make "telephones" for talking and listening. They should work in pairs and insert the string through holes in the bottom of each cup and knot it. The children can take turns speaking into the cups and listening. Have the children compare the sound quality of several different combinations of cups and strings. Help them discuss their results and come to a consensus about which "phones" were easiest to hear through. Which were hardest to hear through?

Questions. "What are some times when we hear sounds through the air? Through water? Through solid objects?" Make a list of the children's responses.

Evaluation. Make note of any children who do not seem to be able to hear as well as the others. You might want to refer these children for hearing tests. Notice the children's interest, cooperation, and abilities to communicate as they participate in the activities.

☐ ☐ ☐   Sending Sounds, Muffling Sounds

Science Processes. Observing, communicating, and classifying.

People send sounds to others in many ways. We project our voices to others in various degrees of loudness from whispers to conversational tones to shouts. We use microphones and loudspeakers to amplify our voices. We send messages over the telephone, on tape recordings, and on records. Discuss some of these examples with children and let them name others. Ask: "When are some times when we want to block out sounds or muffle them?" Record some of their answers. You might also discuss how people with hearing impairments receive sounds and messages from others.

Set up a center where children can work with various devices that send, amplify, and muffle sounds. You might provide a tape recorder, a radio, an educational-listening headset, a stethoscope, earmuffs, earplugs, and other devices. Provide a loud-ticking watch, timer, and other things children could use to muffle its sound. Let them experiment to see if they can muffle the sound by putting the timer in a box or jar, by wrapping it in cotton, or placing it under the table. Let the children work in the center, and then talk, write, and draw about their experiences.

Questions. "What are some things that sounds tell you? What sounds make you feel happy? What sounds help us relax? What sounds warn us of danger?"

Evaluation. Note the children's interest and cooperation. Judge their abilities to discuss situations in which sounds travel and ways sounds are muffled. Look at the children's papers to see if they have conveyed ideas accurately. To see how much they understand have the children divide a paper in half and then draw some devices that convey sound on one half and devices that muffle sound on the other half.

MACHINES HELP PEOPLE

Scientists associate work with movement. Machines help people apply effort and move objects. Thus, work is done as people transfer effort or force from one place to another by using machines. For instance, as we turn the handle of an eggbeater, the eggbeater's blades move rapidly through the mixture. Machines sometimes increase the force we apply. When a person pries open a paint can using a screwdriver as a lever, she pushes on the screwdriver handle with moderate force. The lever action, however, increases the force that is exerted against the paint can lid. Machines can also help us change the direction of force. In the paint can example, the person pushes down, but the lever moves the lid upward. When we stand at the bottom of a flagpole and pull down on a rope and pulley device, we cause the flag to move upward. Some machines also

Children have a natural curiosity. They are eager to explore machines to find out how they work.

increase the distance and speed of a force. When a person uses a broom to sweep the floor, he moves his hands a shorter distance than the bristles of the broom move.

To familiarize children with the many ways machines help people, educators can discuss examples that the children use as they work and play at school. They can also work with children to set up situations in which machines are used. As the children work with the machines, they will begin to understand and appreciate the machines in the world around them.

Outdoor "Chores"

Science Processes. Observing, communicating, and using time and space relationships.

Take the children outdoors to use and observe several machines. Gather devices such as brooms, rakes, shovels, hoes, or trowels for the children to use. Perhaps some children could bring some tools from home or you could borrow some from the school custodian. Demonstrate how to use each of the tools safely. Caution the children not to swing the tools around or hit others with them.

Have them take turns using the tools in various locations. Circulate as they work and point out that they are doing work—moving leaves, dirt, and other materials. Help the children see how the tools let them transfer force from one place to another. Explain that the shovels and hoes also let them increase the force they apply. Perhaps they could plant flowers or vegetables during this activity.

You could take the children to a park or part of the school grounds where adults are using mechanical tools—lawn mowers, hedge clippers, lawn edgers, or trash pickers. Have the children sit where they can see safely. Discuss the machines they see, any safety precautions the workers take, and how much work is needed to keep our physical surroundings neat and safe.

Questions.   "What are some other machines or tools people use to do work outdoors? Indoors?"

Evaluation.   Note the children's abilities to apply the rules for safety you have set up. Note the ease and enthusiasm with which the children work and discuss their work.

☐ ☐ ☐   Pulley Power

Science Processes.   Observing, communicating, and using time and space relationships.

Show the children some pulleys in your school. Show them the pulley on your flagpole. Point out how awkward it would be to put up the flag by using a ladder or by climbing the pole. Help the children identify the wheel or curved part of the pulleys in the flagpole. Have them notice how the long rope or wire fits around the pulleys. Look at drapery pulls or the pulleys on venetian blinds or shades in your school and help children identify the curved parts and cords and how the cords fit around the pulleys. Be sure the children notice that as you pull down, the flag or blinds go up. Explain that the pulleys have changed the direction of the force.

Help the children set up and use several kinds of pulleys. You might purchase a large pulley at the hardware store and mount it above the children's heads. The children could help to thread a rope around the pulley and use it to lift bundles of books. You might mount two pulleys on opposite sides of the room, just above the children's heads. The children could fit a rope around both pulleys and tie the rope tightly to form a device like a movable clothesline. Some children might use clothespins to pin a message onto the line, and work the pulleys to send the message to children on the other side of the room. An easy substitute for a metal pulley is a toilet tissue roll mounted on a string attached to the wall. Rope or nylon cord can go around the roll, as shown in Figure 12.3. Although this type pulley is not very sturdy, it is easy to make.

A child can also use a pulley-like device to exert enough force to move another child. Use two chairs on a smooth-surface floor. Tie a long rope around the round parts of the back supports of one chair. Loop the rope around the round supports of the other chair. Have a child sit in each chair with the chairs about a meter (yard) apart. One child should take the end of the rope and pull hard. The chairs will come together. Let children change roles. They should notice the changing direction of the force and the movements of the chairs. You might also try two such pulleys looped around both back supports of the chair. The children might be able to compare the force they exerted while pulling one one- and two-rope pulley devices.

Questions.   "What are some other things we could do with pulleys?" (Try to follow up on the children's ideas.) "How do pulleys help people in everyday life?"

Evaluation.   Note the children's cooperation and interest. Observe which children can suggest examples of pulleys used in their environment and which children can identify parts of pulleys and the directions of force and movement. Have children draw and write about their experiences with pulleys.

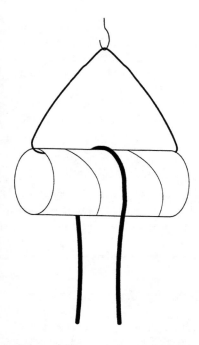

Figure 12.3
An easy-to-make pulley.

Wheels in Motion

Science Processes. Observing, communicating, predicting, using time and space relationships, and using numbers.

Load an old suitcase with books or other heavy materials. Lay it on its side, and let children take turns dragging and lifting it. Stand the suitcase on end and have children drag or slide it this way. Have children discuss any differences in the way the suitcase felt or the force they had to exert to move it. Probably most will be able to feel that more force is needed to lift the suitcase or drag it on its side than to drag or slide it on its end.

Ask: "How could you move the suitcase more easily?" Try some of the children's suggestions. If they do not suggest it, ask the children about using wheels to move the suitcase. Perhaps the children could use a wagon, wheeled cart, or even a large, wheeled toy to help move the suitcase.

Help them discuss more vehicles with wheels that help move things and people. Make a long list of vehicles and other devices with wheels. Examine some wheeled vehicles—toys, wagons, and tricycles. Help the children see how the wheels move smoothly on axles. Explain that an axle usually connects two wheels. Help the children find out how axles are held in place. Have the children notice that wheels touch the ground at a relatively small part of their circumference; thus, friction with the ground is reduced.

Place a marker—an adhesive dot or piece of tape—on a wheel. Ask: "How will the marker move as the wheeled vehicle moves forward?" Let them move the vehicle to test their predictions.

Use a tricycle or bicycle and help the children focus on the direction the pedals move. Point out that the rider moves her feet in a circular path. Ask: "Which way do the wheels turn if the pedals are moved in a clockwise direction?" After the children predict, have them check their predictions. Ask: "When the pedals move around one turn, how many times do the wheels turn?" Again, after the children predict have them check their predictions. Ask: "How many turns of the pedals will be needed to move the cycle from one location to another?" Have them record their predictions and then count the number.

Questions. "How many devices with wheels do you have at home?" Have children predict, count, and share their results. Add the items to your list of things with wheels.

Evaluation. Note on a checklist the children's willingness to participate and share their observations. Have the children fold a paper in half and draw devices with wheels on one half and devices without wheels on the other. Check the papers for accuracy.

Ball-bearing Scooters

Science Processes. Observing, communicating, predicting, measuring, and using time and space relationships.

Show children some marbles and ask them to describe the marbles' characteristics. Because marbles are smooth and round, they are very "rolly." Let children demonstrate how the marbles can roll.

Metal "marbles"—ball bearings—are sometimes used to make rollers. Show children how they can use marbles contained under a metal lid or canning jar ring to make a device that rolls easily over a smooth surface (Figure 12.4). Have them use the device to move a small object such as a book.

Have children place small objects on top of their ball-bearing scooters and give them a push. Direct the children to predict how far their scooters can travel without dropping their loads or before stopping. Measure some distances and compare them to common objects. For example, Marquita's ball-bearing scooter might travel about two arm's lengths—between 1 and 2 meters. Fredo's scooter might travel about 8 of Fredo's foot lengths—just a bit shorter than his body length.

Figure 12.4
Making a roller.

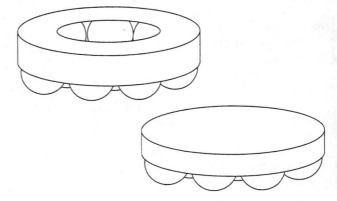

Questions.   "Will more marbles make a scooter go farther than a scooter with just a few marbles? How can we find out? What toys and tools have you seen or used that have rollers or ball bearings?"

Evaluation.   Note children's interest, cooperation, and abilities to predict and measure distances.

PEOPLE USE MANY KINDS OF MACHINES

It's early Saturday morning. You turn off your alarm and rewind the clock. You stumble to the kitchen, open a can of coffee, and pry off the lid of a can of frozen juice. You turn on the tap water to make your beverages. You walk down some stairs and a ramp to get your newspaper. You make some pancakes and use a spatula to turn them. You cut two pats of butter with a knife and loosen the screw top of the syrup container. As you go to your porch to enjoy your breakfast, you open the blinds to let sunlight into your apartment. You relax and enjoy your food and paper.

These activities might be part of a relaxing Saturday morning. They also demonstrate the use of some of the many simple and compound machines that make life easier for us. The six simple machines are the lever, inclined plane, wheel and axle, pulley, screw, and wedge. Perhaps your alarm clock has a lever on-off switch and a wheel and axle winding device. A hand-operated can opener has a wedge in its blade, levers to force the wedge into the can, and a wheel and axle to turn the blade. A can opener used for prying is a lever. Think of your water faucet handles; they may be wheel and axle or lever-type. Stairs and ramps are inclined planes. A spatula is used as a lever. The bottle cap has a screw opener. Most blinds and drapes are closed with pulley-type pulls. Thus, you have used many machines in your brief period of morning activities.

As children investigate machines, they can find examples of each type of simple machine and identify two or more simple machines that make up compound machines. Awareness of simple machines may lead children to understand more about the ways that common tools work and appreciate the many ways that tools help people. The children will explore machines in the activities that follow.

Machines Around Us   ☐ ☐ ☐

Science Processes.   Observing communicating, classifying and using time and space relationships.

Collect one or two examples of each of the simple machines. Show the machines to the children and let them take turns demonstrating how they work. Discuss characteristics of each machine. Ask the children to look around the classroom and find more examples of each machine.

Record the main points of your discussion as you go along. You might make a chart like this one.

Machine	Characteristics	Examples
Lever	Long bar or bars; moves through a fulcrum; you push one place, the lever pushes another place.	Broom Chopsticks Scissors' blades
Wheel and axle	A big, circular wheel and axle that is turned by the wheel.	Pencil sharpener handle Tricycle pedal and wheel Steering wheel to car
Inclined plane	Let us go up at a slant; high at one end, lower at the other end.	Wheelchair ramp Slanted curbing
Wedge	Thin at one end, wider at the other; spreads objects apart.	Knife blade Nail tip Ax blade
Screw	A spiral; has parts that go around and around.	Screw bottle Wood screws Base of light bulb
Pulley	A rope or string goes over a round part; people pull on the string to move things.	Part of flagpole Curtain rods

At a table, provide more devices for children to try out. They can place the simple machines on a mat, classifying them by type. Invite the children to contribute more objects to the collection and to classify them.

Questions. Say: "Show me how this tool works. How do you know what type of machine it is? How does this help you do work?"

Evaluation. Record on a checklist the children's abilities to discuss, identify, and classify the simple machines.

□ □ □ Machines at Home

Science Processes. Observing, communicating, using numbers, and classifying.

Help children fold paper into six columns and then head each column with the name of a simple machine. Direct the children to take their papers home and look for household devices that are examples of each of the simple machines. They can record or draw the machines they find in the columns of their charts. If children find devices that have more than one machine, they can note them on the backs of the sheets.

Have the children discuss their results. Ask: "Did you find more of one kind of machine than others? Which machines were difficult to find?" Organize the class into groups of three or four and have them pool their results and make a graph.

Questions. "What did you look for to find levers (inclined planes, wheels and axles, screws, wedges, or pulleys)? What do wedges and inclined planes have in common? How are screws and inclined planes related?"

Evaluation. Check the children's papers and verbal explanations.

NOW IT'S YOUR TURN

In this chapter, we have presented many concepts of heat, sound, and machines. Now it's your turn to do some further investigation and creative thinking about these topics. Choose from the suggestions listed here or develop some teaching-learning suggestions of your own.

1. Make a list of sounds that affect you in different ways. Perhaps some sounds excite you while others soothe you. Maybe you can identify some sounds that make you happy and some that make you sad. Plan a way to share some of your reactions to sounds with children and to get their reactions to different sounds.

2. If you had a child who couldn't hear, how could you make the concepts related to sound meaningful in some way to that child?

3. Have a child or two help you tape record some familiar sounds and some sounds that will be more challenging for other children to identify. Make pictures to go with the sounds on your tape. Give each child a picture. Play the tape and let the children show the correct pictures when they hear the sounds. Ask the children to suggest other sounds for you to record on a subsequent tape.

4. Listen to some popular or classical music and find examples that illustrate different characteristics of sound: pitch, intensity, and quality. Plan some experiences for children that involve listening and signaling when various characteristics are heard. For example, children might raise their hands when they hear high pitches and lower their hands for lower pitches. They might listen for soft passages and hold their fingers to their lips when they hear them.

5. Create a special story with sound effects or voice effects. You might select and tape record mood music to go with a story. If you play an instrument, you might select or create some music to play as you read a favorite tale or an original story. You might also practice using your voice in unusual or dramatic ways as you tell a story. Practice your "sound effects" and then present your story to children or colleagues. After your story, ask your listeners to discuss some of the ways you used sound to convey ideas and emotions.

6. We suggested three simple experiences with food and heat. Plan another experience in which children use heat to prepare a snack or an art product. Suggest appropriate safety precautions for working with heat.

7. To help children investigate and experience the effects of friction and heat as they work with tools, set up a "workshop." Gather tools for the children to use. Ask several parents or volunteers to help so you will have enough supervision to keep the children safe. Let the children put screws into soft wood, hammer nails, and use saws and drills. As the children work, help them find examples of friction and the heat it creates. Talk about the simple and compound machines in the tools. Report on your workshop experience to your colleagues.

8. Invite one or more community helpers who use special tools and machines to your classroom. Have the workers demonstrate the use of their tools and respond to the children's questions.

9. To increase the awareness of simple and compound machines that affect your life, make a tally of the simple machines you use at home and in your classroom. The tally will let you see what kinds of simple machines are around you and how often you use each one. Analyze some compound machines—for example, write down that a hand-operated can opener has two levers, a wheel and axle in its turning handle, and a wedge in its blade. Devise some ways to share your findings with adult colleagues or with children.

10. David McCauley's book *How Things Work* (Houghton Mifflin, 1988) is an excellent adult reference on machines and technological devices. To broaden your own background, browse through the book. Then choose a particular topic or two to read carefully. Share what you learn with adults or plan ways to simplify the ideas to share them with children.

11. Everyone has access to simple and compound machines in their homes and workplaces. City dwellers see some unique machines whereas other machines are more commonly found in rural areas. Survey the machines where you live. Plan ways to help the children see and understand some of these machines and the ways they help people.

SELECTED CHILDREN'S BOOKS

Bains, R. (1985). *Simple machines.* Mahwah, NJ: Troll Associates.

Baker, B. (1981). *Worthington Botts and the steam machine.* New York: Macmillan.

Bramwell, M., & Mostyn, D. (1984). *How things work.* Tulsa, OK: EDC Publishing.

Gibbons, G. (1982). *Tools.* New York: Holiday House.

How things work. (1984). New York: Simon & Schuster.

Newman, F. R. (1983). *Zounds! The kids' guide to soundmaking.* New York: Random House.

Rius, M., & Parramon, J. M. (1985). *The four elements: Fire.* Woodbury, NY: Barron's.

Rockwell, A., & Rockwell, H. (1972). *Machines.* New York: Macmillan.

Satchwell, J. (1982). *Fire.* New York: Dial Books.

Scarry, R. (1987). *Things that go.* Racine, WI: Western.

Vaughan, J. (1990). *Can you believe it?: The world of machines.* New York: Derrydale Books.

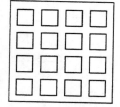

Chapter 13

Magnets and Electricity

IN our modern world magnets and electricity in our cars, games, telephones, door latches, and computers help us at work and play. Young children can explore some of the properties of magnets and electricity in concrete ways. They can begin to gain insight into some of the predictable—and surprising—ways that magnets and electricity work.

This chapter includes the following six concepts for magnetism and electricity:

- Magnets attract some materials but not others.
- Magnets attract through some materials.
- People can make magnets.
- People can work with current and static electricity.
- Some materials conduct electricity.
- Electricity can help or harm us.

For each concept hands-on activities will help the children explore the concept and use a variety of science processes.

MAGNETS ATTRACT SOME MATERIALS BUT NOT OTHERS

Magnetism is a force that acts between certain materials that are called magnets. Lodestone, a natural material, is magnetic. It attracts objects made of iron, steel, nickel, and cobalt. The Earth contains a large amount of magnetic material and acts as a huge magnet. People can make magnets too; we use magnets in household devices

281

and in business and industrial machines. Magnets are also used to help generate electricity.

As the children explore magnets, they will discover that they come in a variety of sizes, strengths, and shapes. They will find the places on magnets that have the greatest strength, the poles. When the poles of two magnets are placed in a certain position, the children will feel the magnets attract, or pull toward each other, and, finally, "stick together." When the poles are placed in other positions, they will feel the magnets repel each other or push apart.

□ □ □ What Do Magnets Attract?

Science Processes. Observing, communicating, classifying, predicting, and inferring.

Divide the class into groups of four or five. Give each group two magnets and a bag containing small objects such as paper clips, pennies, staples, nails, safety pins, and bits of yarn, plastic, foil, wood, and sponge. Have the children take turns handling the magnets and feeling them "stick together" and "push apart." Introduce the words *attract* and *repel*. Encourage the children to lay one magnet on a smooth surface and to bring the other magnet near it (but not touching it) to see if the second magnet attracts or repels it. Ask: "What do the magnets feel like to you as they attract and repel each other?"

Direct the children to fold a piece of paper in half and mark the halves "attracts" and "does not attract." Have the children take turns predicting whether the objects in their bags will be attracted to the magnets or not, testing the objects and putting them on the appropriate places on their charts. If the children want to gather other objects to test, encourage them to do so.

Discuss the results with the entire group. Ask: "What objects were 'easy' to predict? What objects 'fooled' you? What objects were attracted to the magnets? What are they made of?" All of the groups should agree on the results. For example, if one group found that a paper clip was not attracted to the magnet while the others found that it was, have all the children retest the paper clip.

Ask the children to take turns suggesting other objects in the classroom that might or might not be attracted to the magnets. Let them test objects such as items of clothing, your gold or silver jewelry, table legs, cabinets, and windowpanes. Help the children generalize that magnets attract some metal objects but not others.

When the children return their magnets to you, show them how you store the magnets placing them so they won't fall and so the poles attract. If any of the horseshoe magnets have keepers—metal bars that can be placed across the "legs"—help the children place the keepers on the magnets.

Questions. "What are some things in the hall or on the playground that might be attracted to our magnets?" Plan a time to follow up on the children's suggestions.

Evaluation. Note the children's interest in and their abilities to communicate about their experiences with magnets. Observe the children's abilities to predict results, test objects, and place them in the correct category.

Magnet Sort

Science Processes. Observing, communicating, predicting, using numbers, and classifying.

Set up variations of the "What Do Magnets Attract?" activity for the children to use independently. One way to do so is to let the children place small magnets or bits of flexible magnetic tape on the surface of a steel file cabinet. Then direct the children to label a box "These Things Don't Attract." Let them gather a variety of small objects and test them to see if they are attracted to the magnets or not. If the objects are attracted, they will stick to the magnets on the file cabinet. Place the box on a table below the magnets so that the objects tested that are not attracted to the magnets will fall into the box.

For another "magnet sort," attach two or more strips of flexible magnetic tape to a poster board. Show children how to test small objects for magnetic attraction by placing them on the strip of magnetic tape to see if they are attracted to it or not.

The children can make a picture graph of their results of either version of the "magnet sort" activity. Help them do so by providing small squares of paper. As the children test the objects, they can draw pictures of them on the squares of paper and sort the pictures into "attract" and "doesn't attract" piles. After they are finished testing, the children can arrange their papers to form horizontal or vertical bar graphs. They can use another paper to write a title for their graph. Help the children count and compare the numbers of objects shown on their graph.

Questions. "As you predict whether objects will be attracted to the magnet or not, what helps you decide? If we added these two objects (perhaps a pencil and nail) and tested them, how would our graph look different?"

Evaluation. Observe the children's abilities to cooperate, predict, and classify objects based on their observations. As part of your evaluation give each child a piece of construction paper to fold in half to make a magnetic collage. Have the child choose small objects (paper clips, staples, pieces of foil, bits of paper and wire, and so on) and decide whether each will be attracted to a magnet or not. After he has tested each object, the child can glue or tape the objects in a pleasing design on the "attracts" and "doesn't attract" halves of the paper. Check the collages for completeness and accuracy.

What Places on Magnets Are Strongest?

Science Processes. Observing, communicating, and using numbers.

Prepare several ziplock plastic bags with a small amount of iron filings in each bag. As the children work with the bags, caution them to leave the bags closed. Explain that the bags have small bits of iron inside and that the iron filings are not dangerous, but they are somewhat "dirty."

Organize the class into small groups and have each group examine a pair of magnets. Review the idea that when the magnets are placed in certain positions, they attract; in other positions, they repel. Help them discover places on the magnets that don't seem as strong. Point out that the strongest places are called the magnet's *poles*.

Show the children how to shake their iron filings to distribute them in a fairly even layer inside their bags. Direct the children to put a magnet on the table and then place the bag of filings over it. The children will see that the filings "react"; they form patterns as they are placed near the magnets. If the children move their bags a little bit, the filings will move too. Have the children describe what they see. Help them discover that the filings "stand up" and cluster together the most at the areas of the most magnetic force—the poles of the magnets. If you have magnets of different shapes, have the children compare their results.

Help the children make a crayon rubbing of one of the magnets they are using. Then the children should remove the paper and place the bag of filings over the magnet. Show them how to draw the pattern of the filings on their crayon rubbing picture of the magnet. Each child can also write about the experience.

Next the children can work in pairs to experiment with their magnets and paper clips. One child should hold a magnet while another child places paper clips on the magnet in various positions. The children will find that more paper clips are attracted to the poles of the magnets than to other places. Help the children notice that some paper clips are attracted directly the magnet's surface while some cling to those paper clips. Explain that the paper clips that touch the magnet become temporarily magnetized and they attract other paper clips with this induced magnetism. Direct the children to count the paper clips that are attracted to their magnets and compare their results. They can also draw their results (Figure 13.1). Perhaps the children can label their drawings with arrows pointing to the magnet's poles.

Questions.   "How did we find out where the magnets' poles were? Were any magnets stronger than others? How could you tell?"

Evaluation.   Note the children's abilities to handle the materials and discuss their results. Notice the detail and accuracy shown in the children's drawings.

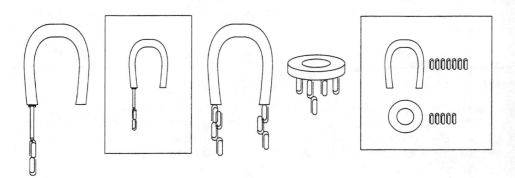

Figure 13.1
Representations of magnetic activity.

Magnet Fishing

Science Processes.   Observing, communicating, using numbers, and ordering.

Ask: "Have you ever been fishing? Have you caught a fish? What did the fish look like? Did you ever pull up anything else on your hook?" Help the children draw, color, and cut out fish and other things that people might catch with a fishing pole (seaweed, old shoes, and driftwood). Then have the children fasten paper clips, staples, and other small iron or steel objects to some of their drawings. They should also fasten bits of wood or paper to some of the drawings.

Let the children use magnetic fishing poles (short sticks or dowels with a piece of yarn with a magnet tied to the end) to try to catch the fish. The children might line up the fish they catch along a meter stick to see how many fish it takes to make a meter length. They might make a graph of what they catch using categories of "big fish," "little fish," "shoes," and "plants."

Have the children explain how they caught the fish and other things. Say: "The magnet attracted the iron or steel objects on some of the drawings. Did it attract any drawings that had wood, plastic, or other materials attached?"

Vary the fishing game by letting the children arrange what they catch in order from the longest to the shortest object. You might also put vocabulary words or number facts on the fish and have the children say the words or answer the facts as they catch the fish.

Questions.   "What else could we attach to our fish and other drawings so that we could catch them with our magnetic fishing poles?"

Evaluation.   Observe the children's care and creativity as they make their fish and other drawings. Note their cooperation in carrying out the activity. During the activity see which children seem to understand that magnets attract iron and steel but not other materials.

MAGNETS ATTRACT THROUGH SOME MATERIALS

When people "stick" papers to their refrigerator doors with magnets, the magnets attract the steel in the doors through the thin layer of paper. Even a heavy, cardboard poster can be attached to a refrigerator with a magnet strong enough to attract the steel through the thicker layer of paper. People use this property of magnets every day. In the simple activities in this section the children can explore the idea that magnets attract through many materials.

Is There a Limit?

Science Processes.   Observing, communicating, predicting, using numbers, and using time and space relationships.

Introduce the lesson with the following surprising demonstration. Hold a manila folder or cardboard rectangle at an angle to the table. Ask: "What will happen if I drop

These young fishermen are finding out that magnets attract some things but not others.

a paper clip down this surface?" The children will probably predict that it will slide down. Demonstrate that it does. Now say: "I will use a magic word and stop the paper clip from falling." Conceal a magnet in your hand behind the folder. Tell the children that you will say the magic word "mmm . . ." and the paper clip will stop. Demonstrate. Try to be sure the magnet "catches" the paper clip as it falls. Say: "Was it really magic that caught the paper clip? No, it was a 'mmm . . . .' " Perhaps the children will guess that you had a magnet behind the folder. Explain that it wasn't magic. Help the children understand that it was a steel object acting in a predictable way—being attracted to the magnet even through the folder.

Let children volunteer to hold the magnet behind the folder and move the paper clip around. Ask the watching children to describe the directions it goes—"up and down" or "across" or "in a slanted or diagonal path."

Discuss the fact that magnets can attract materials through many other materials. Divide the class into groups and give each group a magnet and paper clip. Let them find and test various materials in the classroom to see if the magnet attracts the paper clip through them. Have the children share some of the things they have found. Probably they will find that magnets attract through thin layers of paper, wood, cardboard, plastic, or glass. They may be able to discover that the magnet will not attract the paper clip through iron or steel.

Ask each group to predict whether the magnet will attract the paper clip through 10 pages of a book; then have them test it out. Encourage them to test other thicknesses. Ask: "Will the magnet attract through 100 pages of a book, through a book and its covers, or through three books?" Have the children share their findings.

Finally, have the children see if their magnets will attract the paper clip through another substance—air. Show them how to hold the magnet a short distance above the paper clip to move it along. Have them move the magnet farther and farther away from the paper clip to help them realize that there is a limit to the distance through which the magnet can attract and move the clip.

Questions. "What are some places in everyday life where magnets attract something through another substance?" Elicit some answers to this question. Then have children look at home and bring more answers to school tomorrow.

Evaluation. Note on a checklist the children's interest, their abilities to follow directions, and their motor skills as they work with the activities.

A Magic Wand

☐ ☐ ☐

Science Processes. Observing, communicating, and classifying.

Prepare some cards that can be sorted into two piles. To make the cards, fold rectangles of paper or index cards in half. Draw or glue a picture on one outside half of each card. You might use pictures of plants and things that are not plants, living and nonliving things, or insects and mammals. Tape a paper clip inside of the cards that will be sorted into one pile. Now tape all of the cards closed without adding a paper clip to the cards for the second pile. Also prepare a "magic wand" by attaching a magnet to the end of a short dowel or cardboard strip.

Show a group of children how to work with the cards and wand (Figure 13.2). Explain that they should sort the cards and then test them with the magic wand. Point

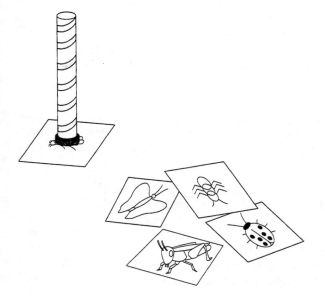

Figure 13.2
The magic wand lifts the pictures of insects.

out that the wand should lift each of the cards in one pile but not the cards in the other. Discuss with the children how the wand works. Help them understand that it uses "magnet power" instead of magic to attract the paper clip through the paper.

Encourage the children to make sets of cards for each other to use. They could make different sets of cards in different colors to prevent them from getting mixed up.

Questions. "How does the magic wand work? What other categories could we use for sorting cards? What other games could we make to use our magic wand?"

Evaluation. Observe the children's interest in and their abilities to make and classify the cards.

☐ ☐ ☐ Magnet Projects

Science Processes. Observing, communicating, and using time and space relationships.

The children can make a variety of projects that "work" because magnets can attract objects through materials such as paper, plastic, air, and water. Show the children examples of the following projects. Then let the children work alone or in pairs to construct a project.

Magnet Boats

The children make boats out of plastic foam and attach a paper clip to each one. They move the boats with "magnet power" by holding a magnet above, but not touching, the boat and its paper clip or by holding a magnet under the shallow container of water (Figure 13.3).

Magnet Boxes

The children draw a picture on the bottom of—or draw on paper that is placed in the bottom of—a clear plastic sandwich or salad box (Figure 13.4). They use iron filings or bits of steel wool to arrange as "hair" on their drawings by moving them with a magnet held under the box.

Magnet Puppets

The children cut out small paper figures and fold the paper at the bottom to make a base (Figure 13.5). They attach a paper clip to the base and put the figure on a cardboard stage. They hold a magnet under the stage and move the magnet to make the puppets move.

Magnetic Path

Have the children draw a path on paper or light cardboard (Figure 13.6). They can make a puppet—a person, a car, an animal, or other creature—to move along the path. Have them fold some paper under at the bottom to make a base for their puppet and attach a paper clip to this base. The children use a magnet under the paper to move the puppet along its path. For a variation of this project have the children tape the paper clips on the underside of the paper and then use a small magnet attached to

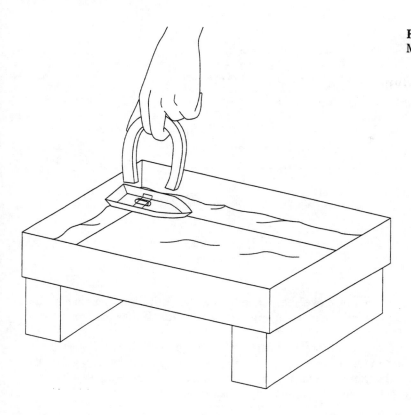

Figure 13.3
Magnet boat.

Figure 13.4
Magnet box.

Figure 13.5
Magnet puppet.

the puppet. As the children move the puppet along the path with their hands, they will feel the magnet attracting the paper clips along the path. If they wander from the path, they won't feel this force.

When the projects are completed, invite each child to describe his project. Divide the class into groups of four or five and let them try out each others' projects. Circulate and ask individual children how and why the projects work; emphasize that all of the projects use magnets attracting through other materials.

Questions. "What other magnet projects could we make?" Follow up on some of the children's ideas if possible. "What magnet games do you have at home?" Perhaps some of the children could bring and display some examples.

Figure 13.6
Magnetic path.

Evaluation. Notice which children did a careful, thorough job on their projects. Observe the children's interest in and their abilities to explain their projects. Have each child write about how he made his project; judge the compositions for thoroughness and detail.

PEOPLE CAN MAKE MAGNETS

Most of the magnets we use are made by people. Some commercially made magnets are manufactured in a process that lets electric current flow through steel; the steel eventually becomes magnetized. In their homes or classrooms, people can magnetize steel objects such as paper clips by stroking them with a commercially made magnet. In this section we will describe this process in detail and also present ways that temporary magnets can be demagnetized.

Let's Make Magnets

Science Processes. Observing, communicating, predicting, using numbers, ordering, and inferring.

Divide the class into groups of three or four. Each group will need a strong bar magnet, 6 or 8 large paper clips, and many small paper clips. Have the children test their large paper clips to see if they will attract any of the small paper clips. (Probably they will not.)

Show the children how to take turns holding a large paper clip tightly and stroking it with the magnet, consistently moving in one direction. Direct the children to stroke the clips firmly, making contact with the magnet for the entire length of the paper clip. After several strokes of the magnet, the large paper clip should attract some smaller ones. It may not lift the small clips, but it should attract and move them.

Now ask: "What will happen if you each stroke your large paper clips different numbers of times with the bar magnet? Will the large clips all lift the same number of small clips or will they lift different numbers?" Help the children ascertain that their large paper clips are not magnetic before they begin stroking them. Then instruct different group members to stroke their large paper clips 20, 40, 60, or 80 times. After a large clip is magnetized, the children should test it to see how many paper clips it will move or lift. The children can record their results on a chart. Help them arrange their large paper clips in order from the strongest to the weakest according to their results. Lead the children to discuss and compare their results. Help them infer that, in general, the more times we stroke a paper clip, the stronger its magnetism will become.

Questions. "What other things might we magnetize?" (Nails, knitting needles, or even steel scissors can be magnetized by stroking.) You might let children test some of the things they suggest. "How many small clips might this large clip attract if we stroked it 200 times?"

Evaluation.   Observe the children's coordination as they stroke the paper clip. Help those who need it. Note the children's abilities to follow instructions, record results, and discuss their findings.

☐ ☐ ☐ Magnets Can Lose Their Power

Science Processes.   Observing, communicating, predicting, inferring, and using time and space relationships.

Substances that people magnetize can also lose their magnetism. Repeatedly dropping or jarring homemade and commercially made magnets causes them to lose their magnetic power. Heating magnets also decreases their power. If magnets are stored with their poles in positions that repel, they can also become weak. Share some of these facts with children.

Help the children test out some of the ways magnets become demagnitized. Have two groups choose the "strongest" paper clips it magnetized and show how many small paper clips each can lift or move. Then have the children take turns dropping their large clips or hitting the clips several times on a countertop to jar them. Have the children test their large paper clips again. Probably the clips will have lost some of their power.

Help a child choose a "strong" magnetized paper clip and show how many small paper clips it will attract or move. Supervise as the child holds the large paper clip with tongs with insulated handles over a hot plate and heats it for about 2 minutes. Cool the clip and have the child test it to see if it has lost some of its magnetism.

Ask: "What do these demonstrations and discussions tell us about how we should treat and store magnets?" Help the children conclude that we should treat magnets gently and keep them away from excessive heat if we want them to last. Remind them that magnets should be stored with attracting poles together—the way they tend to arrange themselves. If you have horseshoe magnets with keepers, small metal bars that go across the magnet's legs, show the children how to place the keeper in the proper position (Figure 13.7). Encourage responsible care of magnets as the children work with them.

Figure 13.7
Storing magnets.

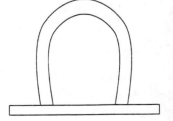

Some magnets also wear out over long periods of time. You might want to have the children select their strongest paper clip magnets and see how many small clips each attracts. The children could write the date and number of small clips on a card and set their large clip aside. After a month or two, the children could test the paper clips to see if they have lost any magnetism over time.

Questions. "How do the ideas we have learned apply to magnets you have at home? What other items do you use at home or at school that we could try to magnetize?"

Evaluation. Note the children's interests and abilities to describe ways to care for magnets. Have groups make miniposters about aspects of magnet care. Check the posters for creativity and accuracy and place them in your science center or magnet center.

WE CAN WORK WITH STATIC ELECTRICITY AND CURRENT ELECTRICITY

Electricity concerns the "behavior" and movement of small particles—electrons. When these minute, negatively charged particles accumulate and stay on a substance, static electricity is built up there. We notice this phenomenon when we see lightning flash or hear the crackling sound then nylon fabrics that cling together are pulled apart. Sometimes we walk across a carpet and then touch an object and feel a tiny shock. Why? Because static electricity has built up in our bodies and moves to the object as we touch it. As objects become charged with static electricity, they gain a negative charge. Negatively charged objects repel each other, but a negatively charged object attracts a positively charged object (one that has lost a substantial number of electrons) or one that is neutral (neither negatively nor positively charged).

Scientists think of current electricity as a flow of electrons. Current electricity travels in a continuous path or circuit—from a power source, such as a battery or generator, through a conductor, such as a wire, to an appliance, and back to the power source. People take current electricity for granted and use it every day—in cars, homes, businesses, and recreational facilities.

Young children can explore some simple ideas about electricity. They can charge objects and see how the objects interact with other objects. They can set up simple circuits to begin to understand in concrete ways how current electricity works. As they work, the children will use physical skills and use a variety of science processes.

What a Charge!

Science Processes. Observing, predicting, and communicating.

It is best to do static electricity activities in cold, dry weather. Help the children charge objects with static electricity. For example, they could rub plastic combs with nylon or wool cloths and then hold the combs near the hair on their arms or their heads. The children can see and feel the effects of static electricity as it attracts their hair. Some children's hair will react to static electricity better than others.

Help the children make static electricity boxes. They will need small boxes with clear plastic lids or clear, plastic sandwich boxes. The children can cut and tear small bits of tissue paper and place these inside their boxes. Ask: "What will happen if you briskly rub the plastic top of your box?" As they do so, the children will notice that the pieces of tissue paper move about; some will cling to the lid. Explain that the plastic has beome charged with static electricity. The static electricity attracts the lightweight bits of tissue paper. Have the children describe what they see and feel.

The children can also make tiny figures of lightweight paper. They can fold the paper, draw a figure, and cut it out (Figure 13.8). Then the children can make the figures move with static electricity. To do so they rub a comb with a piece of nylon or wool and then bring it near the figures to make them "dance" or "race."

Lead the children to discuss the idea that static electricity can be built up in objects. Point out that these objects then can attract other objects. Let the children describe other experiences they have had with static electricity.

As the final part of this activity, inflate a balloon and draw a funny face on it with permanent marker. Briskly rub the "face" of the balloon and bring it close to the cheek of a volunteer child. The charged surface of the balloon will attract the hair on the child's face. The balloon may have enough static charge to cling to the child's face or to a wall. Provide turns for any other children who want to get a "kiss" from the balloon, recharging the balloon's surface as necessary.

Ask: "What will happen if you charge the faces of two balloons with static electricity and bring the balloons close together?" As you do so, the children may be surprised that the balloons do not attract each other; two charged surfaces repel. One balloon may "turn its face" away from the other.

Questions.   Say: "We don't see static electricity. How do we know it's there? Working with static electricity can be fun, but sometimes it's bothersome too. Does static electricity ever bother you at home or other places? What do you do about it?"

Evaluation.   Have the children draw pictures and write about their experiences with static electricity. Check their work for detail and accuracy of information.

Figure 13.8
Using static electricity.

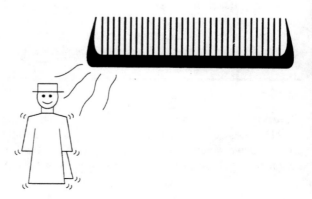

"Look at this! After we rub the balloon, it sticks to the wall!"

Complete Circuits

☐ ☐ ☐

Science Processes. Observing, communicating, predicting.

A complete circuit usually includes a power source such as a battery, an appliance such as a light bulb in a socket or doorbell, and conductors to carry the power from its source to the appliance. Conductors are usually wires. Small flashlight bulbs and sockets can be purchased at hardware stores or school supply companies. A 6-volt battery or 1½-volt flashlight battery is inexpensive and safe. The wires may be any thin-coated or uncoated steel or copper wire. If the wire is coated or insulated with plastic, use scissors to strip off the ends of the insulation leaving a 1 to 2 centimeter (½ to 1 inch) section at each end of the wire. Attach this uninsulated part to the battery or socket. A 6-volt battery has terminals on the top to attach the wires. The children can hold the ends of the wire firmly to the ends of the flashlight battery. Flashlight battery holders are also available from school supply companies. These have places to attach the ends of the wire so it does not have to be held in place.

Help the children to work in groups to set up a simple circuit (Figure 13.9). Show them how to connect the power source, appliance, and wires as shown. Ask: "What will happen if the wires are disconnected at a point like A or B? What will happen if the wires are switched at A or B? What if the wire is loosened at C or D?" Help the children trace the circuit or path of electricity from one terminal (or end of the battery), to the appliance, and back to the battery.

Show the children a flashlight and let them find its appliance, power source(s), and conductors. Ask: "What will happen if you unscrew the light bulb, switch the positions of the batteries, or move the flashlight's switch?" Let them try these things to test their predictions.

Let the children who are interested see if they can hook up a complete circuit independently. Caution the children that although classroom-size batteries and light bulbs are not dangerous, they *must not experiment* with larger batteries, electricity

Figure 13.9
A simple circuit.

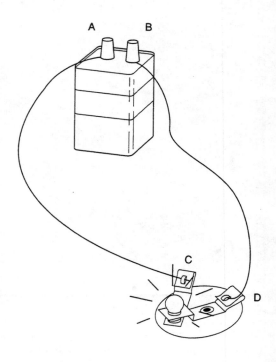

Making a complete electrical circuit is not a hard job. These children have drawn a picture showing how to connect the battery, bulbs, and wires.

from a wall socket, or other appliances. Tell them that they *must not taste* any liquid or crumbly substance that may accumulate on a battery.

Questions. "What are some other devices that use a power source, appliance, and conductors? On this hot plate (or other classroom appliance), where are the power source, the appliance, and the conductors?"

Evaluation. Have each child make a picture of how to connect the battery, bulbs, and wires. Check the pictures for accuracy. Note the children's interest and their small-muscle coordination as they work with this activity.

SOME MATERIALS CONDUCT ELECTRICITY

Electricity flows through most metals freely. These materials are good conductors of electricity. Carbon and solutions of water and some acids, salts, and bases also conduct electricity. They also allow electrons to move freely through them. Electricity travels poorly through many other materials. Plastics, cloth, wood, paper, glass, and rubber are poor conductors; often they are called insulators. Pure water and dry air are also poor conductors of electricity. People use insulators to stop the flow of electricity. For example, we want electricity to flow from a wall switch to a lamp, but we do not want the electricity to flow to our bodies when we touch the cord. Therefore, we use a good conductor—typically copper wire—to conduct electricity; however, we coat the wire with plastic to inhibit the flow of electricity anywhere but to the lamp.

Through concrete experiences children can discover for themselves which materials are good conductors of electricity. They can apply this knowledge as they think about everyday electrical appliances and make projects that require a flow of electricity.

Is It a Conductor or Not?

Science Processes. Observing, communicating, classifying, predicting, inferring.

Have a child set up a simple circuit using a small light bulb, battery, and wires. Detach one of the wires and replace it with two wires attached to the bulb and battery but not to one another. Help the children dicuss why the light was on in your first circuit, but is not now. Lead them to understand that the circuit is broken. Ask: "What will happen if the wires are placed firmly back together?" Help a child put the wires together to see. Tell the children that you are working with a battery of very low voltage; they will not be hurt by handling the wires. Caution them that they *should not* handle the wires from a larger battery or wires that lead to a household electrical power source!

Have the children predict what will happen if you put various objects in the place where the wire is separated. Use objects such as scissors, a pencil, an eraser, and a penny. Have children hold the ends of the wire firmly against the surface of each object. The metal objects should conduct electricity and the bulb should light up.

It's awkward to hold the wires in place, so show the children how to use a small board with two nails to test objects and see if the objects complete the circuit or not

Figure 13.10
Testing objects for conduction of electricity.

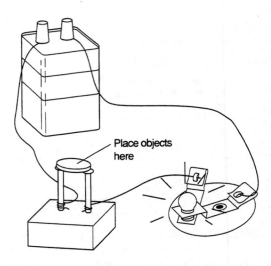

Place objects here

(Figure 13.10). The children should select objects, predict whether each will conduct electricity or not, and then firmly place the objects across the two nails to see what happens to the light bulb. As the children test objects, have them sort the objects into two piles—those that conduct electricity and those that do not. Introduce the words *conductor* and *insulator* and encourage the children to use them. Be sure the children use a variety of metals—steel, copper, silver, aluminum—and several nonmetal objects. After testing many objects, help the children infer that metals conduct electricity while most other materials do not.

Questions. "What helped you predict whether or not an object would conduct electricity? Why are most electrical wires in our classroom and homes coated with plastic?"

Evaluation. Mark on a checklist the children's abilities to predict and to classify objects.

Simple Switches

Science Processes. Observing, communicating, predicting, and inferring.

Have a child set up a simple circuit. When the bulb is lit, ask the children to suggest some ways to turn off the bulb. They may mention loosening the wire or unscrewing the light bulb. Discuss whether these are the procedures they use at home for turning off appliances. They probably will not be—the children most often use switches to shut off lights and other appliances.

Cut one of the wires and show the children how to insert a simple switch (Figure 13.11). One switch design uses a small block of wood, thumb tacks to hold the wires, and a piece of foil folded-over to open or close. Another simple design uses a piece of thick cardboard or plastic foam, nails to wrap the wires around, and a paper clip bent to make a switch. Still another design uses cardboard and thumb tacks to hold the wire and a piece of bent metal to open and close. Have a child volunteer to "install" the switch and see what happens to the bulb. Point out that if the switch is "open"—

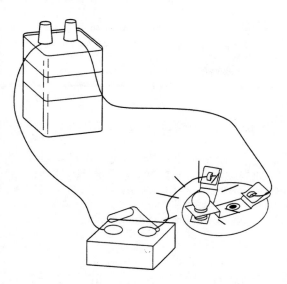

Figure 13.11
A simple switch.

not touching the metal nails on thumb tacks—the bulb should not light. If the switch is "closed," its metal parts complete the circuit and the bulb should light.

Provide materials for groups of children to set up their own circuits and switches. They can take turns opening and closing the switches to see what happens to the light bulb. Circulate as the children work. Encourage them to tell whether their circuits are complete or not and to describe the role that the switch plays. Let them experiment with two switches.

Questions. "What would happen if we installed two switches? (See Figure 13.12.) Would the bulb light if one switch is open? What if both switches are closed?"

Figure 13.12
Two switches.

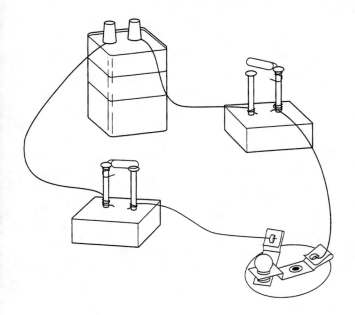

Evaluation.   Note the children's interest and small-muscle abilities as they connect the circuits and make and install their switches. Check their abilities to describe what they are doing and the role that the switch plays in the circuit.

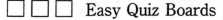 Easy Quiz Boards

Science Processes.   Observing, communicating, using time and space relationships, and inferring.

Children can make easy, inexpensive quiz boards with file folders, aluminum foil, and tape. Prepare a sample quiz board (Figure 13.13). Cut or punch holes along each side of a file folder. Write or draw questions and answers, mixing them up. Now cut strips of aluminum foil. Use a strip inside the file folder. Join a question and its answer with foil leaving foil covering the hole. Tape the foil in place. Join another question and

Figure 13.13
Making a quiz board.

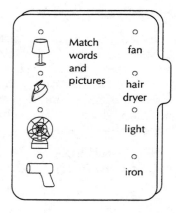

outside

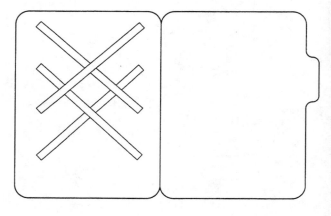

inside

answer and cover the foil with tape. Proceed until all the questions and answers are joined.

Show the children the quiz board and how to place the loose ends of wire on the foil in the hole for a question and answer to make a simple circuit. Explain that if the bulb lights, the answer is correct (Figure 13.14).

Instead of the battery and bulbs, you might also use an electric continuity tester (an inexpensive device that includes power source, light bulb, and wires and alligator clips on the ends).

Organize the children into groups of three or four. Each group can make a quiz board. The children can trade quiz boards and use them, or the quiz boards may be placed in a learning center with one battery, bulb, and wire setup (or continuity tester) for the children to take turns.

Questions.   "Why do our quiz boards work? Where is the complete circuit? What conducts the electricity? How else could we use our quiz boards?"

Evaluation.   Note whether the children's work is careful and complete. Are they able to make good matching questions for each other? Can they explain how the quiz boards work?

ELECTRICITY CAN HELP OR HARM US

People use electricity in hundreds of ways. Electricity powers appliances that cook our food, heat and cool our homes, style our hair, and entertain us. Electrical devices greatly improve our quality of life. Electricity is a wonderful force, but producing electricity is becoming more and more expensive. People are investigating ways to conserve electricity by creating power-saving and power-efficient appliances. People can also conserve electricity by limiting their extravagant use of it.

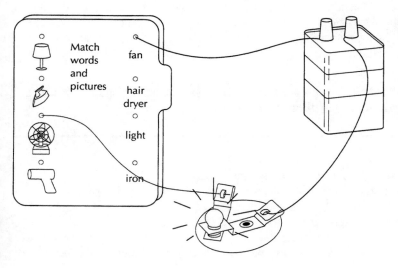

Figure 13.14
Using the quiz board.

Electricity can also be dangerous. Lighting can harm people and start fires. Current electricity can cause annoying and life-threatening shocks. Unsafe use of appliances can result in burns, fires, or other accidents. The activities in this section will help the children understand that they must respect electricity and learn to use it wisely.

□ □ □ Ways We Use Electricity

Science Processes.   Observing, communicating, using numbers, classifying, ordering, and inferring.

Help children start a list of the many ways they use electricity. After they name several things, begin to categorize their answers. You could use categories such as electrical things that make us hot, things that make us cool, things that help us work, things that help us play, and "other."

After this initial discussion, ask the children to complete one of these assignments at home.

- Count all the electrical appliances and devices you find in each room.
- Talk to adults to see what other uses of the electricity they can name.
- Find five electric appliances. Draw them. Put the pictures in order from the largest to the smallest appliance.

Back in the classroom, have the children share their findings in small groups. All of the children in each group should organize some of their data on a graph. They can then share their graphs with the entire class.

Lead the children to discuss the need to save, or *conserve,* electricity. Have each group talk about the uses of electricity that they found and select the appliance that they think is the most important and useful. They should also discuss the appliance that they consider the least important—one that would be easy to give up. Each group can present their choices and give reasons for their judgments.

Questions.   Using appliances named by the children, give clues and ask the children to identify the appliances. Start with general clues and then give more specific ones, pausing between clues for their guesses. For example, say: "This appliance is found in the kitchen. It's usually quite large. It has one or more doors. It keeps food cold. What is it?" (refrigerator)

Evaluation.   Note the children's abilities to name, discuss, and categorize appliances. Check the care and accuracy with which the groups made their graphs.

□ □ □ Safety First

Science Processes.   Observing and communicating.

Review some of the ways electricity helps people. Help the children discuss the need for cautious and correct use of electrical appliances and devices. Let them offer their ideas on safety precautions for using electricity.

Let each child make a safety poster about electricity or add to a class safety booklet. Encurge the children to draw and write about proper ways to use electricity as well as things *not* to do. Children might create an electrical safety character to use in their artwork. They might use the circle and diagonal slash design as they draw safety cautions.

Display the children's work in the hallways or offer your completed classbook to another class to read. The children might also display and explain their posters for another class.

Questions.   "What ideas does your poster (or book page) show? Which of these ideas can you use at home? How can you use them?"

Evaluation.   Note whether the children work carefully and complete their work. Do they show sound and independent thinking in what they discuss and portray?

Electricity in Your School

Science Processes.   Observing, communicating, predicting, classifying, and using numbers.

Electricity is used many ways in any school. Ask the children: "How many electrical devices do you think you will find in our classroom?" Then have the children look carefully around the room and help them list all the electrical devices. Together decide on a classifying scheme and categorize all the things they have found. Perhaps you could categorize them as "Things That Give Light," "Things That Give Heat," "Things That Help Us Learn," and "Others."

Ask your school custodian to give the children a special tour of some parts of the school to talk to them about electrical appliances in the school. The custodian might show the children how he changes florescent and conventional bulbs, where the fuse box and circuit breakers are, and what electrical tools he uses. Ask the children to notice the safety aspects of the custodian's work.

Have the children work in groups to make large pictures of the many electrical appliances used in the school. Each group should write or dictate a few sentences about its picture. Then, group members can explain the details in their pictures to the entire class. Display the pictures, along with thank-you's to the custodian, in the hallway.

Questions.   "Which one or two electrical devices are most important to us—the ones we'd miss the most if our electricity didn't work? Why do you think so? Which of our appliances do you also have at home? Which are special things used only at school?"

Evaluation.   Note the children's interest, cooperation, and counting abilities. Note the detail shown in their pictures and written work.

Life Without Electricity

Science Processes.   Observing and communicating.

It's almost impossible for most of us to imagine life without electricity. It provides the power to appliances that entertain us, give us light, cook and cool our food, and heat and cool our homes. Spend part of a day without electricity. Before the children arrive, turn off the light and any electric or cooling systems. Put away any projectors and other electrical learning materials.

When the children arrive, talk with them about the differences they notice in the classroom. Discuss the many benefits electricity provides. Encourage the children to give examples of how they have coped without electricity at times when it has gone off in their homes. Discuss what people did 100 years ago when most did not have electricity in their homes. Let the children offer ideas of what whey would do if they had to decrease their electric power consumption somewhat—one or two electrical appliances they would give up.

Have each child draw and write a page or two for a class book entitled, "Life Without Electricity." Have a committee bind the book pages together and then display it in your library or science center.

Questions.   "What would you miss most if we had no electricity?" Make a graph of the children's responses.

Evaluation.   Note the children's contributions to the discussion and the detail shown in their drawings.

NOW IT'S YOUR TURN

It's your turn again. After reading our information and activities for magnets and electricity, you should be ready to put your mind and hands to work. Extend and vary our suggestions with your choices of the following activities.

1.   How many magnets can you find among your possessions and in your home? Predict a number; then conduct a search. Find several unique magnets or magnetic devices that you could share with the children. Plan a way to show the magnets. Then give the children a chance to manipulate them.

2.   Review the magnet projects that are described in this chapter. Plan another magnet project that young children could make and use. Perhaps you can add something especially appealing to children's sense of touch or to their need for physical activity. Actually make up your devices and share them with the children or with your classmates.

3.   Read more about the history of people's knowledge of electricity. Have people known about electricity, its nature, and ways to make it work for a long time or a relatively short time in history? Make a time line and put some important "electrical" events and their dates on it. Share your findings and time line with your peers.

4.   If you live near an Amish community, visit that settlement to observe life without electricity. Share your discoveries.

5.   Design and make an electric quiz board for the children you teach. You may use a variation of the quiz boards described in this chapter or create a new design of

your own. Use questions that will reinforce knowledge that your children need to work on, or devise items that will offer a special challenge to some of your students who need it.

6. We read and hear so much today about energy conservation. Find out more about the ways that electricity is generated, reasons why electrical power today is limited, and ways to conserve electricity. In relation to conservation of electricity, investigate electrical blackouts and brownouts. Think of ways to share some of your findings with the children.

7. Knowing ways to conserve electricity is not enough. People need to act on their knowledge. To help you become more aware of your consumption of electrical energy, each day for a week list the electrical appliances you use and note the approximate number of times or minutes you use them. Now make and carry out a plan to cut your electricity consumption by 10 to 20%. Share some of your methods of conservation with your peers. Discuss ways to modify this project to use it with young children.

SELECTED CHILDREN'S BOOKS

How things work. (1984). New York: Simon & Schuster.

Keen, M. (1976). *The know how book of experiments with batteries and magnets.* New York: Grosset and Dunlap.

Kirkpatrick, R. K. (1985). *Look at magnets.* Milwaukee: Raintree.

Santrey, L. (1985). *Magnets.* Mahway, NJ: Troll Associates.

Wilkes, A., & Mostyn, D. (1983). *Simple science.* London: Usborne Publishing.

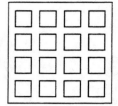

Index